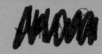

The family home

Relaxed, informal living for all ages

Joanna Copestick

RAINCOAST BOOKS

Vancouver

For my family: Brian, Hannah and Julia, and my five sisters.

And in memory of my parents, who taught me that families are

more important than pristine homes.

First published in Canada in 1998 by
Raincoast Books
8680 Cambie Street, Vancouver
BC V6P 6M9
(604) 323-7100
Web site: www.raincoast.com

First published in the UK in 1998 by Conran Octopus Limited

ISBN 1-55192-188-X

Canadian Library Cataloguing-in-Publication Data is available
from the publisher.

Printed in China

author's acknowledgments

A book such as this always owes its existence to a lot of hard work
by a solid, stoic team of people. Many thanks go to Denny Hemming
for seizing the idea and Juliet Burton for smoothing the way;
Gillian Haslam, model editor – calm, encouraging, fun and careful
with deadlines; Alison Barclay for imaginative design; Clare Limpus
for tireless picture research; and Alison Wormleighton who tied
together, and made sense of, numerous batches of copy with her
usual expertise.

Grateful thanks and big hugs to Brian, Hannah and Julia for extra
patience while I monopolised the computer for a very long time –
normal family life can now resume. My parents-in-law, Doris and
Harry Copestick, were, as always, endlessly supportive. Thanks also
to my five sisters, Mary, Patricia, Maureen, Sally and Lesley and their
families, for many years of inspiration, insight and good company.
And to Susie Ross and Leanne Walters for introducing me to
Anjie Davison and her many talents.

A big thank you to the six families who allowed us to photograph
their homes for the family features.

And the following people who offered advice, encouragement
and playmates for my children over many weeks and months:
Dorothy Turner, Wendy Copestick and the cousins, Karen, Harry
and Joel Saunders, Laura and Alice Cronshaw, Meryl Lloyd, Janice
Norwood, Sarah Rogers, Laura Garnish and everyone at Wainscot,
Carmel Morgan, Debbie Williams, Julia Miller and Karen Hewish.

CONTENTS

INTRODUCTION

When children enter your life, your perspective of the world shifts dramatically. One minute you are coasting – going to work, dashing to catch a movie, arranging dinner with friends, or embarking on a weekend of decorating a room. Travel occurs whenever time and money allow, and weekends can be spent in indulgent entertainment, exercise, or shopping.

Then Junior appears and parental responsibility stares you in the face. There are always far too many things to do, and you lurch from one time-management compromise to another. You learn a whole new vocabulary and lifestyle. Within weeks you are comparing one brand of diaper against another, and deliberating long and hard over the relative merits of different strollers. You begin fretting about education and you bore friends with the natural genius of your offspring. Life becomes one big routine, on a loop.

And then there is your home. When babies appear, previously serene spaces become cluttered with baby gyms, building blocks, and gaudy plastic toys. Precious upholstery and rugs develop a coating of dried crackers. Glass-topped tables rapidly assume life-threatening status, trailing stereo wires become trapezes, and display china is suddenly an enormous liability. The easiest (and least stressful) solution is simply to remove all the

LEFT: This converted barn provides ample space for children to dash about safely, while parents can relax, knowing they have adopted a damage-limitation approach to decorating. Using color on walls to enliven and define a space in which furniture is childproof and under-stated is a good low-main-tenance solution.

BELOW: Altering a living space so that it divides loosely into separate zones, each with its own function, means you can go with the organic flow of a home. Adapting each space as children grow and the family's needs change obviates the need to move every few years.

hazards, albeit for a short period – along with the precious white upholstery and expensive rugs.

The whole business of parenthood is so overwhelming that interior decoration can become a low priority. Even when the children get older, and life settles into a more manageable routine, the home still tends to receive little attention. Yet the home actually becomes *more* important with the onset of family life. It is the hub of the family unit and the place in which daily life reverberates. New mothers can suddenly find themselves spending much longer at home. Making it comfortable and practical should therefore be a top priority.

To most people a family home means a place of comfort, relaxation, and nurturing – a physical focus for the family, and a gathering place and refuge from the wider world, offering a chance for reassurance and renewal. Making a family home at once comfortable, inviting, functional, and easy to maintain is the principal challenge – and what this book is about.

Some books focus on specific aspects of decorating without taking into account the daily life within those carefully colored walls and thoughtfully furnished rooms. This book, however, includes ideas for making your home low in maintenance and high on convenience, enjoyment, and a little luxury. Creating, maintaining, and adapting a family home so that everyday living is more stress-free and at the same time stylish is a challenge. For a family home to work, it must be looked on as an organic entity, forever evolving – and it is the realization of this ideal that is at the heart of this book.

ABOVE FAR LEFT: Toys may only be around for a few years, but storing them so they can be seen, used, and put away becomes a vital part of family life for a while. A chrome trolley on casters can be moved from room to room as required, and promotes a sense of order in the younger generation.

ABOVE LEFT: Not only do children love keeping a record of their heights as they grow, but it is also a significant way of monitoring how quickly the early years progress.

RIGHT: This open-plan space makes a perfect kitchen, dining area, and family room. The linoleum floor is hard-wearing and anti-bacterial and will retain its good looks. Painted kitchen units and woodwork in soft eau-de-nil are an ideal backdrop for wood and wicker.

ROOM TO MOVE

ROOM TO MOVE

The demands made on today's family home are very

RIGHT: Making good use of
the area under the eaves
is always a successful way
of creating space. Here,
the equivalent of a
whole bedroom has
been slotted into a hallway.
Two beds, complete with
integral shelving, have
been built between
floor-to-ceiling cupboards.
Sited under small windows,
the beds function as
windowseats by day.

It is not uncommon for the family home to be empty for

most of the day, with the adults out at work and the children

at school or at daycare. Yet this does not make it any

less special. Home is where you and your family can shut

out the rest of the world and recharge your spirits,

and where you can invite friends to enjoy your hospitality.

A comfortable, nurturing atmosphere is important, not only

for its contribution to the family's quality of life but also

because it will determine the image of home your children

carry with them into adulthood.

LEFT: In this large, opened-up apartment each space is separated from its neighbor by a brightly painted wall with a wide, square opening. The apartment has the best of both worlds, as each activity zone, though separate and distinct, is in touch with the others and can easily change its function as needed. The same wooden flooring throughout the apartment helps to link one room to the next.

LEFT: Battered pine and a friendly old piano are the epitome of a comfortable country home. A mishmash of unfitted kitchen units and individual storage items fills one wall, leaving ample space for a large family table. This is a room perfect for dining, doing homework, chatting, entertaining and working, with everything stored close at hand and plenty of room for both family and friends.

different from those of a generation, or even a decade ago.

The definition of a family today is much broader than it was a generation ago. A high proportion of families are now single-parent, and many lifelong family relationships are formed out of marriage. Stepchildren and siblings often coexist happily in a loose arrangement of weekend sleepovers.

Some families are multigenerational, sometimes with aging parents cared for by offspring who became parents themselves well into their 30s or 40s and find they have the responsibility of caring for a generation on either side of them. Neverthe-less, it can be a boon for working parents to have their children's grandparents on hand, not only for babysitting but also for enriching the children's lives generally.

Working patterns are more flexible today, with both parents working in the majority of families. It is now not unusual for the father to stay at home to look after young children while the mother goes out to work. A growing number of people work at least part of the time from home.

VERSATILITY AND FLEXIBILITY

With these changing social patterns, the family home has inevitably altered too. It is now required to fulfill a diverse range of functions, depending on the number and age of the inhabitants and how long they spend at home. As everyone expects to claim a portion of space for themselves, a clever use of this limited commodity is vital. Multifunctional rooms, and furniture, free-flowing layouts, and careful clutter control are all ways of achieving this. The home has to run itself if busy parents are to cope.

HAPPY MEMORIES

Despite – or perhaps because of – this fast-lane approach, people still tend to retain an idealized image of the family home and family life, with a sentimental concept of a mother at home sewing and making jam. Many people try to preserve and reinvent these romantic ideals – which were proba-bly not perfect but whose appeal is strong nevertheless. Visions of children playing outdoors unfettered by worries about safety and riding bikes on traffic-free roads are all part of our nostalgia for that homely idyll.

Still, the emotional pull of "doing the right thing" is a strong one. Families are often fragmented, by relationships or by geography, but the notion of a family living under one roof, however chaotically, endures as a natural bond.

CHOOSING A STYLE

Everyone wants their home to look good and be comfortable and functional at the same time. But these criteria can seem mutually exclusive when the family living in the home comprises two or three generations and a variety of interests and requirements. Nevertheless, it is perfectly possible to create a home that not only reflects your personality and is full of things you like, but also is a place where everyone can put their feet up and relax.

BEYOND FASHION

When you are decorating or furnishing a home, you are bombarded by the latest fashions and trends in interiors, which these days seem to change every season. Don't let

these fads of color, shape, or texture dictate to you. They obviously will be sources of inspiration when you are choosing decorating schemes and furnishings; but don't be afraid to choose an approach or scheme that you love but that is not currently chic – you may just be ahead of your time! Similarly, have the confidence to reject anything that is not "you" or is inappropriate for your family or your home.

For example, "country style" is often regarded as the ideal family environment: cozy patchwork quilts, plain wood furniture, nurturing Aga stoves, home-baked cookies, and homespun values. But if you live in a small urban apartment, the rustic wood

ABOVE: Cozy and homely, this comfortably furnished cabin makes a delightful retreat. A wood-burning stove is both heat-provider and architectural feature.

LEFT: Here, traditional style combines seamlessly with modern needs. The working area – which would once have been the scullery – is separate but not completely cut off from the main eating area, giving it a timeless appeal.

RIGHT: Converted spaces, especially barns, make good family homes with generous space and light.

LEFT: This contemporary approach to a traditional barn environment exudes controlled efficiency. No discarded cookies behind radiators here, only a calm approach to uncluttered family living. A utility area, a food preparation counter and an island dining unit are all self-contained pools of activity in a space delineated with stone flooring.

RIGHT: Sunrooms and conservatories are versatile adjuncts to a living space. Here, natural light enhances an area devoted to relaxation, where simple matting and rattan furniture add to the atmosphere of comfortable informality.

could look incongruous next to, say, delicate plasterwork or a marble fireplace, while an Aga might completely overpower your kitchen. And do you really want the discolored, unsightly bottoms of your cooking pans hanging in full view?

Another fashionable approach, the latest version of modernism, could be equally inappropriate. Even modernists have children eventually. The revival of pure, sparse design in white and other impractical colors means that at least one room given over to toys, primary colors, and constant clutter is the necessary compromise for the smart, design-led parent.

INSPIRATION AT HOME

Sometimes it is difficult actually to identify beforehand precisely what *will* work for your own family, or even what you will like. As well as poring over books and magazines to find ideas, you could try some original research.

Take a look around your home as it is now, imagining you are a photographer taking close-up photographic details for an interiors magazine. Find particular combinations that you feel really work – a lamp creating a pool of light on a table, an inviting sofa under a window, the contrast of rich wood against a particular rug or wall,

the vivid pink tulips next to the deep blue curtains, a pleasing group of pictures. Analyze what it is you especially like about them, and then try to reproduce these elements elsewhere.

ESTABLISHING PRIORITIES

Always base your decorating schemes and furnishings on comfort, convenience, and practicality. There will always be the home-furnishing equivalents of stiletto heels, but don't be tempted by these ephemeral fads, however beguiling they are. Let form follow function in your home. Practicality does not preclude taste and style.

SPACE MANAGEMENT

Practically every family finds itself needing more space than it has. Living space, working space, and storage space are all high priorities in any family home.

When a couple starts a family, they often become aware of an urgent need for more space. One or two people can occupy a one-bedroom apartment or house quite happily, but add an energetic toddler, along with his or her toys and equipment, to the equation and the home suddenly shrinks; it contracts even more when friends come to play. Families also discover a pressing need for extra space when children become teenagers and seem to outgrow their bedrooms.

Apart from moving to a bigger home or extending your existing home, it *is* possible to increase the space in your home through good space management. This involves a three-pronged attack on the problem:

- Reduce the number of belongings that take up space.
- Increase the efficiency of the existing space.
- Create the illusion of more space, so that your home *feels* bigger.

PARING DOWN

The search for space must begin with reducing the amount of furniture, accessories, books, videos, gadgets, collections, mementos, sports gear, clothing and general junk you cram into the home. Start by looking critically at all of it. Devote a weekend to throwing out, recycling, or giving away unwanted, unused, or unloved objects. Work out whether you need additional storage for what is left. (You will find room-by-room storage ideas throughout this book.) When you add something new, try to get rid of something to compensate, so that you are not continually adding to the total amount.

USING SPACE WELL

The efficient use of space involves making every part of your home function in ways that will best suit your family. Most people these days find that the traditional roles of each room are no longer relevant. The full and varied lives people now lead, along with changing work patterns and more fluid mealtimes, have led to changes in the ways rooms are used.

The kitchen, in particular, has partially taken over the roles of both living room and dining room. As a result, you need to ensure that the kitchen is organized and furnished so as to cope with this wider role (see the chapter on Cooking, Eating, and Entertaining) and also that you are not left with redundant rooms – dead spaces people simply pass through or never visit at all.

Sometimes all that the rooms require is to make them more functional. For example,

a living room so fancy that everyone prefers to sit in the kitchen, or a family room that is such a mess no one can even get through the door, would be relatively easy to improve once the problem was recognized.

Other rooms may be devoted to purposes for which they are only occasionally required. One option is to change a room's use completely. A rarely used dining room could become a playroom, family room, or study, for example. Alternatively, you could make the room dual-purpose.

DUAL-PURPOSE ROOMS

Some dual-purpose rooms can be used for different functions at different times. For example, a conservatory that no one sits in after dark could become a dining room; a guest bedroom could turn into a workroom when the guests have left; a garage could become a games room or exercise studio during the day when the car is gone.

It may be possible to make a room dual purpose simply by choosing furniture carefully. A sofa bed will allow a living room or study to double as a guest room, while large cupboard doors will hide a desk and computer workstation. (Multipurpose furniture for each room is discussed in the following chapters.)

Other dual-purpose rooms are divided into separate areas so that one room can fulfill either function, or both, at any time. One corner of a living room could become a study area, or part of the kitchen could be a family room. The approach you take will obviously depend on the size of the room and the purposes it will be put to.

OPEN-PLAN LAYOUTS

A common approach is to remove some interior walls – or leave them out when building a house – in order to create open-plan, multifunctional spaces. Now that people's lives are not so compartmentalized, the barriers are coming down. The kitchen is no longer Mother's domain, nor the study Father's, and children certainly will not agree to stay in the nursery. There is therefore less need for these separate boxlike cubicles devoted to particular purposes. A large, open-plan area often provides a more functional, versatile, and comfortable living space suited to modern lifestyles.

Make the most of open-plan living by creating separate activity zones using furniture groupings, area rugs, screens, open shelving, etc. Cooking smells and noise can be problems in large, open-plan areas, so install good ventilation to eliminate odors, and soft surfaces (rugs or carpets, curtains, upholstery or soft covers, cushions) to absorb sounds.

COMMUNAL VS PRIVATE SPACES

There is a lot to be said for open-plan rooms, with their flexibility, free-flowing space, and large, multi-purpose areas. However, before you take a sledgehammer to your walls, think carefully about whether communal living is right for your family. You may well prefer to shut the door on the mess of the family room, the dirty dishes in the kitchen, the incessant blare of the television, or the children's boisterous games. And, of course, each member of the family will want a room they can retreat to when they need privacy or peace and quiet.

The most functional family homes combine a feeling of space yet retain an element of privacy. Even just one room closed off from the kitchen or family room means that there is a chance to escape the noise every so often.

A mix of open-plan communal spaces, with rooms off them to provide some privacy, can work particularly well, although needs do change as a family grows. For example, if a parent works from home during the children's preschool years, it is wise to keep a work room away from the general mêlée of family life so that children can get on with their routine unperturbed by the fact that Mummy or Daddy is in the house but not available for comment. However, once the children are at school and ready to use the computer, it is handy to have it sited in a communal, accessible area. Children of this age can usually work fairly quietly (at least for short spells), so their playroom could possibly be converted into one large family work area.

THE ILLUSION OF SPACE

A light and airy decor will always make a room seem more spacious. Use a pale color on the walls and ceiling. (If you want the

ceiling to seem higher than it is, it should be a little lighter than the walls.) Glossy finishes and other reflective surfaces will add to the illusion. Floor-to-ceiling windows overlooking a great view will almost double the apparent size of the room. Flooding a room with light or placing large mirrors on one wall will visually widen and brighten the whole area.

COZY ROOMS

There is also a place for cozy, intimate rooms decorated and furnished in rich

BELOW LEFT: Positioning bookshelves in the area between one room and another provides a browsing library for all the family. The walls are painted white to enhance the sense of space.

RIGHT: Glass bricks around a doorway keep adjacent rooms separate without making them seem cut off. A room that receives only limited natural light will benefit from the borrowed light.

colors. People sometimes assume that small or dark rooms can never carry off this type of decor, but in fact they are often the prime candidates for such an approach. You could, therefore, use the light colors in the airy, open-plan areas, while emphasizing the coziness of the smaller, private rooms with a rich palette of jewel colors.

SHOULD WE MOVE HOUSE?

It is always difficult to decide to move house, but sometimes family homes reach the point at which all inhabitants start to tread on each other's toes. Storage is at full capacity and the only way is out the door and on to the next house – or so it seems.

ONE LAST LOOK

Before deciding that you have outgrown your current home and bringing in the real estate agents, ask yourself a few questions:

- Is there space to build an extension, a conservatory, or a garage? Can you extend into the roof? Loft conversions can often yield another bathroom and a bedroom or playroom. If you do add on a room, try to make it dual-purpose.
- Can you increase the usable space by knocking through walls to provide a communal family area?
- Is your garden large enough for your children as they grow? If not, is increasing the size of the garden important enough to you to make a move worthwhile? Would you have to sacrifice location or house size to have a larger garden?

DUE CONSIDERATION

Avoid making any firm plans to move until you have considered all the options and figured out where you may have to move to in order to get the property you need. Be sure to find out what the local schools are like; many people actually move house in order to be near good schools. Look to the future, too – if you are likely to have any more children, or perhaps elderly relatives living with you, the property ought to be suitable for them, too.

If you live in the center of a city but you yearn for a complete change of lifestyle in the middle of nowhere, consider whether the attractions of the rural idyll outweigh the convenience and amenities of the city. Will you mind not having close neighbors or youngsters nearby for your children to play with? Are you willing to spend a lot of time in the car ferrying and shopping?

Similarly, if you currently live in the country but are considering moving to the city, find out exactly what the traffic congestion and noise are like at various times of day near the proposed new home. After you have weighed up the pros and cons, and perhaps looked at some possible properties, you may see your existing home in a much more favorable light.

LOW-MAINTENANCE LIVING

Low maintenance is an apt mantra for a family home. In a space that is either unoccupied for most of the day or swamped with children and their belongings, it is the ease with which everything can be accessed, dealt with, and tidied away that makes for less effort and housework.

An uncluttered environment, practical finishes on walls, floors, and furniture, removable covers on upholstered seating, unfussy window treatments, and a flexible layout, along with careful time management and good organization, are the essential components of low-maintenance living.

WALLS AND FLOORS

Choose easy-care finishes like paint; or, if you prefer wallpaper, use vinyl wallcoverings or at least spongeable wallpapers. Also go for low-maintenance floors like varnished wood, vinyl, linoleum, or sealed cork tiles. (There is more detail about these in the relevant chapters.)

FURNISHINGS

Keep the floor area as clear as possible through the use of built-in storage. Reduce the number of accessories and collectibles you have on display in order to create a

cleaner look as well as easier-to-clean surfaces. Avoid silver, copper, and brass unless you love polishing.

Loose covers cause less fretting than fitted ones when children are clambering around waving biscuits; however much you enforce the rules, there will always be accidents. Where possible, choose washable fabrics, and avoid any that stain easily or are delicate. New rugs, carpets, matting, upholstery, and even loose covers should be treated with a stain-repellent finish such as Scotchgard before the children are allowed anywhere near them. (For more advice on low-maintenance soft furnishings, see page 100.) Shutters, Venetian or wooden blinds, and simple fabric blinds are neater and less fussy than curtains, making cleaning bills a thing of the past.

CLUTTER CONTROL

There is a famous law of physics that states that, with every passing day, the universe becomes more and more disordered; be in no doubt that this law applies equally to the home. You have to decide, therefore, just how long you can tolerate the inevitable descent into chaos before you attempt to reimpose a semblance of order.

The "lived-in" look resulting from a small amount of disorder is reassuringly normal – indeed, cluttered rooms are many children's idea of heaven. But if you can

LEFT: Pared-down walls and floor are brightened with contemporary classic dining chairs and graphic prints in pop-art shades and there are no dust-gathering objects in sight.

RIGHT: Limited display, chic wooden flooring, and furniture on casters make for easy cleaning, flexible seating arrangements, and a sense of effortless order.

resist the natural inclination to fill every bit of space with furnishings, accessories, and clutter, you will make the job of maintaining order a great deal easier.

GETTING ORGANIZED

Messy corners piled with magazines, snap-shots, and a supposed "in box" always produce a muddled approach to chores. If you have to spend half an hour looking for the bills you are meant to pay, a spare light-bulb, a pen that actually writes, or the lid for a particular casserole dish, then life

could be made a lot easier. Contain, clear out, conceal, or catalogue everything, so you can find and use each item you need with a minimum of disruption.

For natural hoarders of circulars, maga-zine articles, and other paperwork, a brutal approach to editing the quantity of paper that is kept is essential. If parting with yellowed pieces of interesting information is too much for you, give a corner of the attic, garage or under-stair cupboard over to the "pending" file and resolve to sort it out later on (you never will).

Rather than investing in elaborate guilt-inducing files and other containers for paperwork, use a computer to save paper and do the work for you. Spend a weekend (boring, but worth it) keying in all essential addresses, telephone numbers, annual itin-eraries, birthdays and timesaving lists such as instructions for house-sitters, medical histories, or what to pack for holidays. Keep a printout of it all somewhere handy and then don't forget to put a note of where to find the printout on the bulletin-board – your life on a floppy disk.

the chathams, **loft living**

Several years before Manhattan's SoHo area had become the style capital it is today and a long time before the seriously fashionable and expensive stores and restaurants had moved in, architect Walter Chatham

and his wife, designer Mary Adams Chatham, bought and carefully restored the top floor of a dilapidated former power plant, with the intention of creating a stylish but comfortable family home in an urban environment.

Walter, a modern architect with a flexible view on design, discovered that the arrival of their three children had a major impact on his contemporary aesthetic. Having studied painting, he has always been interested in color, but the arrival of the three small children gave him design ideas that had hitherto not featured in his everyday work. He positively embraced the artificial colors that children love, unlike many parents who, appalled at the unsubtle colors and materials used by toy manufacturers, hide away all the primary-colored plastic toys that their children hold dear and replace them with tasteful wooden bricks and houses

Above: A floor-to-ceiling window floods the dining area with daylight. The tubular steel legs of the extendable dining table sit well against metal-framed chairs reminiscent of utilitarian school furniture.
Left: The Chathams gathered on the unobtrusive steel staircase that links the main living space with the work area and roof terrace upstairs.
Right: A narrow study tucked off the living room works as an extension of the living space. Housing the computer where the children can have easy access to technology is important when they are of an age to gain knowledge in this way.

that are, in truth, seldom played with as eagerly in the early years. Walter believes you should encourage rather than stifle them in their quest for brightness and went about designing his loft so it would appeal to all ages.

Walter maintains that color and light are the most joyful aspects of architecture, and not only did he incorporate zingy colors but he also added four large skylights and a wall of windows to the space. A restored concrete floor, cased beams running through the apartment, and a brightly painted industrial stairway leading to the studio provide visual reference to the building's original use as a power plant. It hadn't been used for over 15 years before the Chathams decided they could make a home out of it.

In order to accommodate their growing family, the Chathams created a huge space all on one level, organizing it in such a way that both generations have their own separate spaces, while still retaining the basic open-plan design. Near the entrance to the loft is the children's zone. This giant play space doubles as a corridor, with doors to the three children's bedrooms, their bathroom, and a utility room all opening off of it. Being sent into the corridor was

never more fun, as the floor space is large enough to accommodate a basketball game, skittles match, complete gymnastic workout, or a session on the trapeze that swings from the steel girdered-ceiling.

Each of the children's rooms has built-in bunks that help accommodate sleepover guests. As they have grown, so their belongings have graduated from skittles to electric guitars and the play zone is now taken up with a large air hockey table. The built-in storage of each room has it contents sifted through and edited before new belongings take their place. Walter says that architects are often criticized for not providing enough storage in family homes, so he has made efforts to incorporate as much display space, shelving, and cupboards as is practical in an open-plan loft. The family is also lucky to have a basement that acts as garage and storage area for out-of-season belongings.

The play zone leads into the kitchen/dining area, which works as a buffer between the generations, separating the living room from the children's wing. There is communality between the two zones, but when privacy is required, the children's area may easily be closed off from the kitchen/dining area by means of tall metal doors.

Above left: Children's bunks span a room with floor-to-ceiling shelves against painted walls that match the architectural style elsewhere in the loft. Toys are displayed, stored, and used for decoration in an otherwise perfectly white room.

Above right: The central open plan area that takes up the majority of the apartment effortlessly combines the activities of cooking, eating, and general family life in one large, flowing space.

House Rules

* Open up the space into flexible zones for
work, play, and sleep.

* Don't use glass doors until the children are
old enough to respect them.

* Throw out your old style and embrace primary
colors, and the children's toys won't look out of place.

* If possible, create a play zone in a wide corridor
for indoor games.

* Paint the inside of open shelving in bright
colors to create instant impact.

* Families enjoy space, so don't create too many small
rooms that limit communal action.

These doors have really been put to the test now that the two boys have formed their own rock band. They are able to practice behind two layers of closed doors (those of their bedrooms and the living space) with scarcely a comment from adults in the dining area – soundproofing at its best.

As part of the open-plan approach, the kitchen area has been designed to be as unobtrusive as possible, more of a workstation at the end of the living room. The hob and sink are discreetly integrated into slimline worktops, one of which doubles as a breakfast bar. The kitchen is fitted with open shelving for display and easy access – ideal in a family home where nothing stays still for long. The insides of the shelves are painted sharp apple green to provide a shot of color.

The shelving extends through to the living room, where the color becomes a vivid lemon yellow, an effective background for the ceramics and books on the shelves. Drawers below the display shield clutter from view. In fact, the same shelving reappears in most areas of the loft as a reminder that furnishings can be functional but still make a graphic statement.

Above left: The kitchen is specifically designed to integrate into the living space. Nothing shouts utility in this corner of the loft where a breakfast bar and food preparation island could just as easily be a storage unit in a dining room.

Above right: Using the generous hallway as a children's activity space is an inspired architectural solution. Huge sliding doors, vestiges from the building's former use, make a vital soundproofing divider when sound levels inevitably increase during playtime.

"Devote as much space as possible to discreet storage – families always seem to accumulate far too many belongings."

A narrow study tucked neatly off the living room is an extension of the living space when the door is open but can be closed off when necessary. A family computer is housed in here, allowing the children easy access to it – an important consideration when youngsters get to an age when they want to use the family technology.

In the master bedroom, sited at the opposite end of the loft from the children's bedrooms, the antique four-poster bed is strategically placed so the Chathams can view the entire home in comfort – great for keeping an eye on the kids. Also in here are more open shelves painted apple green on the inside to continue the look. Mary designed her own harlequin dressing cabinet when she couldn't find the right piece of furniture for the space, so the bedroom displays a bold mix of old and new, built-in and unfitted, in a scrupulously contemporary setting.

Upstairs, on a separate level, Mary has her work studio, where she designs and makes hats. This is the only truly self-contained space of the apartment, aside from the roof garden, which leads off from the top-floor studio. Here, climbing plants, a sturdy picnic table and chairs, and the children's colorful play equipment happily coexist with the giant skylights. Walter also plans to add a sauna to the roof terrace as an escape from the hectic daily life in the heart of the city.

This apartment is proof that, give or take a few compromises, family living can be adapted to almost any kind of architectural belief and lifestyle. The Chathams have turned an urban loft in the least likely city environment into a calm, beautiful, and functional family home. Their views over downtown Manhattan are the only giveaway of its city location.

Above and right: On the roof terrace, a grown-up eating area
merges into a miniature playground set against the New York skyline.
Left, above and below: A romantically enclosed four-poster bed fits neatly
into the parents' bedroom space and provides a good viewing spot for
keeping an eye on the children at the far end of the loft.

COOKING, EATING, and *entertaining*

COOKING, EATING,

and *entertaining* The kitchen has usurped

RIGHT: A kitchen large enough to include a generous table close to the cooking zone allows family life to mingle with the chores. This knocked-through room contains Shaker-style units that emphasize the architecture of the room rather than producing a tightly fitted atmosphere. A small peninsular unit divides the cooking zone from the eating area, and there is enough storage room for toys and games as well as display space for artistic achievements.

The kitchen is the one area of the home where the entire family assembles to cook, eat, and just *be*. Nowadays, food preparation, cooking, and eating are all part of daily family life, taking place in full view of, and often with the help of, partners, friends, and children. But the kitchen is not only a refueling post where members gather briefly to eat and then disperse in their own directions. It is also host to discussions and plans, work and play, and the inevitable tantrums and tears. In fact, the kitchen is fast replacing the living room as the very core of family life.

34

FAR LEFT: Clutter control is essential in this large, airy room. Unusual stepped kitchen cupboards blend organically into the wall space, while an Arts and Crafts butcher block serves as both counter and decorative center-piece. The comfortable sofa, curtain fabric, and china on the hutch all echo the color of the painted wood splashback, helping the living, dining, and kitchen areas to blend effortlessly together.

LEFT: A country kitchen always seems tailor-made for a family. Here, a traditional Aga offers an enveloping warmth and varied cooking options, while a battered pine table is a prerequisite for a variety of activities, from baking or eating to doing homework or paying the bills – all of family life is here. Stripped wooden floorboards are both rustic and practical, while dark floor tiles delineate the cooking area.

the living room as the very core of modern family life.

All family members are instinctively drawn to the kitchen. It is both the social hub and the inner sanctum of the home, where ravenous teenagers construct colossal sandwiches; a snacking toddler leaves an unmistakable trail of cookie crumbs; or a hungry partner, returning from work, searches in the fridge for "something to keep me going" till dinner.

And then there are the guests: the daytime "droppers-in" who linger for a cup of coffee and a leisurely chat while you load the washing machine, empty the dish-washer, start the ironing, and receive a few telephone calls; or the dinner guests for whom all traces of the previous daytime activities of the children have to be expunged before you embark on a "grown-up" evening of quiet sophistication.

THE IDEAL KITCHEN

The best family kitchen is one that works for you, is easy on the eye and quick to maintain, and is, at best, a comfortable reflection of your lifestyle and collective personality – a place where you are happy to draw in family and friends for entertaining and relaxing.

Nowadays, when many people lead frenetic lives and time is at a premium, everyday chores need to be dealt with in the simplest manner possible. Food is often prepared quickly and eaten in the same room for convenience. The custom of cooking in one room, eating in another, and enjoying a relaxing conversation in yet another is just too impractical for many busy families. They find it much easier to have one room as the focus for all daily life,

with such essentials as a telephone, a bulletin board for family messages, time-saving appliances, and space to cook, eat, and play, all close at hand. Cooking is very much part of living in this type of kitchen, where food can be served effortlessly from oven to table.

Other people, however, like the cooking activities to be tucked away in a small room, or behind a subtle partition. If you prefer to be a "secret chef," unwilling to share your flat soufflés with friends, this arrangement could suit you better than a completely open-plan kitchen/eating area.

TOUCHING BASE

The traditional family breakfast has all but disappeared in households where both parents or single parents go out to work.

BELOW: As this kitchen demonstrates, white cupboards, walls, and tiles do not have to look austere. Here the effect is crisp and snappy because of the black granite counter and pendant lights and the occasional flashes of color. Whimsical touches like life buoy bar stools and fish help prevent a clinical look.

RIGHT: Basement kitchens can often be warmer and more inviting than those swamped with natural light. A reassuring cooking range, natural wood, simple tones of ever-popular blue and white, and a casual informality make this a comfortable place for breakfast or any other family meal.

FAR RIGHT: Even a small corner of a family kitchen can be adapted to provide play space for children.

The morning "getting ready" frenzy too often consists of snatched cups of coffee, checking that the children have everything they need for school, and hurried conversations about who is collecting whom during the day and what time everyone wants dinner. When time is short, it is worth setting the breakfast table the night before, so that even just a few minutes of manic toast-crunching provides a chance for family members to touch base before they rush away to their daily routines.

Yet many families do manage to eat together on the weekends, and if a little time and effort go into these family occasions they can more than make up for the usual weekday chaos. Psychologists frequently remind us of the importance of breaking bread together as a means of family bonding. Sharing a meal is an important time for exchanging news and views and reinforcing relationships, not to mention a chance to enjoy your cooking,

appreciate your best decorating efforts, and take pleasure in your everyday china.

PRIORITIES

If the kitchen is to be the main focus of the home, it should be both comfortable and inspiring, while meeting the modern requirements of practicality and ease of maintenance. You may have inherited a kitchen whose layout fits your needs perfectly, or you may want to customize the cupboards or the space to suit your own requirements.

Fashion invades the kitchen in the same way as decorating fads influence other rooms in the home, but a family kitchen needs to be functional above all else. An industrial-style stainless steel scheme will look impressive but it will also provide a lot of extra polishing work. Similarly, a slick white mass of units will show every streak and mark.

The cooking and storage area can boast discipline and order or a quiet, unfitted informality. As long as there is plentiful storage, adequate appliances, and natural daylight, the decorative touches of furniture, fabric, paint, and accessories will add color and make the room appear welcoming and cozy.

KITCHEN PLANNING

Even in newly built homes, the kitchen can often be one of the smallest rooms, yet it needs to accommodate more items, equipment, and work space than anywhere else in the home. Therefore, when planning a family kitchen, it is important to ask some basic questions before you begin:

BELOW: A kitchen that merges comfortably into the architectural style of a home makes a good family room. This cottage-style arrangement of shelves, dresser, and range tucks neatly into a space around the back door. The range is set into a peninsular unit rather than the more conventional position in an alcove or against a wall.

- Will your kitchen be large enough to double as your main family room? If not, is it worth knocking through into an adjacent room, extending outward, or adding an extension to provide an eating area?
- Is it a place where family members can carry on other activities while you cook?

- Is your home furnished in a specific style and does the kitchen need to match this?
- Are your children of an age that you will want to incorporate activities within the kitchen space? Or are they at a stage when dirty gym clothes will be magnetically drawn to the recently cleaned floor?

ABOVE: A converted industrial building gains in natural light what it loses in the view. Sharp white walls, units, and pendant lights are a graphic statement in a space that is large enough for a generous island unit and a good-sized pine table. The mellow wood table and floor and the blue doors and striped chairs provide effective foils for the white.

RIGHT: Flooded with light, this contemporary kitchen revisits the country style in a successful fusion of comfort and color. Industrial shelving and a hanging rail make use of the floor-to-ceiling area, while the wall of glass bricks stops the room from looking too narrow. A long, rustic table is a nod to country living. Opposite, the sink and appliances run along the wall in a single line.

SPACE PLANNING

Planning or altering a kitchen layout to suit your demands is one of the most important tasks in a family home, so consider all options. An eye-level oven is invaluable for a family with small toddlers. A dishwasher is an additional cost, but think of the time it will save. Adequate storage space is ideal for keeping small appliances and a large *batterie de cuisine* out of sight, while generous countertops are a must for keen cooks.

A well-planned and spacious food-preparation area is particularly important, since preparing food is an integral part of family life, whatever the size of your family.

Once you have established priorities and an achievable goal, whether a weekend revamp, gentle face-lift, or complete refurbishment, space planning is the next step.

A family kitchen does not need to be huge in order to work smoothly and save you time. The main considerations are ease of use, the best possible use of space, low maintenance, good ventilation, space for laundry activities (if not sited elsewhere), appliances that save you time, plenty of work surfaces – and a large trash can.

A small kitchen can work very well if you plan to use it solely as a food-preparation area. Floor-to-ceiling storage and a strict rule about banishing unused paraphernalia will impose its own order on your kitchen contents. If you do not have a utility room, try to place laundry appliances somewhere other than the kitchen (see page 72). Make the space seem bigger by maximizing natural light with bare windows and yellow or cream walls and ceiling, light-colored units, and a floor neutral in tone.

Think about the future, too. At some stage you may have to cater to the needs of more offspring, domestic help, or aging parents. For instance, a stove sited where you will be able to glance up from cooking and check children playing in the backyard, at the kitchen table, or in an adjacent room is a real boon. Counter height is another important consideration in a kitchen used by more than one generation.

Making the best use of limited time and energy is crucial, which is why the so-called "work triangle" devised by time-and-motion experts half a century ago is still relevant today. Think of the working part of the kitchen in terms of three different zones: food storage, preparation, and cooking. The imaginary lines between the fridge, sink, and stove form the work triangle. To be efficient, each side of the triangle should be 4–7ft (1.2-2m), and the total of the three sides no more than 22ft (6.5m). Despite the fact that kitchen design has undergone much reinterpretation, the basic tenets of the work triangle still hold true.

LEFT: With the family table placed in the center of the room, it becomes the natural focus of daily life. The tables with the most character are frequently those scarred by hot drinks, school homework, and crafts, a visual reminder of the routines and rituals of family life.

RIGHT: Sleek, beautiful, and uncompromising in steel and stone, this narrow U-shaped kitchen dares you to be inefficient. Display and storage are as one, and pitted pine would find a place only in the chrome trash can.

These layouts offer classic solutions to kitchen planning that are tried and tested, but you should still gear your layout to your own needs. If you work from home at the kitchen table, incorporate a cupboard unit for storing papers and equipment. If the family is perpetually in and out of the back door with toys, sports equipment, or gardening tools that end up in the way, then allocate some storage space to improve matters.

U-shaped layout

Arranging kitchen units or freestanding elements in a U-shape around the walls creates a cozy, workable layout. Because there is often only one door, this arrangement offers a continuous run of countertop.

L-shaped layout

Arranging the units along two adjacent walls provides an efficient use of space, leaving room for an eating area near the other two walls. For safety and convenience, site the sink and stove on the same side. Where rooms are large or long and narrow, where there is a shortage of wall space, or where awkward corners or doors interrupt space flow, an L-shaped kitchen is ideal.

Galley layout

A galley arrangement has to be economical with appliances as well as clutter. It is a practical layout for a small kitchen or for those who prefer the business end of a family kitchen to be contained, away from the more relaxed eating and communing area. Usually a galley consists of two parallel runs of units, on opposite sides of the room. Allow at least 4ft (1.2m) between the units so that cupboard doors on both sides can be opened simultaneously.

In larger rooms, remember to plan the work triangle so that you don't have to keep turning around or walking a long way. Do not position the fridge at the dining end of a kitchen, for example. Avoid bottlenecks caused by siting appliances like the stove and the dishwasher next to each other.

Think about safety. A stove should be positioned with adequate counter space, ideally in a heatproof material, on either side. Avoid siting it in a corner, where access is limited. (However, a stove placed *across* a corner can work well.) Never put a stove by a window. The best position for the main countertop is down one side of the triangle, between the stove and sink.

CLASSIC LAYOUTS

When designing units and storage, stick to a simple plan. Think about what you need to store and how you want the result to look. Remember that plumbing is usually the most expensive aspect to alter in a refurbishment, so you may wish to leave the sink where it is and design around it.

There are several classic layouts for kitchen units. You can incorporate elements of more than one if you wish (and if space permits), or you can economize and free your creative instincts by installing the bare essentials of sink, stove, and fridge and then filling in the gaps with other freestanding pieces (see page 47).

The best work triangle for this layout is to place the fridge on one side and the sink and stove on the other. The galley layout is often used in rooms where doors open out into the backyard, so bear safety in mind when opting for this scheme, since the work space may double as a main thoroughfare.

Single-line layout

Often the only option in a small room, the single-line kitchen can be extremely efficient, though fitting in enough countertop may be tricky. The sink should be in the middle of the run, between the stove and fridge. Try to use floor-to-ceiling storage so you can cram in as much as possible. This could mean having wall cupboards specially made to maximize storage space. Place little-used items high up and edit your kitchen contents before planning the space.

Island layout

An island unit, whether fixed or movable, provides additional work and storage space in a U- or L-shaped layout. It works best in a larger kitchen, where its presence does not impede movement around and to the sink, stove, and fridge. The island provides a possible site for the stove or sink (though both are better on an outside wall) – or for a second sink. For keen cooks or for large families, additional burners may be added to the unit, allowing two people to prepare separate meals, maybe one for each generation. Remember, however, that a sink, stove-top, or power points will require plumbing, gas, or electricity. With a stove you might want an overhead extractor, or a downdraft type of extractor built into the stove itself. You could also incorporate a small eating bar for snacks and breakfasts.

DEFINING AREAS

Once you have settled on your layout, there are ways of defining a space or demarcating cooking, eating, and relaxation areas. You can vary the floor covering, wall color, and styles of decoration. Folding doors or screens work well, as do waist-high dividers in glass bricks and curved counter-tops of wood, laminate, metal, or mosaic.

KITCHEN STYLE

Kitchen style is a matter of personal preference, although the demands of a busy family make some styles more appealing. If you aim for simplicity in all things, you should be able to save time and effort.

The country look

For many, the relaxed style of the country kitchen, with its range, ceiling airing rack, and informal furnishings, is the epitome of the family kitchen. Roomy, not too polished in appearance or radical in its structure, it is a nurturing, comfortable environment.

In many homes, country style has gradually given way to a simple, soft, modern approach. Painted units or hutches have evolved into wood-and-white rooms, where unnecessary embellishment is banned. Nevertheless, country style will endure, as it does suit family life. Mismatching, battered tables and chairs, simple curtains, and the reassuring warmth of the range are irresistible to many people.

This look is easy to create. Standard wooden units can be painted or stained. The "unfitted-kitchen" approach (see page 47) works well for a rural ethos. A butler's sink surrounded by a wooden work surface and curtained storage works well with an armoire or hutch for food and dishes, while utensils are displayed on the walls. A stove can be countrified with a surround of earth-colored or brightly clashing wall tiles. Decorate the table with checked or floral accessories; dot storage baskets around the room; suspend smaller baskets and kitchenalia on hanging racks; arrange china on a hutch or sideboard.

Urban sophistication

In most households, absence of clutter is a state aspired to but never quite achieved. The modern mantra of light, space, and simplicity, however, can work well in a simple family home, as long as the strict rules of minimalism are not taken too seriously. Urban chic need not mean soulless steel or minimal style taken to extremes.

Color, fabric, and tiles all have a place in urban schemes. Simple blinds look right, while tiles in black and white, blue and biscuit, or orange and lemon work well. Work surfaces in granite-effect laminate or in beech cut into wavy shapes would be neat options. State-of-the-art appliances now come in curvy shapes and bold colors as well as streamlined stainless steel.

KITCHEN APPLIANCES

Appearing on the market are ever more appealing appliances in diverse shapes, sizes, and colors, all designed to lighten the kitchen workload. They can be genuine time-savers if chosen with care. Some are indispensable, others fairly useful, and still others purely indulgent.

OVENS, STOVES, AND RANGES

For keen cooks, choosing the right oven is of paramount importance. Even if you spend the minimum amount of time required to cook a family meal, well thought-out cooking appliances will be both efficient and practical for all to use.

When children are small, eye-level ovens, which are out of their reach, are the best solution. Many people prefer these anyway as they are easy to use without bending down. The downside of ranges – oven and stove in one unit, keeping all cooking activities in one place – is that they are less safe with young children around and require frequent bending down.

Double ovens are invaluable for families. The smaller oven usually includes a broiler, so you can prepare an early meal for children while cooking the adults' dinner in the main oven. Similarly, you can batch-bake cakes and cookies in both ovens if the desire for an old-fashioned baking day overcomes you. Many ovens are available now with a combined broiler, rotisserie, fan option, and microwave capability.

Many British homes boast an Aga-type range (as shown above), despite the heavy initial investment. You can cook virtually anything on such a range once you have become accustomed to its individual cooking methods. Agas are powered by solid fuel (wood or coal), oil, gas, or electricity. They produce a constant heat source, and some will also heat radiators and water.

Semiprofessional, heavy-duty cooking ranges are also on the increase. Versatile but expensive, they often combine gas burners with hot plates, built-in griddles, broilers, and ovens with rotisseries. They make sense if you have a large family and plenty of space in the kitchen.

Stove-tops can be separate from ovens, but more typical is a single unit combining the stove and oven. Some units have two ovens, one of which contains a broiler. If you have young children, make sure that the controls are out of reach and that the oven door(s) is well insulated so that it remains cool in use.

Gas burners are always popular because the heat can be adjusted instantly. Some gas stoves have fold-down lids. A dual-fuel stove with two electric rings and two gas burners is versatile but can be limiting if you are used to using four gas burners at once. Electric burners – either radiant rings, sealed or solid hot plates, or ceramic – are less responsive than gas, but some people prefer not to have an open flame. A magnetic induction ceramic stove-top generates magnetic energy so that only the pan (which must be ferrous) and its contents become hot; the stove-top stays cool. A halogen ceramic stove-top cooks by light and will heat up and cool down very quickly. Whatever type of stove you have, do use a stove guard while your children are small.

EXTRACTORS

Heat extraction is a must in a busy family kitchen, to prevent the buildup of both

LEFT: A steam oven, with a slide-up door concealing the steamer, is combined here with a conventional oven. Ovens built into units at eye level are safe and efficient for old and young alike. Placing them within reach of the table and counters makes serving meals easier.

steam and cooking odors. The most efficient models are ducted and therefore work best if attached to an outside wall, in order to keep the ducting as short as possible. If this is not possible, for example on an island unit, you can install an expensive hood with a powerful motor. Also available are downdraft extractors that are built in on either side of a stove, with only the metal grills visible.

MICROWAVE OVENS

In a busy family kitchen with meals being eaten at different times, microwave ovens are most frequently used for instant heating, reheating, or defrosting, or for quick and nutritious meals such as baked potatoes. Buy the most powerful version you can afford, since a 650- or 750-watt microwave oven is much more versatile and faster than the standard, less expensive models. Older

Siting appliances

Always try to avoid siting a dishwasher, boiler, stove, or radiator next to the refrigerator or freezer, because the heat they give off will force the fridge or freezer to work harder.

*

The most efficient extractors expel air outside and so work best when on an outside wall, so that the ducting is as short as possible. A stove and extractor should therefore be sited on or adjacent to an outside wall where possible.

*

A dishwasher and a washing machine should be placed as close as possible to the water source, i.e., near the kitchen sink to avoid expense when installing plumbing. Most tumble dryers will also need ducting to an outside wall.

*

To make the most of limited space in a kitchen, build in a microwave oven or replace a conventional oven with a combination oven/microwave.

*

Avoid having a door between the sink and the stove.

LEFT: Solid and timeless, a four-oven Aga slips neatly into a bright alcove for cooking with a view. Constantly warm, it is always at the ready for a quick bake.

RIGHT: Whatever else you have near your stove, an extractor of somekind is essential. Here an extractor hood forms a modern still-life with an orderly row of utensils of exactly the same width as the stove and extractor.

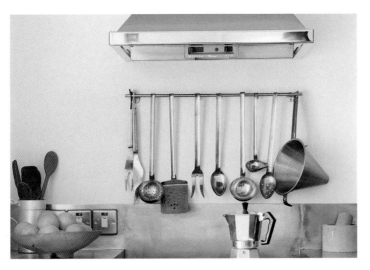

children love cooking their own popcorn, and built-in models will give them easy access when they want to help themselves.

DISHWASHERS

Some appliances really do change your life, and this is one of them. Once you have owned a dishwasher, it is difficult to contemplate ever again facing a pile of dirty dishes after a meal. If you don't have enough room for a full-width one, a slim-line version will still help you escape the drudgery of washing dishes (though they can be more costly than standard versions). Make sure that there will be room to walk around the door when it is open. Many models also have a built-in timer so that the machine can be run at night.

You will have to make sure you have enough glasses, dishes and cutlery to enable you to run the machine only once a day or so. Make it a policy only to buy china and pots that are dishwasher-safe. And be sure to train older children and teenagers to rinse and put dirty dishes straight into the machine rather than simply stacking them on the counter.

WASHING MACHINES AND DRYERS

In apartments, where space is at a premium, the kitchen is also the laundry room. Clothes washing is a major chore in a family home, making a washing machine one of life's indispensables. The bigger the family, the more important the machine's role in the domestic scene. Top-loaders tend to have a larger capacity than front-loaders. A combination washer–dryer makes efficient use of space but is rarely as effective or fault-free as a conventional washing machine. And, of course, washing and

drying more than one load in a combination machine will take longer than a washer and separate dryer working simultaneously.

Since family washing machines are generally used at least once a day, it pays to buy a robust model, though it does not have to be the most high-tech machine. A wide range of settings is not important, since in practice most families only use the same two or three settings. More important is to choose a model economical on water and power. Extras worth having include a half-load setting and a quick-wash option. Child locks can be attached to washing-machine doors for the early years to prevent the mysterious disappearance of the pet cat or Junior's favorite teddy bear.

Most laundry rooms also have a dryer; hanging the laundry out to dry is not an option for most busy families. However,

powerful dryers do shrink certain fabrics, so always line-dry any delicates such as silk, linen, or shrinkable cotton.

REFRIGERATORS AND FREEZERS

Today's fridges and freezers are compartmentalized in ingenious ways to cater to the different kinds of foods and packaging supplied to us by supermarkets. Can holders, bottle holders, jar containers, and fresh-fruit and chilled-meat compartments are all now found in a standard fridge. It is the size and configuration of fridge to freezer that vary so much. Self-defrosting models are improving and more widely available.

When choosing a fridge and freezer, decide what kind of cook you are. If you regularly cook batches of soups, stews, cakes, or desserts that freeze well, make sure your freezer compartment will be able to store these items. It is good to keep a permanent store of convenience food – pizzas, oven-bake French fries, frozen vegetables, and ice cream – for when your children have unexpected visitors.

Fridges, freezers, and combination fridge-freezers range from enormous free-standing models to tiny individual drawers. Buy the largest you can find room for – it will never seem empty. One option is the model with freezer compartment above the refrigerator. With the increased popularity of frozen foods, however, this is often replaced by the side-by-side model, offering as much freezer space as fridge space. For a streamlined kitchen, choose a built-in model that is flush with other units. Some of these models have constant supplies of chilled water and crushed ice, deep door space with sensible compartments for storing large cartons of milk and fruit juice

LEFT: The doors or fronts of appliances like fridges, dishwashers, and laundry equipment can be covered with panels that match the cupboard doors in the rest of the kitchen. It is often more visually appealing to look at a neat line of regular units than at a space punctuated with shiny white appliances to remind you of the chores.

LEFT: Some smaller appliances save time and effort in the cooking process. To make them as accessible as possible, store them in an appliance "garage" at the back of an extra-deep countertop so that they can simply be slid out instead of having to be lifted. A cupboard door or roll-up shutter keeps them clean.

and big bottles of water, as well as a lot of space for food in the fridge section.

A good spot for an extra fridge or freezer is in the garage or under the stairs. A chest freezer here can be used for large cuts of meat, out-of-season fruit, and large batches of fresh-frozen food or cooked meals for emergencies. In hot climates, a fridge devoted to cooling drinks is a good idea.

GARBAGE-DISPOSAL SYSTEMS

If you are planning a kitchen from scratch, it is worth considering a garbage-disposal unit for organic waste. It reduces the amount of trash you have to put out each week and is a fast way of clearing up after food preparation. If, however, you save organic waste for a compost heap, a garbage-disposal unit is much less useful. Electric trash compactors are available, too. These compress inorganic waste into flat packs that are easier to dispose of.

SMALL APPLIANCES

Don't bother with so-called time-savers such as electric carving knives or electric can openers. However, the ultimate time-saver, a food processor, is invaluable in a family home. Store it where it is easily accessed and use it often for chopping, grating, and creating winter soups, cake batters, sauces, and much more. A blender is indispensable for puréeing baby food and creating summer smoothies — from milkshakes to fruit punches and cocktails.

Less of a necessity but nice to have are an electric juicer, mixer, filter or espresso/ cappuccino coffeemaker, coffee grinder, and toaster or toaster-oven. Toaster-ovens will toast, broil and oven-bake small amounts of food. They are freestanding but do not take up much space on a countertop.

STORAGE

Kitchen storage is a complex affair, with kitchen designers forever inventing new ways of storing spice jars, pans, and wine bottles, not to mention all the usual tableware and cooking utensils.

FITTED UNITS

Fitted units still remain the most space-efficient means of containing the myriad bits and pieces vital to the smooth functioning of a kitchen. If everything you are likely to need has its own easy-to-find home, the huge amount of time you spend in the kitchen will become much more enjoyable. For example, a pull-out larder in a fitted scheme saves space, promotes ease of access, and also encourages a regular turnover of tired jars that are reminders of past culinary misadventures.

When fitting a kitchen, make a list of absolutely everything you will need to store, and if starting from scratch, incorporate a variety of cupboards to cater to all the different elements. Ready-made kitchen units are available in a bewildering quantity of sizes, configurations, and materials, so it is best to start with a fixed idea of the look you are after before embarking on a great style hunt.

Apart from the luxury, custom-made end of the market, the unit carcasses are usually made from inexpensive painted or laminated wood and finished with an infinite choice of doors, ranging from solid wood such as beech, oak, or ash to colored laminates, hand-painted MDF (medium-density fiberboard), wood veneer, and, for the chic industrial look, stainless steel.

Work out your overall budget and choose your materials accordingly. Family kitchens take a good battering from children and their toys, so keep a practical eye on your choice of finishes, forgoing the hand-painted and finished cupboards if your children are still young. If you are worried that a long run of units may look rather bland, think about enlivening it with one or two wall cupboards comprising glass doors, interior lighting, and a stylish collection of glassware or china.

SIMPLE FACE-LIFTS FOR UNITS

Existing units can be given a face-lift without the expense of replacing them. New doors can be put on the old carcasses, or the old doors can be removed, sanded down, and then painted and varnished. (If the units are faced with laminate, you will need to use a specialist paint or primer.)

Basic cupboards can be cunningly lifted from mundane to interesting by cutting out

each central panel with a router so that a lip is left on the inside. Attach chicken-wire, glass, or a metal grille to the lip, and back the opening with fabric if desired.

Even just adding decorative beading or cornicing can make a plausible transformation when finished off with new door hardware. In fact, replacing the handles alone sometimes creates a whole new look. Door hardware can be as rustic as simple wooden knobs or as flashy as chrome pulls, more sculpture than handle. Old shop handles look good, as do long stainless steel handles.

Choose door hardware that each member of the family will be able to use without effort. People with arthritis or rheumatism will cope more easily with push-action magnetic catches than with spindly drawer handles. Special ergonomic handles are also available.

UNFITTED KITCHENS

As kitchens become more multifunctional, the conventional concept of fitted units arranged in one of the traditional layouts (see page 40) is increasingly open to interpretation. Influential kitchen designers have produced custom-made kitchens that barely look like cooking areas. Relaxed, graciously proportioned spaces furnished with flowing curves, delicate woodwork, and sympathetic color disguise function while highlighting comfort and cohesive decoration.

The advantage of an unfitted approach to kitchen units is flexibility. Once the sink and stove are in position, the rest of the space is yours to lay out as you please. In some countries, people always take their kitchen with them when they move house, and this idea is gradually gaining ground.

ABOVE: Neat pigeonholes positioned above a solid counter work as a storage area, combining function and display.

LEFT: A compact alcove is home to the kitchen sink, wall-mounted metal racks for china, and terracotta pots for utensils. The racks allow china to drain straight into the sink.

An unfitted kitchen can be dismantled and rearranged over the years according to the current needs of the family. You may start with a modest hutch for storing china and progress to a series of freestanding console tables and dramatic armoires or

a range of tough chrome shelving where display is everything. An unfitted scheme is flexible enough to accommodate the family's prevailing work-flow – the routes taken between the work surfaces, sink, appliances, and doors.

CUPBOARDS AND SHELVES

A freestanding cupboard, meat safe, or armoire, or even an old wardrobe, is ideal

ABOVE: Simple wooden unit doors are each painted a different vivid color to break up a run of uniform cupboards on a wall of strong color. Ordinary emulsion paint needs to have several coats of dead flat acrylic varnish applied to protect it from condensation and also to make it easier to keep clean.

Freestanding cabinets and wrought-iron baker's racks are decorative in their own right. Loaded with piles of china, table linen, gleaming pans, chunky candles, interesting ceramics, and generous bowls of fruit, they quickly become major features in a kitchen. They will inevitably also become home to school letters, unpaid bills, junk mail, and car keys, but their basic function is sound, their innate beauty reassuring. However, remember how easily dust can gather, and only display frequently used items that have no time to turn into "clean me" guilt-trippers.

Open shelving is another versatile storage option. Use shelves to store cookbooks within sight, to house mugs on cup hooks, and to hold small baskets of bills

and receipts. Fitted with rails or pegs underneath, open shelves provide homes for pots, pans, or china. Pigeonhole units, either freestanding or wall-mounted, can be used to store items such as children's assorted craft materials, sewing repair kits, magazines, napkins, candles, and baskets of vegetables.

STORAGE SOLUTIONS

Small-scale storage provides a pleasing change of scale and good space management in a kitchen.

Specialist items

Tall, narrow wine racks can be built in vertically between wall units or slotted into a standard cabinet space or a narrow gap

LEFT: Purpose-built storage will fit a space perfectly and allows you to incorporate into a scheme elements such as baskets, neat drawers, pigeonholes, or wine racks. Here, deep wicker baskets fit into pigeonholes under a counter, disguising anything from vegetables or piles of table linen to large toys or muddy shoes. A similar effect can be created using freestanding wooden furniture and basket drawers.

RIGHT: Simple cupboard doors may reveal surprisingly organized interiors. Cooks in large families need many pans, and pull-out storage below the stove-top is more accessible than shelves inside cupboards. Partitions in the top section are ideal for lids.

for storing everything that doesn't fit into wall cupboards or a pull-out larder and works equally well in either a fitted or an unfitted kitchen. Similarly, a walk-in pantry built into a corner of the room makes a splendid larder. Fitted with deep, wide shelves, it is instantly practical and visually appealing, particularly when stocked with intriguing storage jars and homemade preserves. If space is tight, turn an old cabinet with a glass door into a wall larder where your most-used ingredients will be immediately visible.

RIGHT: In this small, colorful kitchen, open shelving and wall-mounted cabinets with glass doors allow a lot of china to be crammed into a tiny space, showing it off to best advantage. Beneath, there is still space for utensil storage and an egg cabinet, allowing the work space to remain clear when cooking is in progress.

beneath a counter. Butcher blocks often provide space underneath for slotting in wine bottles, while freestanding chrome wine trolleys are good for transporting bottles around the room.

Don't store wine too near a heat source such as the oven, however, since it needs to be kept at a constant temperature. Ideally this is around 55°F (13°C – much cooler than most kitchens – so it might be better to keep only a few bottles in the kitchen and any further stocks in a cool bedroom, entrance hall, utility room, or basement.)

Herbs and spices should be kept in the dark, but they have to be accessible so make a feature of wooden, chrome, or stainless steel containers. A revolving tray, or lazy Susan, placed inside a cupboard allows easy access to the cook's full range of herbs and spices.

Cooking equipment

Pots and pans need to be close at hand and near the stove. Suspend them upside down from their handles on a hanging rack or wall-mounted curved metal hanger. With an oven set at eye level, open shelves or built-in drawers are also useful. Casseroles and other large pans look attractive arranged on sturdy open shelves or underneath a butcher block, or on industrial-style metal shelving.

Tableware

Store everyday tableware as close as possible to the dishwasher and sink, either on a wall-mounted open plate rack, from which they can drain straight into the sink, or in a cupboard. Decorative china looks good on a hutch, though if you want to use it occasionally, you will probably have to wash it first. Basic cutlery, especially children's cutlery, can find a home in a table or hutch drawer. Keep serving dishes near the oven, jugs for juice near the fridge, and cutting knives near the main counter.

Pantry ingredients

Store much-used food where it is easily accessible to the whole family, apart from the very young. If your eating area is well away from the cooking zone, consider having two smaller pantries – one to keep cereal, condiments, and other provisions near where you eat, and the other to store cooking ingredients near the stove.

User-friendly kitchens

When children are small, try to incorporate a safe corner for them in the kitchen. Give them a cupboard of their own where they can rummage among old pots, pans, and wooden spoons in imitation of your culinary creations.

*

Store frequently used items at waist-height or above to minimize bending.

*

Have a "hold-all" container handy for teenage clutter – sports equipment, shoes, school books, and so on.

*

A combined radio, tape recorder, and CD player is a good companion for kitchen users of all ages, to play classical music, educational tapes, toddlers' story tapes, the news, or loud rock, according to the generation. Include CD storage in the form of a box, a shelf, or a freestanding unit to minimize clutter.

Odds and ends

Reserve a space somewhere in the kitchen (or under the stairs, in the garage, or in a shed) for nonperishable items that are more economical bought in bulk, such as bottled water, toilet paper, paper towels, bottles of juice, lightbulbs, and cleaning materials. Always include a pack of candles in your long-term storage and remember where your matches are in the kitchen (up high, out of reach of the children) in case you have a power outage. Keep a flashlight handy, too.

In a family kitchen it is worth devoting one cupboard or drawer, preferably well out of children's reach, to snacks, treats, and cake-decorating paraphernalia. You will inevitably accumulate novelty cookie cutters, cake pans, and cake decorations, so store these alongside cookies and candy bars reserved for special occasions.

FEEDING A FAMILY

Preparing meals for a family can be a repetitive business. No sooner is a chaotic breakfast eaten and cleared than thoughts turn to lunch and an evening meal. What most family homes need are conveniently stored food, easy-to-access cooking equipment, and a comfortable place to prepare a meal at speed and with ease. Good organization is essential if you are going to achieve the time-efficient, healthy meals that are the key to surviving modern family life.

PREPARING FOR THE CHOP

Chopping ingredients forms a major part in the food-preparation process, so take some time to think about utensils and equipment.

A good, sharp set of knives is essential, as long as they are kept in a safe place, preferably in a knife block, well out of reach of young children.

Next in importance is a solid wood chopping board. Research has shown that a wooden chopping board keeps bacteria at bay just as well as an ugly synthetic one. Reserve separate boards for vegetables, meat, fish, and garlic or onions. Always clean thoroughly in soapy water after use.

Keep a marble slab handy for rolling out pastry if you haven't built in a marble surface within a countertop.

If work surfaces are limited, a butcher's block on casters provides an additional preparation area. Knives can be stored in it if children are old enough to be careful with them, and baskets underneath can be used for keeping vegetables fresh and out of the light.

EVERYDAY UTENSILS

Regularly used utensils can be stored in pots or hung on butcher's hooks from rails or from wall- or ceiling-mounted racks. Not only are items like colanders, sieves, cake racks, whisks, spatulas, and slotted spoons close at hand when you need them, but they make interesting decorative items in their own right. Another benefit of storing them within sight is that dinner guests are positively encouraged to roll up their sleeves and help with the meal.

FAR LEFT: A base-unit door with an extra top section creates a useful counter extension, with a caster underneath providing a movable support for it. The inside of the door is fitted with curved racks.

LEFT: Grow fresh herbs all year-round in pots on a windowsill or other warm, sunny spot.

RIGHT: A solid butcher block with knife storage makes a convenient food preparation area. Deep drawers and cupboards house cutlery and utensils behind doors that match the adjoining units. Varying counter heights and materials according to the activity for which they are intended makes good ergonomic sense.

BELOW: Racks fitted to the ceiling above an island stove-top allow pots and pans to be stored close at hand. They also serve as decorative devices in an otherwise neat, ordered kitchen. The generous counter space surrounding the stove allows plenty of room for food preparation, making the island particularly useful.

SENSIBLE SHOPPING

Keeping a constant supply of staple foods will enable you to feed your offspring's friends after school and to cook instant dinners for unexpected visitors, as well as provide a quick fallback for days when your time is short or your energy failing.

An ongoing shopping list in an accessible place is a necessity. Encourage the rest of the family to write down those things that

LEFT: In this spacious kitchen, custom-made cupboards extend right up to the sloping ceiling, tracing the architectural lines of the space. The huge amount of storage allows much paraphernalia to be hidden from view, but a distinctive collection of stainless steel pans and utensils is displayed around the room.

51

are running out and their personal requirements. You can decide whether to ignore demands for catering-size quantities of chocolate-chip cookies. If you have a computer, keep a permanent list of perennial requirements, then print out lists every so often and simply check or highlight the items you need. It saves having to resort to scraps of paper torn from the bottom of bills or from children's precious artwork.

Examine your eating habits, taking into account any special dietary requirements and what produce is in season, then shop and store accordingly. Try doing one huge shop each month for pantry staples, then stock up in between just with fresh produce. This is a good way to reduce the quantities of surplus food you are tempted to buy whenever you visit the supermarket.

LIFESAVERS FROM CANS

Many a delicious supper emanates from a can. Tuna, anchovies, canned tomatoes, borlotti beans, lima beans, olives, or chickpeas can become fresh pasta sauces, Provençal salads, or Italian minestrones. And you can use the can afterwards (provided there are no sharp edges where the lid was removed) for storing paintbrushes, pencils and tiny odds and ends.

Baked beans, canned spaghetti (when you are desperate), and canned fruit salad can often save the day when you have stepped through the door with tired and emotional offspring suffering from low blood-sugar levels.

The inevitable ketchup for youngsters, culinary treats such as properly aged balsamic vinegar, mushroom ketchup, soy sauce, and chili sauce can enliven most pantry concoctions.

ABOVE: Store condiments where they are needed – in this case, next to the TV in a beech unit that looks more like a piece of furniture than a cupboard. A slimline pull-out unit fits neatly into a tight space and is ideal for storing small jars, cans and bottles, as it allows access even to those seldom-used items right at the back.

FRIDGE AND FREEZER STANDBYS

Fresh ingredients really do make the difference, even in hastily prepared dishes. Fridges keep peppers, fruit, salad ingredients, and vegetables fresher for longer.

There are a few cheats you can use instead of fresh ingredients. Keep a supply of bottled lemon juice, fresh-frozen herbs, and fresh ginger in the freezer (simply slice off a frozen piece). Keep loaves of sliced bread, focaccia, ciabatta, and pita bread in the freezer – great for off-the-cuff snacks.

Other freezer standbys include minestrone, watercress, or vichyssoise soup for filling suppers; mild to medium curries (chili dishes somehow get hotter when

defrosted and heated), lasagne, and moussaka; individual servings of pasta sauce; and pizza bases. Frozen vegetables such as green beans, spinach, peas, and corn are staples of many a child's supper. Another standby is a chicken dish braised in tomatoes and peppers. Serve it to children with potatoes and to adults jazzed up with paprika, sour cream, and saffron rice.

BAKING DAYS

Baking can coincide with entertaining the children, particularly if your kitchen allows you space to accommodate youngsters who want to help. The days when pies were batch-baked at the beginning of the week and bore different decorations according to their "eat-by" days are long gone, but the idea of baking for the family is a ritual enjoying a comeback. To encourage budding chefs, keep a supply of flour, sugar, eggs, paper cupcake liners, and chocolate sprinkles alongside quick and easy recipes. The best concoctions are those that can be mixed together in a bowl, such as an all-in-one chocolate cake recipe that can be used for a standard cake or cupcakes. Bake several batches at once and freeze some.

MEAL PLANNING

Family members by necessity often eat on different timetables from one another. To avoid having to cook three different dinners at three different times, try adapting one dish to feed all comers, such as schoolchildren at 5pm, a middle sitting (two older children and one parent) at 7pm, and a late arrival or still-hungry teenager between 8 and 9pm. Choose recipes that don't suffer when kept in the oven or reheated in the microwave. Adding "grown-up" ingredients like sun-dried tomatoes or wine is sometimes all that is needed to turn the bland flavors preferred by children into something interesting enough for an adult palate.

Talk to children about the relative merits of protein, carbohydrates, and fiber and they will eventually realize that it isn't necessary to eat vast quantities of vegetables every day in order to stay healthy. To children the old adage about eating carrots to see in the dark may be less of an incentive than "If you eat a banana each day your feet may soon grow enough for new shoes."

LEFT: Simple floor-to-ceiling open shelving, finished off with decorative cornicing at the top and a small baseboard at the bottom, makes a fitted kitchen corner more informal and accessible. A tiny island unit also includes one side of open shelves.

BELOW: Pasta, pulses, and garlic combine with glass and steel to make a striking still life on these simple shelves.

BELOW: A walk-in pantry makes the perfect spot for keeping nonperishable foods in one place. A mixture of deep and narrow shelves on three sides provides adaptable storage, so you can always see what you have and whether it is running out or fast approaching its expiration date. Glass doors increase visibility even more. A perpetual shopping list hung on the wall could send you into efficiency overdrive!

ENTERTAINING

Entertaining in a family home is always easier to handle if you know your limitations and don't let ambition overtake the time you have available. When you have small children, the idea of spending all day preparing a sumptuous four-course meal complete with imaginative table setting and a sparklingly clean house does not seem quite as appealing, or even remotely possible, as it once did. However, the same impression can be created with a careful choice of menu.

One theory is that if you always invite someone over one day or one evening each week, your house will at least have to be straightened up, however cursorily. Make it a rule to go out on a regular basis, too. Getting a friend to babysit encourages you to take a critical look at the indecently high ironing pile and the stove that has seen cleaner days.

MULTIGENERATION PARTIES

Try inviting another family for breakfast or brunch instead of lunch or dinner. Children are often at their best in the morning and a change of routine is usually welcome. A spread offering smoked salmon, bagels and a range of flavored cream cheeses will please all palates, young and old alike.

RIGHT: More formal entertaining, such as an adults' dinner party, can be carried out with a minimum of fuss. Friends come to see you rather than your latest culinary marathon involving long absences before and during the meal, so make sure that the food does not take over. A comfortable, relaxed atmosphere, well-considered table, and dimmed lighting are also important.

LEFT: More informal entertaining means that children and adults can enjoy themselves to the same degree. Decide how many people your home and/or yard can hold and work from there. Invite a range of ages and serve food that can be prepared in advance or assembled on the day of the event.

Another way to escape the routine of mealtimes is a picnic. Leave the house behind, forget about mess (existing or potential), and enjoy the fresh air. Pack clothes, food, and drinks appropriate to the weather.

Throw a multigeneration cocktail party starting late morning or early afternoon. A cold spread is always easier to prepare and present than a formal sit-down meal. You can offer a variety of nonalcoholic drinks,

including fancy punches. Mixing the generations means that younger teenagers can be put in charge of the little ones' entertainment, so that the hosts get to talk to all their guests. Allocate a room for the children, a general gathering space for all guests, and a quiet room for those who want to sit down.

A potluck party also works particularly well when you want to have a get-together but don't have a lot of preparation time or money. Each invited family brings a dish with them, be it appetizer, salad, vegetable dish, or dessert. The hosts decide in advance what they themselves will prepare and then wait for the offers to come in. If everyone brings their own culinary success story, the result is very often a gastronomic extravaganza. (The hosts can eat the left-overs, too!)

TABLE SETTINGS

For an exclusively grown-up gathering, choose crisp white table linen, understated white china, pristine glasses, and gleaming cutlery. Finish it off with a simple arrangement of white flowers and greenery highlighted with white candles and handwritten place cards. Stylish and serene.

At the other end of the scale, informal entertaining is all about creating a sense of welcome with mismatched plates, jugs of garden flowers instead of elegant vases, a couple of checked tablecloths overlapped on a large table, and a mishmash of napkins, napkin rings, and unstemmed glasses reflecting a thrown-together but homey atmosphere. Be careful that you are not so laid-back that all the chipped china makes its way onto the table, though. Baskets containing seasonal pots of flowers such as snowdrops, hyacinths, winter berries, and lavender make delightful centerpieces, but make sure their scent is not so intoxicating that it upstage the food.

Entertaining for celebrations such as birthdays or holidays is more memorable if tiny gifts are prepared for the guests. Hand-painted pots containing homemade chocolates or preserves, dried hydrangeas tied with ribbons, herb-scented olive oils, or hand-decorated boxes of potpourri will make guests feel special.

Creating a welcome

Always have a vase of fresh flowers somewhere near the eating area. Even some simple greenery cut from the garden will show that you care about your surroundings.

Keep bottles of wine, juice, and mineral water, as well as olives or other nibbles, handy for unexpected evening visitors.

*

Candles transform the atmosphere and place the accent firmly on a table and the conversation. Keep a supply of night-lights, pillarcandles, oversized round ones, and a variety of candle holders. Use at least four candles when there are four to six diners, and six candles for eight people.

*

Music is an important backdrop and can enrich or ruin a special atmosphere.

*

Replace the plastic tablecloth with a freshly laundered linen cloth with a basket of fabric napkins for an instant transformation.

*

Always check special dietary requirements of guests beforehand. Keep a note of friends' particular allergies, such as strawberries, shellfish, or nuts.

*

The best children's parties for enjoyment and ease of organization are themed ones. Make perennially favorite games such as large pictures of treasure maps, a donkey with a detachable tail, and a giant hopscotch mat and reuse them year after year.

KITCHEN WALLS

The walls of a family kitchen, as the nerve center of a busy home, need to be welcoming, cheerful, and tough as they have to withstand harsh treatment. Temperature changes, cooking oil splashes, food and drink spills, and knocks from toddlers' toys mean that kitchen walls are the most vulnerable in the home.

SUITABLE PAINTS

BELOW: Not so much a wall, more a color extravaganza in this compact kitchen. Bright blue tiles and mosaic borders merge into orange shelves for a simple but funky space-saving device. The stepped top of the splashback behind the stove avoids having too many horizontal lines.

Kitchens generate steam and moisture in the same way that bathrooms do, so choose paint accordingly. Hard-wearing oil-based paints such as eggshell and gloss or specialist kitchen paints work best as they withstand constant exposure to condensation. Vinyl silk emulsion is also a good choice. Vinyl matte emulsion is not as easy to clean, but can be used over a large area as long as you seal it with matte acrylic varnish.

If you want to change the color scheme of your kitchen, painting the walls is a less drastic option than painting the units. It is only a day's job to transform walls with a pot of Monet yellow or Modernist turquoise, but quite another thing to remove all the cupboard doors, sand them down, and apply a radical change of color and mood.

OTHER WALL COVERINGS

A vinyl wall covering can be used, but avoid ordinary spongeable wallpaper in the kitchen, as condensation will quickly cause it to attract mold and peel off. The splashback area between wall cupboards and counters calls for a robust, easy-to-clean surface such as tiles, stainless steel sheeting, laminate, or varnished wood paneling.

TILES

Tiles can be expensive and handmade, cheap and cheerful, or somewhere in between. They can be placed above sinks and behind stoves for the practical purpose of resisting splashes (though the grouting can be difficult to clean), or along a run of units to provide interest and color.

Mosaic tiles usually come as small tiles stuck to a 12in (30cm) paper square, which is peeled off after they have been secured in place, so that the chips do not have to be stuck on one by one. Use mosaics on their own or to break up expanses of conventional tiles. To liven up a plain tiled surface,

ABOVE: When counters and cupboards are all steel or one color, brightly colored walls provide a room with a sharp uplift. Here, deep primrose kitchen walls contrast subtly with a shade of apple green in the dining area.

RIGHT: Midnight blue walls above the units focus attention on the neat lines of wood and stainless steel in this streamlined contemporary kitchen.

Decoration ideas

In a weekend you can retile splashbacks or apply a completely different material to give your kitchen a new look.

✳

Mix materials for interest. Plain wood cupboards are more striking for the addition of a dark slate splashback or bold wall color, while painted cupboards look good against either plain white tiles or a neutral backdrop.

✳

Paint the walls with either oil-based eggshell or vinyl silk emulsion, then add decoration in the form of stencilled single line borders, stamped geometric motifs, or painted dado-height panels of different colors.

✳

Add a wall panel either of cork or plywood painted with blackboard paint for shopping lists and reminders and for displaying children's artwork and party invitations (see pages 88-89 for ideas).

✳

To avoid having to decorate a new extension, leave bare plaster exposed and rub in diluted red paint pigment to give the effect of a colorwash. Or, for a chalky effect, mix the paint into the plaster before it is applied. Seal the wall with a coat or two of matte varnish.

---

stencil or hand-paint a motif onto them (using specialist tile paint or primer so that it will withstand repeated washing).

COLOR IN THE KITCHEN

Color is an economical, effective way of transforming walls. By separating the work space from the eating area using color, you can create two different atmospheres. Food-preparation areas may be white, clean, and efficient, while an eating area could be relaxed and informal – try a welcoming aqua green or cheerful yellow. The notion

that blue is too cold for a north-facing room while red encloses and shrinks the space is true to some extent. But the right tone used with its complementary color – such as blue with orange, lavender with yellow, or mint green with rose – can look spectacular. In multifunctional rooms, you could define each area with a different color. To make a kitchen feel brighter, use whites and creams on the ceiling and walls and liven it up with shots of colorful accessories such as enamel pans. Stone and chrome add sparkle to the darkest of rooms.

WORK SURFACES

Technology has caught up with the humble work surface. Where once wood was the obvious option, tough stainproof, heatproof materials are being developed, ranging from granite, terrazzo, solid hardwood, and tiles to laminates, stainless steel, and solid-surface materials. Different materials can be inset, such as marble or granite in a wooden counter, a wooden chopping board in a tiled counter, or stainless steel next to the hob in a wooden counter.

SOLID WOOD

Solid timber, which is available either oiled (fed with linseed oil) or lacquered (protected with a sealant), is a marvelous choice for the kitchen. Despite some controversy, wooden counters (and chopping boards – see page 50) have been proved to be anti-bacterial and are certainly hard-wearing. Hardwoods are preferable, as softwood will dent (and will stain if not protected with polyurethane varnish). When marks or scratches do occur, they can usually be removed by sanding and oiling the surface.

LAMINATE

Synthetic boards topped with a sheet of laminate are available in every color and effect. Their reasonable price and relative durability, and the fact that they are water-proof and easy to clean, make them popular. Although they will not completely resist hot pans, harsh cleaners, or sharp knives, they are better in these respects than they used to be and will endure a good few years of heavy use before showing signs of wear and tear. However, they don't last forever and can look grungy once chipped or scratched.

TERRAZZO

Terrazzo is made of fragments of marble and granite poured into concrete and polished to a high sheen. Available in a huge range of colors and patterns, this is a costly surface but is durable and pleasing to look at. It should only be used on sturdy units, because of its weight. A smooth and reflective surface to work on, terrazzo is a luxury finish and only worth installing if you plan to live in your home for some time.

BELOW: Well-designed counters can double as eating surfaces, though they work best if an overhang creates some knee room. This island unit provides space for a sink, food-preparation area, stove-top, and breakfast bar, which is ideal for quick breakfasts and easily prepared meals at the heart of the home.

ABOVE: Wooden counters age well, are tough, and are relatively hygienic. They also combine well with other materials and never go out of decorating fashion. Protected with oils, they last a lot longer than some laminates and are easier to keep clean than tiled surfaces. However, they are not heat-resistant and will require occasional sanding down and re-oiling.

RIGHT: Gleaming stainless steel needs frequent buffing to maintain its sheen, but if you can find the time, it does look impressive. Such a scrupulous, unforgiving surface brings the perfection of a professional kitchen to the home.

GRANITE

Granite is probably the most indestructible of surfaces. Highly polished in appearance and available in many colors and patterns, it is waterproof, stain-resistant, scuff- and scratch-resistant, and heatproof. It is perfect for pastry-making since it is always cool so the pastry doesn't stick to it. Granite can be mistaken for marble but does not stain in the way marble does. Naturally heavy, it should only be applied to sturdy units. It is expensive, so make sure you won't want to change your kitchen too soon.

STAINLESS STEEL

The choice of professional chefs and fans of industrial style, stainless steel is both heatproof and hygienic. Brushed-finish stainless steel is slightly more expensive than the highly polished type but does not show every fingermark. It wipes clean easily, but needs regular cleaning and buffing to maintain its good looks. Small scratches can be buffed out, although you should always use a chopping board because it scratches quite easily. Stainless steel can be noisy to work on. It does not curve around corners very well so is better finished with a thick edging.

TILES

Tiled counters can look suitably rustic in a farmhouse kitchen or beautifully elegant in an all-white, minimal kitchen. Color combinations and a mixture of plain and patterned tiles can be used to form borders or decorative panels. Tiles are hygienic to use, but you must use a grouting that is resistant to acids and cooking liquids. Even then, grouting can become discolored and dirty, so set tiles as closely as possible. This is more

difficult with the beautiful handmade tiles, part of whose charm lies in the uneven edges. Slate tiles have a pleasing patina and are extremely cheap, but are best used only on small areas as their steely grey color absorbs natural light.

SOLID SURFACES

A "solid-surface" material such as Corian is a synthetic composite in which the color goes all the way through the surface. Although expensive, it is extremely hard-wearing and is heat- and stain-resistant. It will not chip, and scratches can be repaired. Available in many colors, it can be formed into any shape, so integral sinks can be joined invisibly to the counter.

COUNTER HEIGHT

Current opinion suggests that for maximum comfort counters should not all be a uniform height. For food preparation, a surface should be 2-4in (5–10cm) below flexed elbow height; on a surface where appliances are being used, the surface should be 7-10in (17–25cm) below elbow height. Installing one low counter is a good idea for kneading pastry or other industrious jobs, and children will find it easier to work at. Higher-level surfaces are useful as serving areas, where food can be taken from the oven and dished up. Also bear in mind when planning a kitchen from scratch that particularly tall or small families may need higher or lower work surfaces in general.

FLOORING

Kitchen floors need to be hard-wearing and easy to maintain as well as nice to look at. For a family home with young children, practicality is obviously more important than aesthetics.

STONE AND TILES

While terracotta tiles and textured slate are undoubtedly elegant, they are very unkind to children's heads and limbs. The same applies to quarry and ceramic tiles, stone, and terrazzo – all look lovely in country kitchens and eating areas but are unsafe until children are older. Opt for a softer flooring, or anchor a soft rug (using a non-slip undermat or double-sided carpet tape) to areas where children are running around. Ensure the rug is washable, as buttered toast is sure to land butter-side down.

LINOLEUM

One family-friendly choice is linoleum. Made from natural materials such as cork and linseed oil that have been sealed under heat to a jute backing, this classic flooring is enjoying a phenomenal revival, and rightly so. Not only is it warm underfoot but it needs little maintenance other than washing and wiping. It comes as sheets or tiles and is available in myriad colors and patterns.

WOOD

Wood is another natural choice that works well in the kitchen. Existing floorboards can be renovated or a new floor laid (using new or reclaimed boards). Floorboards that are less than perfect can be painted with a durable oil-based paint and then varnished for extra protection.

Another stylish wood flooring is wood strip, which comes in beech, oak, cherry, and many other types and various widths. This form of flooring is not entirely water-resistant. If water penetrates underneath the floor, the surface can buckle and be ruined.

If your children are still quite young, a wooden floor is probably not the best option. Floorboards are not particularly comfortable for crawling babies, who may even pick up splinters. Also, a wooden floor is likely to take a battering from children's tricycles and toys (and increase the noise levels, too).

scheme. It is available in both sheet or tile form and is water-resistant. However, it will show cigarette burns and scorch marks. The studded variety is not practical for a kitchen because it is hard to clean around the indentations.

VINYL

The most readily available and cheapest of all options is vinyl sheet flooring, which comes in a huge range of colors and designs and either cushioned or flat. Vinyl tiles are available that are fairly realistic imitations of a variety of surfaces, from parquet to marble inlaid motifs and block patterns. Better-quality vinyl tiles tend to be more expensive but are durable, stain-resistant, and easy to clean. Though not as warm underfoot as natural linoleum, vinyl is a good compromise surface.

MATTING AND CARPET

Natural matting is not generally recommended for areas that may get damp. However, for a family with children old enough not to spill juice and crumbs, it can be used in the eating area if it has been made stain-resistant. In a combined kitchen and eating area you can use the flooring to delineate the space. Kitchen carpet and carpet tiles are available, finished with a protective, stain-resistant coating. After a few years, though, they can become very shabby, not to say bacteria-laden.

ABOVE LEFT: Flooring can differentiate zones within a room. Here the original kitchen tiling has been preserved around the food-preparation and cooking area but blends into linoleum in the hallway and stone tiles elsewhere in the kitchen.

LEFT: The warmth and texture of mellow wood – in the form of strip flooring, counters, wall units and a Venetian blind – stop this white kitchen from looking clinical. Easy to clean and sleek in appearance, wood is durable and makes a good basis for kitchen planning.

FAR LEFT: Stone tiles are attractive companions to these fitted units. Although hard and cold underfoot and therefore not ideal for families with very young children, they are easy to maintain (providing they are sealed) and can take heavy use.

LEFT: Classic black-and-white checkerboard flooring is elegant, even in a tiny kitchen, adding graphic definition to any style of decoration.

If you already have a wooden floor, consider laying a plywood base over it and using sheet vinyl or linoleum as an interim floor covering, until the children are older.

CORK AND RUBBER

A surface that is kind to children's feet and limbs and will survive a hard pounding is cork, which comes in several colors. It is easy to fit, economical to buy in sheet or tile form, and, once sealed, resistant to water and staining. Rubber flooring has similar properties and works well in a modern

LIGHTING

Adequate lighting is important all around the home, but the family kitchen, as the busiest room and the one where accidents are most likely to happen, simply has to be well lit. You can never have enough lighting options in a multifunctional room. The best solutions offer flexibility for all the practical tasks and enough different forms of lighting to create atmosphere for eating and entertaining. A mixture of good task lighting, soft background (or ambient) lighting, and a little accent lighting – combined with generous quantities of candles for the evening – should cover all options.

RIGHT: A row of pendant lamps above a dining table is at once graphic, decorative, and functional. A dimmer switch allows lighting levels to be varied according to what is happening on the table.

The most successful schemes include some form of spotlighting for sink and stove; directional lights, such as under-cupboard lights, for counters; and overhead lights for eating areas. Make the most of available natural light by siting the sink, main work surface, or table adjacent to the window where possible.

Illuminate the eating area at night, but leave the kitchen itself (and the dirty plates) in darkness save for one or two halogen spots. Dimmable overhead lighting will also serve this purpose, provided that the work zone and eating areas are on different circuits, so you can control them separately.

TASK LIGHTING

For counters, under-cupboard lighting, hidden either by a cornice or other trim that

ABOVE: Halogen spotlights on chrome tracking can be twisted to provide directional pools of light at various places around the kitchen, so that stove, table, and counters are all adequately illuminated. The light built into an extractor hood augments this over the stove.

RIGHT: Natural light is harnessed through a skylight to throw pure daylight into the heart of a kitchen. Recessed halogen ceiling lights cast light into the room at night. These are supplemented by under-cupboard strip lights and a light in the extractor hood, ensuring that cooks never have to work in their own shadow.

matches the cupboards, not only creates safe, shadowless illumination for chopping and preparing, but also provides subtle background lighting for the evening. This is the one (and only) place where strip lighting finds its natural home. Tungsten tubes are available or you could use fluorescent tubes, which are longer-lasting than tungsten, in warm white or ultra-blue.

Low-voltage halogen lights – either recessed into the ceiling or in the form of track lighting – can also be used for lighting work surfaces. Their bright, white light gives a truer reflection of color and light quality, which is important if you are preparing food or supervising children's painting sessions. It is so close to daylight that it can be switched on during overcast weather without casting a yellowish glow. Be sure to position the lights immediately above the work surface or you will be working in shadow. This form of task lighting is also ideal for lighting the sink, the stove if it does not have an extractor hood with lights above it, and an island unit.

The family table is best served by a single pendant light (or two if the table is long) that is both dimmable and height-adjustable. Supplement it with generous quantities of candles, both on the table and on surfaces such as a hutch or sideboard.

Angled work lamps such as an angle-poise lamp can be used in other areas where task lighting is essential – near the telephone and bulletin board, for example, on a small desk, or close to a butcher block that doubles as a hobby space.

BACKGROUND LIGHTING

Halogen downlighters or track lights provide a good general light, too. For addi-

Well-designed lighting

Always plan the kitchen lighting before having new units installed or redecorating. The light fixtures themselves, however, should not be attached until the very end of the process when everything else has been finished.

✳

Decide where your main areas of activity are and plan your lighting from there, combining background, task, and accent lighting for the best effect.

✳

Make sure that lighting for work surfaces is adequate. Light as many surfaces as you can in the kitchen in order to give maximum flexibility.

✳

Attach dimmer switches to as many lights as is practically possible. (However, remember that halogen lights need special inductive dimmers.)

✳

Light the family table with a pendant light that can be dimmed when you are eating and used on full brightness when someone is working at the table and needs to be able to see clearly. If possible, choose one with a rise-and-fall fitting, which can be easily adjusted to provide sufficient light without creating glare.

✳

Uplighters will provide simple and subtle background illumination in the darker corners of an eating area, and they can also double up as accent lighting if carefully positioned.

✳

Fit an outdoor light outside the back door for reaching the trash and for picking outdoor herbs more easily when it is dark. You will also be able to put away any children's outdoor toys without falling over them first.

✳

If using table lamps in the kitchen, be careful to avoid trailing cords where people could trip over them.

✳

Never leave lit candles unattended or near unsupervised young children.

tional background lighting, wall lights throw light outward or upward into a kitchen. Unless they are halogen, attach a dimmer switch for extra flexibility.

In the eating area of the kitchen, downlighters or uplighters could be used as "wall washers" to create a soft, glowing light over one entire wall.

ACCENT LIGHTING

If your cupboard units do not extend right to the ceiling, some form of uplighter placed on top will create an interesting pool of light and pinpoint any decorative objects such as generous salad bowls or baskets. If dimmable, these lights can be used for atmosphere when eating or entertaining, drawing attention away from the food-preparation areas.

Cupboards with clear or frosted glass can be lit from inside too, to provide additional accents. Colored glass or interesting dishes stored on glass shelves come to life under the sharp glow of accent lights, making interesting displays.

WINDOW TREATMENTS

Window treatments provide one of the best opportunities for making a family kitchen cheerful and welcoming, but they do need to be practical. Avoid elaborate effects such as voluminous curtains, complicated swags and tails, or fussy blinds. Instead, opt for simple lines for both curtains and blinds and washable fabrics that will not be affected by steam or cooking smells.

USING FABRICS

Checks, spriggy florals, and strong, simple motifs all work well in the kitchen. Bold fabric can really lift an all-white decor and add punch to a neutral scheme featuring a lot of wood. It can be used to coordinate with your china, table linen, and pots and pans, pulling together several different elements or colors or creating a pool of color away from the main food-preparation area.

BELOW: In this rustic-looking kitchen, check fabric is a keynote. The café curtains maintain some privacy while still allowing in light, and the same fabric is used instead of built-in cupboards to hide away clutter underneath the work surface.

Fabric can be especially effective in places where you want to create a distinct atmosphere, for example in an eating area or homework space.

Café curtains in muslin, calico, or checked cotton that are mounted halfway up a window frame are good for preserving the light but also providing some privacy. Suspend them from an understated pole using café clips, punched eyelets, or a simple tie or tab heading. Even dish towels or waffle-weave squares can double as curtains for smaller windows.

ABOVE: In an all-white interior a series of semi-sheer Roman blinds stops the window from looking too bare, without detracting from the light, airy look of the room. For privacy at night, white colonial-style shutters can be drawn across the window, folding back inconspicuously by day. Big, attractive windows often look better with simple treatments such as this that do not obscure the architecture.

RIGHT: A Mediterranean color combination of blue and white is continued on the wall around a deep window recess and around the frame itself within the recess. Small windows like this do not necessarily benefit from a fabric treatment. Instead, the painted border emphasizes the window without blocking the light. Given the proximity of the sink, it is also more practical than a curtain would be.

Simply draped fabric is another ultra-practical solution, but only if the window is away from food-preparation or cooking areas in order to keep curtains as clean as possible. Muslin hung in a combination of colors is perfect for warmer climates where keeping warmth in is not a priority. Fabric wound around a thin pole and hung, banner-like, at either side can also be effective. These treatments can be combined with simple blinds if privacy is required.

Tailored blinds work very well in the kitchen because, unlike curtains, there is no billowing fabric to get in the way. Roller blinds are a good solution for a contemporary style of room, particularly if used in a strong, plain color. For a softer, less austere look, Roman blinds are ideal. When down, this type of blind forms a flat panel and then is pulled up into neat horizontal pleats to the desired height.

VENETIAN AND PINOLEUM BLINDS

Venetian blinds in wood, metal, or plastic are not affected by cooking smells or steam and always lend a crisp look to the window. You can pull them up to different heights according to the amount of light or shade you need. Wooden Venetian blinds that are close to a sink will need to be protected with varnish, so be sure to specify this when ordering them if you choose to have them specially made.

Pinoleum blinds, made from thin strips of wood, are also well suited to the kitchen atmosphere. Cord-operated, they are rolled up to the desired height.

SHUTTERS

Perhaps the most practical of all window treatments for the kitchen are shutters. Easy to remove and clean, they look good and can be painted either to blend in with the room or to provide a sharp jolt of color. Colonial-style wooden slats are the most common, but shutters can also be made from just about any material. Unpainted plywood can be punched with tiny port-holes, MDF (medium-density fiberboard) can easily be shaped with a jigsaw, and even panels of Plexiglas attached to hinges will block an ugly view while still letting in the daylight.

THE FAMILY TABLE

ABOVE: Drawing at the family table means peace and quiet all around for a short while. Several children gathered at a table will thoroughly enjoy demolishing a paper tablecloth with sketches and doodles.

PREVIOUS PAGES: A table sited near a window acts like a magnet to anyone in the kitchen. A good-sized one like this can be used for several different activities, often all at once.

The family table is the setting for relaxed meals, but it is also much more. The heart of the kitchen, it is party to much drama and delight. It is the one place in a family home that is host to shared memories and occasions, discussions and plans, and the inevitable tantrums and tears. Often the best family table is one whose pitted and battered surface bears the imprint of several generations' worth of daily rituals.

FUNCTIONAL TABLES

Decide on a style of table that suits your lifestyle, and work from there. If the table also has to cater to other activities such as homework, creative crafts, and paperwork, take this into account. A table with drawers has the advantage of storing place mats, napkins, and cutlery, not to mention being a handy repository for discarded pizza crusts and comfort blankets.

TOP: Dog heaven – a large cushion ideally placed for the inevitable crumbs during children's meals.

ABOVE: A weathered table is always at home in a family kitchen, even when it is a neat, contemporary space like this. The more battered the surface, the more relaxing the atmosphere around it.

A family table works best placed next to the strongest source of natural light, either a window or French doors. Consider the position of your table at the earliest planning stage. A dresser, pigeonhole shelves, cupboard, or sideboard placed near the table will enable you to store and access table linen, cutlery, glasses, and china when entertaining – a natural time-saver.

If you entertain often and have the space, then a rectangular or oval table will work best. For a small space, a round table is invaluable. One that is about three feet (just under a meter) across will allow four people to eat in reasonable comfort. A gateleg or fold-down table is a good solution where space is very tight, or, for an awkward corner, consider a custom-made table.

A breakfast bar, too, can work surprisingly well in a room with limited space. It can be wrapped around an island unit or across a narrow room, where it will form part of the counter.

TABLE LINEN

For everyday use, a plastic-coated tablecloth is excellent. Children can spill and pour as much as they like and you will still manage to preserve your surface and sanity.

Place mats are a good compromise between a bare table and a cloth that needs frequent washing. Use decorated plastic mats for young children, graduating to cork, padded fabric, rush, and sisal in assorted colors when they are a little older. Match the mats to your own scheme.

THE DINING ROOM OR DINING AREA

For many, the kitchen table has become the only place in the home where family meals and entertaining take place. Nevertheless,

LEFT: Round tables are excellent in small spaces and awkward corners, particularly as they seat more people than a square or rectangular table of the same size. Those that can be extended, forming an oval shape, are even more versatile. If there is not enough room for a centerpiece, it can be placed nearby.

a dining room can be an ideal place for preserving an adult space, where the grown-ups can ban toys, decorate for themselves, and indulge in refined food and conversation. Children will also appreciate the odd meal in a grown-up atmosphere; it helps them to learn how to behave as civilized human beings so you can take them out to restaurants with a degree of confidence.

The room could perhaps double as a study, with computer and papers hidden behind a wall of storage or simply disguised behind a screen. Sideboards can house both work papers and table linen.

Sometimes a dining area can be created within a larger living room or in an open-plan ground floor where the kitchen is a galley arrangement off the main room. Delineate the space with different flooring, and perhaps also a screen, and choose a table that is suited to the space. Round, generous tables work well in an open-plan setting, where space flows easily around the eating area.

RIGHT: Expandable tables that can fold upward, outward, or downward are ideal in a family kitchen that is also used for entertaining. If the legs also fold down, the table is particularly suitable for a tiny room where space does not allow a permanent table. Even the chairs can be folded away if necessary.

SEATING

Kitchen seating should combine comfort and practicality with a degree of flexibility. Dining chairs, whether formal or rustic, last better if they are made from wood or wicker and if slipcovers or tie-on cushions are washable. Upholstered furniture may also have a place in a family kitchen, but away from the table. If you have a scrupulously modern or utilitarian attitude to decoration, try stacking designer chairs, either molded plastic or aluminum café-style. Tall-backed chairs lend formality, while cane or direc-tor's chairs blend eating and relaxing easily.

CUSHIONED SEATING

Given that the kitchen table is not only used for eating but may also accommodate homework, bill-paying, hobbies, and relaxed conversation, chairs should be comfortable. Some form of cushioning, be it woven raffia or tie-on squab cushions, works best. While the children are tiny, protect cane and wicker with cushions or make a slipcover to fit over the entire chair, since oatmeal tends to solidify into a stubborn and unattractive coating on your best wickerwork.

WINDOW SEATS

Window seats are the last word for space-saving, generous forms of seating, since they can often accommodate more people than a conventional arrangement of single chairs. Those that incorporate pull-out toy drawers or lift-up lids provide a valuable and acces-sible form of extra storage, too. You can never have enough storage, and such drawers can later go on to house sporting equipment and gardening tools or become recycling centers, repositories for plastic bottles, crushed cans, and newspapers.

DOUBLE DUTY

Dual-purpose chairs that can be imported from another room as supplementary dining chairs when you are entertaining include director's chairs, Lloyd Loom box-seated armchairs, and cane fold-ups. Some of these

ABOVE: Bar stools tucked neatly underneath a breakfast bar always work best if facing the kitchen or a window, rather than a blank wall. Their elegant lines add decorative interest when ranged along a run of counter. Here, a generous window seat filled with comfortable loose cushions makes talking to the cook an easy option, while the welcoming armchairs of a family living space are placed nearby.

tables that are solid enough to take the weight of the chair plus child, but they only work on tables that have shallow tops. A traditional wooden chair can be supplemented with a safety rail made from wooden doweling and a pair of restrainers. Once a child can sit, stand, and climb, a booster seat can be strapped to an adult chair.

SEATS FOR RELAXING IN

If you have enough space in your kitchen, the addition of an easy chair or even a squishy sofa will add to the sense of welcome. Visitors and family can make themselves at home while you make a drink and a snack. Alternatively, salvaged church pews and wooden benches with lift-up seats and fabric-covered cushions are simultaneously practical and comfortable.

BAR STOOLS

If you want to encourage help with the food preparation, tall stools placed at a breakfast bar will tempt people into joining in, especially if you place some flowers or an inviting bowl of fruit or nibbles within their field of vision.

chairs can be made more comfortable with cushions for the seats and backs. Make sure that the young and the old sit on the sturdy, comfortable seats – children always manage to disappear down folding chairs and fall off wobbly ones.

HIGH CHAIRS

It is important for little ones not to feel excluded at mealtimes, so choose a high chair that will sit easily at the table. A high chair can take up quite a lot of space in a small kitchen. Clip-on models exist for

LEFT: Not only does placing a table close to the natural daylight make it instantly more inviting as a place to work, read the newspaper, eat, or play, but it also means you can keep a watchful eye on young children playing outside while you are catching up on paperwork or chopping ingredients at the table. Here, an antique high chair sits at the top of the table so the baby can appreciate the view too.

UTILITY AREAS

Creating a separate space for the washing, drying, and ironing of clothes is a good way of screening off these essential yet rather mundane chores from the more creative and enjoyable pursuits of cooking, eating, and entertaining in a family kitchen. Apart from the convenience of having all the laundry equipment grouped together, it means that mealtimes are not accompanied by the sound of clothes spinning round at 1,000 revolutions per minute.

THE DEDICATED UTILITY ROOM

As well as a washing machine and dryer, a purpose-built utility room may also contain a sink, which can be used for washing delicate items by hand as well as cutting flowers and messy garden jobs; a freezer; cupboard space for cleaning materials, a vacuum cleaner, a mop, and an ironing board; plus shoe racks and sports equipment. Shelves are useful for storing ironed clothes and full laundry baskets awaiting attention.

A hanging rail on casters is also handy for hanging up shirts after ironing them and items that are non-iron if hung up straight from the dryer. Or install an overhead airing rack, which is a versatile addition to either a utility room or a kitchen. Use it to dry off clothes that can't be slung in the dryer, to dry herbs and flowers and children's paintings, and – in the kitchen – to suspend birthday streamers.

OTHER UTILITY-AREA SITES

When there is no utility room and the kitchen is small, the washing machine and tumble dryer or washer–dryer could perhaps be sited in the garage or a bathroom if there is space. If you rely on a clothesline a lot, the best place for the washing machine will be as near the back

ABOVE: Utility rooms are very often home to muddy boots, hats, and coats, assorted footwear, pet baskets, and sports equipment. Dedicated storage racks serve to maintain order and prevent it all from ending up in a large messy heap on the floor.

RIGHT: A pull-out ironing board, which is instantly accessible yet invisible when not in use, is ideal in a small utility room.

ABOVE: An organized utility room almost makes you want to tackle the laundry. Presorting laundry according to color, shrinkability, and ironing requirements makes the job easier. A hanging rail provides a convenient temporary home for freshly ironed clothing, from which it can be easily redistributed around the home.

RIGHT: Pigeonhole shelves holding Shaker baskets are invaluable as they provide an attractive home for gloves, hats, and scarves, sunglasses and cameras, sports equipment, and all matter of other household clutter.

door as possible, since wet laundry can be heavy. Many new houses are designed with a laundry room adjacent to a bedroom, so dirty clothes can then be easily gathered from everyone's bedrooms. However, this assumes you will use a tumble dryer, rather than line-drying the laundry.

UTILITY AREAS IN KITCHENS

If there is no room elsewhere for a utility area, the washing machine and dryer can be incorporated into the kitchen layout, either side by side or stacked. Consider covering them with panels that match the cupboard fronts for a unified look. While some designers think this is the equivalent of hiding a television in a mock-antique cabinet, there are advantages to this approach in a kitchen. If the room also has an eating area, you may not want to stare at the washing machine while you entertain friends. Cupboard doors also cut out some of the noise, allowing you to concentrate on food rather than laundry settings.

AVOIDING WASH-DAY BLUES

To make the somewhat Herculean task of doing the laundry and ironing more manageable, encourage the family to presort their dirty clothes into whites and colors.

The traditional notion of Monday as wash day is long gone, but of course it is useful to maintain some sort of washing schedule if you want to avoid gargantuan piles of ironing stuffed into neglected baskets, a sudden lack of clean towels, or a pile of washed but wet bed linen in the middle of winter with nowhere to hang it all out. Ironing is best kept under control with a "little but often" policy. Only iron what you absolutely have to – neat piles of ironed underwear belong to a different generation.

RECYCLING AND HEALTHY LIVING

SIMPLIFYING THE PROCESS

Sorting of waste into separate containers, either outdoors, indoors, or both, is becoming as much a part of the domestic routine as putting out the garbage. There are many ways to simplify the process of recycling and to prevent it from becoming yet another tedious, time-consuming chore. Allocate separate cans or boxes for paper and cardboard, plastics, glass, metals, and organic waste. If you do not have space in the kitchen for storing different recycling containers, use the garage or build a structure on the back porch and incorporate plastic recycling crates that stack.

Always recycle cardboard packaging and boxes, cutting it into manageable pieces. Avoid overpackaged goods when shopping in the supermarket, and look for paper items that have been recycled. Choose

ABOVE: Adapting or planning fitted cupboards as deep pull-out drawers can help to sort garbage for recycling. Various designs of recycling bin are available, including some with separate compartments for each type of waste. Any family produces a lot of material that can be reprocessed: paper, organic waste, glass, aluminum, tin, and plastics are all prime contenders for reuse.

Recycling plays a very important role in creating a healthy family home, one in which the next generation will learn to be automatically less wasteful of the earth's resources and to develop a more responsible way of living. In some countries the recycling of domestic waste is not just second nature but also a legal requirement, and it is now becoming far easier and quicker to dispose thoughtfully of paper, glass, aluminum cans, and other household refuse through special waste collection services and recycling centers.

ABOVE: Recycling does not have to be consigned to concealed bins. Under this table sit large baskets for storing newspapers and bottles on their way to the recycling plant.

LEFT: Containers can be reused for something other than their original purpose. These jam jars make good vessels for storing bright cutlery, but would also serve as pots for pencils, or, with their lids on, as storage jars.

People are at last beginning to realize that speed and convenience are being gained only at great personal cost to the earth's resources, which are finite and not always renewable or repairable.

A HEALTHY DIET

Healthy living is vital for longevity, a sustainable ecosystem, and a sense of well-being. Fresh produce does not have to mean uniform pieces of fruit that taste unlike their organic counterparts, or color-enhanced carrots whose vibrant shade looks almost radioactive.

Growing one's own organic fruit and vegetables, herbs, and flowers in one's own space, however small, is becoming an important part of family life. Many gardens have room for a small vegetable plot, and even if you live in an apartment, you can usually find room on a balcony for a pot of tomatoes or a wigwam of beans, or on a sunny windowsill for a few fresh herbs. Even very young children can be encouraged to take an interest in growing their own food – chapter 6 gives more information for young gardeners.

To maintain a healthy diet, eat not only organic fresh fruit and vegetables but also organically managed meat and eggs. Ensure a balanced diet for the whole family, including plenty of carbohydrates such as whole-grain bread, pasta, and rice, plus pulses for fiber and dairy products.

Recycle organic waste such as fruit and vegetable peelings, coffee grounds, dead flowers, grass cuttings, and annual weeds as compost for the garden. Install a water receptacle next to the house so that rainwater can be collected from the gutters and recycled for watering the yard.

refillable packages of items like laundry detergent or fabric conditioner.

Also, make a conscious decision to cut down on needless electrical equipment in the kitchen. A hand whisk and one all-purpose food processor can usually do the work of several individual blenders, shakers, and mixers.

A move away from ultra-convenient and inexpensive but environmentally damaging food-growing practices, chemical treatments, and wasteful packaging is gaining momentum in many countries worldwide.

Conservation tips

Use old computer printouts for children's drawings and paintings. Cut sheets of paper that have been used on one side only into strips for shopping lists and notes for family members.

*

Save jam jars to use as containers for cutlery, household tools, and so on.

*

Choose natural fibers for tablecloths, floor coverings, and curtains. Natural materials always "breathe" more easily and wear well.

*

Cut up old clothes to use as cleaning rags. Whole shirts can be used as painting aprons by both adults and children.

*

Use up stale lemons as a natural bleach and cleanser.

*

Use natural cleansers and disinfectants around the home when possible.

*

Invest in a few large, sturdy canvas bags for supermarket shopping. Reuse any plastic bags you accumulate as wastebasket liners instead of buying new ones.

*

Only boil as much water as you actually need in a kettle.

*

Never leave faucets running (especially hot water) while you wander off to another task.

*

When the oven is switched on, cook several dishes at once and freeze them for later use.

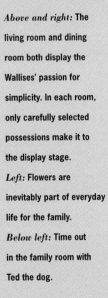

the wallises, **city town house**

The Wallis family bought their London town house ten years ago, when it was a hodgepodge of several separate studio apartments in serious need of conversion back to a spacious family home. Before their two children arrived, the generous basement was given over to Jane's business, the Jane Packer School of Floral Design, so working from home was never easier. But as their children, Rebby, now six, and Lola, four, got bigger, the need for more living space spurred them on to move the school to separate premises and to convert the entire basement into a large open-plan kitchen and family room. The basement is a magnet for the family and the dog, as well as friends and work colleagues who regularly drop by. Jane often entertains down here as well as in the more formal dining room on the ground floor.

With another two successful floristry schools in Japan, Jane has to travel to Tokyo two or three times each year. Because of this and the demands of her flower shops and

Above and right: The living room and dining room both display the Wallises' passion for simplicity. In each room, only carefully selected possessions make it to the display stage.
Left: Flowers are inevitably part of everyday life for the family.
Below left: Time out in the family room with Ted the dog.

school of floral design in England, the family employs a nanny to help with childcare during the day. Each evening, though, Jane and Gary leave their respective businesses behind and enjoy the chance to be quiet at home.

Jane's decorating style, like her attitude to flowers, has a modern confidence about it which is at once simple and appealing. Her taste is eclectic rather than focused on one particular theme. Flowers are, of course, a part of everyday life and always make an appearance at home, even in the children's bedroom, but they are low-key, never a statement. A large alcove cupboard in the family room is filled with a comprehensive collection of vases, old and new. Jane's unfussy approach to decoration is reflected in each room of the home, where color is kept neutral and natural. The only stronger wall color appears in the hall, where a soft shade of eau-de-nil provides a good foil for a tabletop display of some of Jane's most striking vases.

The open-plan kitchen and family room in the basement have a slightly more modern appeal, with plain fitted cupboards, a dog- and child-proof terracotta-tiled floor, and a wooden family table.

Simple furnishings in the form of a sofa, two comfy armchairs, and a large television allow the family room to be a small living room as well as a comfortable children's area after school. A miniature table and chairs are ideal for messing around with crayons and paint. In the kitchen itself, a large refrigerator is just what a busy family needs for storing fresh, cooked, and frozen food. A big fridge becomes more of a necessity than a treat when four or more people live under one roof.

Jane's attitude to food and cooking is strikingly similar to her decorating ideas. Informal meals with friends and colleagues are often conjured up at the end of a busy day with a minimum of fuss but many disparate influences. The family's favorite foods include modern and traditional British cooking along with Mediterranean, Thai, and Indian dishes. Jane, in particular, enjoys recreating specific meals she has eaten in restaurants, but without the obligatory celebrity-chef cookbook. She works from instinct rather than a recipe, whereas Gary, another enthusiastic cook, is more precise in the kitchen, creating equally delicious meals with a more formal approach. Rebby and Lola have been eating food with an

Above left: **With two parents juggling hectic work schedules, the family makes special efforts to eat together, whether it is a weekday breakfast before school or a snatched lunch, whenever the opportunity arises.**

Above centre and right: **Jane is a keen cook and her daughter, Lola, loves nothing more than helping to make a chocolate cake for an afternoon treat – in her view, the more chocolate frosting there is, the better!**

international flavor since an early age. Their particular favorites include hummus, salami, calamari, and olives. (Parents are always delighted when their children suddenly develop a passion for olives. It gives a faint glimmer that there will be more to culinary life than chicken nuggets and pizza in the years to come.) Like many children of her age, Lola also adores candy, with chocolate her current all-time favorite.

While most of the day-to-day family activity goes on in the basement, Jane and Gary spend their evenings in the living room on the ground floor once the children are tucked up in bed. They enjoy entertaining and tend to invite people over at least once a week. Once in a while Jane finds the time to really plan and prepare a meal, but the demands of family life and the couple's two separate businesses mean that informal suppers, often hastily thrown together but nevertheless enjoyable, are the norm.

A traditional British Sunday roast lunch is a regular choice on weekends. Easy to prepare, the meal invariably has enough variety among the meat, gravy, crispy potatoes, and vegetables to please children and adults alike.

House Rules

A large family room provides an area where everyone can be together at various times of the day.

Keep wall colors neutral and add interest with natural textures.

Simple furniture and furnishings need less upkeep.

Make flowers part of everyday life, and use them to add splashes of color to every room.

Entertain a lot so mealtimes don't become too routine.

Put utensils and gadgets on display, close to where they are used, to save time.

Choose antique, adult furniture for children's rooms so it does not date as they get older.

Above left: After the children were born, the basement, which had been used for part of Jane's business, was the obvious place to create a large kitchen and family room with enough space for children to play, work, or eat with discreet parental supervision.

Above right: Frequently used appliances and utensils are stored neatly on metal hanging racks fitted below kitchen cupboards – the ideal way to keep them out of the children's reach and also to keep work surfaces clear.

"Cooking is one chore that is more of a pleasure when all the family can join in the preparation and enjoy the end result, which is an informal meal shared with friends."

Throughout the house, furniture is mostly sturdy and antique. In Jane and Gary's bedroom, the rich, mellow tones of an Arts and Crafts cupboard, an old wooden trunk, and stripped and stained floorboards contrast with a calico-covered chaise longue and an iron bedstead dressed with all-white bedlinen and a muslin canopy. A well-worn rocking horse resting against the fireplace is both ornament and toy.

The bedroom shared by Rebby and Lola is, unlike the rest of the house, painted a strong color, to acknowledge the fact that youngsters enjoy bright surroundings. Nevertheless, Jane has managed to keep it cheerful yet subtle, with a delicate shade of lilac blue. The beds have dormitory style metal frames with soft mattresses for bouncing. Underneath each one is plenty of room for baskets of toys, plastic boxes on casters, and even space for a good game of hide-and-seek. Each child has a personalized box of drawers for precious and tiny items, while soft toys find good homes on the mantelpiece and free-standing wardrobe. Family photos on the chest of drawers and mantlepiece reinforce connections.

In taking their time to convert and renovate what is essentially an urban town house, the Wallises have made a successful family home by adapting the available space to suit their varying needs. An unpromising shell has become a comfortable and accessible home, teeming with activity, in which adults and children, dogs and visitors can happily coexist.

Above and left: The children's room is painted a delicate shade of blue and decorated with small-scale toy boxes, sets of drawers, and a wooden alphabet on the wall.

Right: The parents' bedroom, by contrast, is calm, simple, and uncluttered.

APPLIQUED aprons

RIGHT: The idea of decorating aprons for each member of the family is an appealing one, as it encourages adults to cook and young ones to keep relatively clean while messing around with Play Doh, paint, and cooking ingredients.

BELOW: Appliquéd motifs, such as these vibrant Mexican chiles exploding from a decorated bowl, can be chosen to match the recipient's tastes and interests.

Aprons are easy to make and fun to personalize. They are also absolutely essential for helping young children to stay relatively clean, whether engaging in an enthusiastically messy painting session or helping with the cooking. Children will enjoy decorating their own, and personalized aprons also make ideal gifts for friends and relations who are keen cooks. Either sew the aprons yourself, as shown here, or buy ready-made white cotton aprons from catering suppliers (children's ones are often available from school suppliers) and tea-stain or dye them before decorating if you wish. Use the recipient's particular interests or talents as inspiration for the motifs with which you decorate the apron.

YOU *will need*

* About 1yd (1m) duck (exact amount depends on size of apron)
* Matching sewing thread
* 5 grommets
* 1yd (1m) of thick cream rope (to fit through eyelets)
* 1yd (1 m) of ¾in- (2cm-) wide cream-colored thick ribbon
* Fabric remnants in red, green, yellow, blue, and striped cotton
* Fusible interfacing
* Sewing machine
* Iron

1 Cut out the basic apron shape to the required size. On the top edge, turn under and press ¼in (6mm) and then 1in (2.5cm), and on all the other edges turn under and press a double ⅜in (1cm) hem. Pin in place and then stitch. Following the manufacturer's instructions, insert a grommet at each top corner. Thread the rope through the grommets from wrong side to right side before tying knots in the ends. Cut two lengths of ribbon, tack one end of each in place at the top of each side edge, then machine-stitch in place. Remove the tacking.

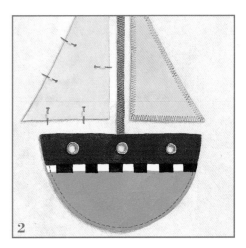

2 For the yacht pocket, cut out pieces from the red, striped, and green remnants that will make up the hull. Join the pieces with right sides together, making ¼in (6mm) seams. Press the seams open. Turn under and press ¼in (6mm) and then 1in (2.5cm) along the top edge; pin and stitch. Turn under and press ¼in (6mm) around the curved edge. Insert three equally spaced grommets across the hemmed top.

Stitch the pocket to the apron around the curved pocket edge using a close machine zigzag stitch and backstitching a few stitches at each end to help reinforce the top edge of the pocket. Iron the fusible interfacing to the yellow and blue

fabric remnants and cut out two yellow triangular sails, a yellow mast, and a small blue flag for the top of the mast. Position the pieces, interfacing side down, on the apron just above the pocket, and carefully iron them in place. Finally, stitch them to the apron using a close machine zigzag stitch and a contrasting thread.

VARIATIONS

- Instead of the grommets and rope at the top, use another length of ribbon, attaching the ends to each top corner. Use a piece of blue-and-white-striped fabric to make a pocket that looks like a mixing bowl and appliqué a fabric "spoon" to the apron behind the pocket.

- Make a pocket from two pieces of yellow fabric with a narrow strip of red and green triangular-patterned fabric between them. Make the chiles by appliquéing green stems to the red chiles and then appliquéing these to the apron so that they appear to be exploding from the Mexican bowl.

- Instead of appliqué, try decorating the apron with a child's handprints. The child simply dips his or her hand in a saucer of fabric paint and then presses it firmly against the fabric. Follow the manufacturer's instructions for fixing the paint with a hot iron.

TIE-ON chair cushion

In a kitchen or dining room where children regularly spill drinks and crumbs, wooden chairs with tie-on cushions are ultra-practical. Not only are they comfortable, but they are much easier to clean than either upholstered dining chairs or chairs with woven cane or raffia seats. These cushions are made from leftover fabric and would make elegant companions for curtains or blinds using one of the fabrics. You can leave the ties off if you prefer, but they do help prevent the children slipping off their seats at mealtimes.

YOU *will need*

* Fabric for bottom of cushion and ties
* Fabric remnants for top of cushion
* 1in- (2.5cm-) thick foam
* Sewing machine and iron
* Felt-tipped pen and large scissors

RIGHT: Tie-on chair cushions are practical, comfortable, and elegant. Here, a gusset has been added to the basic design to accommodate a plumper slab of foam.

FAR RIGHT: Ties that are sewn into the cover make it simple to attach the pad to the chair legs. This means children are less likely to slide off the chair and onto the floor.

1 To make a pattern for the cushion, place a large piece of paper on the seat. Draw around the edge of the seat and around the back struts, cutting into the corners. Mark the position of the ties and of the center front and back.

2 Fold the pattern in half along a line between center front and back. Cut around the marked outline, then check the fit. Cut out the fabric for the bottom of the cushion, adding ⅝in (1.5cm) all around for the seam allowances.

3 Decide on the size of your patchwork squares, adding seam allowances of ⅜in (1cm) all around. Calculate how many squares you will need in order to make up a piece the same size as the bottom

of the cushion. From the fabric remnants, cut out the squares, all to exactly the same size. With right sides together, join the squares into rows, being careful to make the seams all exactly the same width. Press. Now join the rows with right sides together; press. Using the pattern, cut out the cushion top from the patchwork fabric, again adding a ⅝in (1.5cm) seam allowance.

4 Cut out four 12 x 3in (30 x 7.5cm) strips of fabric. Fold one tie in half lengthwise with right sides together, pin, and machinestitch around the ends and one side, making a ⅜in (1cm) seam and leaving a central opening. Trim seam allowances to ¼in (6mm), turn the tie right side out, and press. Slip-stitch the opening. Repeat for the other ties. Attach the ties to the right side of the bottom fabric at each back corner as shown, so the edges are even with the seam allowance. Tack in place.

5 Place the cover pieces with right sides together, sandwiching the ties between them. Pin and stitch along the seamline, reinforcing the stitching over the ties, and leaving an opening at the back to insert the pad. Trim seams and outer corners, and clip into the inner corners (the corners between the ties). Turn right side out and press. For the pad, use the felt-tipped pen to draw around the pattern onto the foam. Cut out. Insert the pad into the cover and slip-stitch the folded edges together.

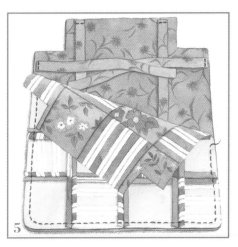

PAPIER-MACHE bowl

BELOW: Papier-mâché is one of those crafts that children find hard to resist, consisting of a gooey mess, lots of water, vigorous stirring, and an end result that needs painting and decorating.

RIGHT: A deckle-edged papier-mâché bowl can be transformed with paint to resemble a watermelon.

Papier-mâché is an ideal way of involving the children in making permanent, useful objects for the home using recycled materials, without having to spend a fortune on craft equipment. This fruit bowl is made using the pulp method, which is relatively simple. You can shred the paper by hand, but it is much faster in a shredding machine. To help the paper bind easily and harden quickly, interior wall filler is added to the pulp. The instructions are for one large bowl; for a smaller bowl, use half quantities.

YOU *will need*

* One 2gal (10L) pan or two 1gal (5L) pans
* Waste paper (not newspaper)
* Shredder (optional)
* Hand-held electric blender or whisk
* Sieve
* 6 tablespoons (90ml) PVA glue (undiluted)
* 6 tablespoons (90ml) interior wall filler (in powder form)
* Wooden spoon and large bowl
* Large heatproof mixing bowl (glass, aluminum, or stainless steel)
* Plastic wrap
* White emulsion paint and flat artist's brush
* Artist's acrylic paints in light green, medium green, yellow, cream, red, and black (or colors of your choice)
* Round artist's brush
* Matte acrylic varnish
* Varnishing brush

1 Shred enough paper to fill the pan, then add water to the top. Bring the water to a boil, and simmer for 15 minutes until the paper is soft and starts to fall apart. Leave in the pan to cool. Use a hand-held blender or whisk to liquidize the contents until the paper turns to pulp; the mixture will be very watery and slushy at this stage.

Put the pulp into a sieve and squeeze out as much water as possible by hand.

2 Break up the clump of pulp with your fingers and transfer it to a large bowl. Add the PVA glue and filler and mix thoroughly with a wooden spoon until firm.

3 Line a large heatproof mixing bowl with plastic wrap, then transfer the pulp into this mold. Press the pulp into the base, packing and smoothing it as you go and kneading it continuously until it is approximately ½in (1.2cm) thick. Take the pulp up the sides, leaving the edges jagged. (Or you can smooth them up to the rim for a hard-edged effect if desired.)

4 Leave the pulp in the mold for a few days to let it set; keeping it in a warm place or outside in the sun will speed up the process. When it is completely set and dry, take the papier-mâché bowl out of the mold, and remove the plastic wrap. It is now ready for decoration.

5 Paint the bowl with a coat of white emulsion inside and out. When dry, decorate it using artist's acrylics. For a watermelon bowl, paint stripes on the outside in light green, medium green, yellow, and cream, blending them into each other at the edges; paint the inside red, then add black ovals for seeds. When dry, apply three coats of varnish, allowing it to dry between coats.

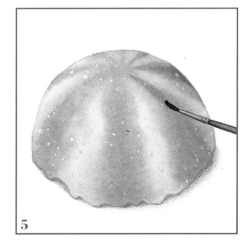

FAMILY bulletin board

A bulletin board is a vital center of information in a busy family home. Once everyone in the family knows that important invitations, phone numbers, lists of things to do and groceries to buy, and messages are stored and displayed in one place, together with a family calendar, they can all refer to the same, up-to-date information whenever there is an appointment to make or meet.

This board is designed to be dual purpose, with one side cork-faced so that it functions as a bulletin board, and the other covered with blackboard paint for shopping lists and messages. It is mounted on the wall with swing-door hinges so that it can be swung around to allow either side to be used. An extension of one of the plywood edging strips serves as a handle.

Here the cork was reused from an old bulletin board, but you can buy sheets of cork at home-decorating stores or you could use untreated cork floor tiles. Small brass cup hooks fixed into the wooden frame at the bottom of the board are handy for storing pens and pencils tied on with string, key rings, papers clasped with a large clip, and other essentials. The bulletin board featured here measures 17 x 24¾ in (430 x 630mm) but you could easily alter the dimensions to suit your own requirements.

ABOVE: Families are often defined by their display of personal photos and memorabilia on bulletin boards, fridges, and shelves. You can tell a lot about a family from what they have in the way of invitations, posters, photographs, and newspaper cuttings and clippings on their bulletin board.

YOU *will need*

* ¼in- (6mm-) thick plywood:
  one piece, 17 x 24¾in (430 x 630mm);
  4 strips 1 x 17in (25 x 430mm); 3 strips 1 x 24¾in (25 x 630mm); 1 strip 1 x 24¾in (25 x 630mm) except for the bottom 6in (150mm) which should extend by an additional 1in (25mm) to form the handle (see photo at right)
* Wood glue
* Emulsion paint, blackboard paint, brushes
* Cork to fit inside frame, approximately 15 x 22⅞in (380 x 580mm)
* Small cup hooks
* 2 swing-door pivot hinges

1

1 Miter the corners on the edging strips by cutting the ends diagonally at 45-degree angles. Cut the top and bottom of the handle at 45-degree angles so that its outside edge is about 4in (100mm) long. Use the strips to make up a frame that fits around the plywood panel, gluing all the pieces together. Allow the glued frame to dry completely before proceeding.

2 Paint the edging strips with emulsion paint, then paint one side of the panel with blackboard paint. You may need to give the panel two coats, in which case leave the first to dry thoroughly before applying the second.

3 Once the blackboard paint is completely dry, cut the cork to size and glue it in place on the other side; leave to dry.

4 Attach cup hooks to the bottom edge of the bulletin board, then attach the board to the wall with the pivot hinges, following the manufacturer's fitting instructions.

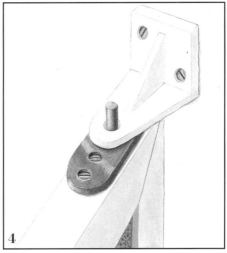

LEFT AND FAR LEFT: Two sides of the same bulletin board serve very different functions. Mounted on a swing hinge, the board can be turned one way for a display of postcards, invitations, and memorabilia; the other way for a blackboard where messages and appointments can be noted, and children can add some decorative artwork in colored chalk.

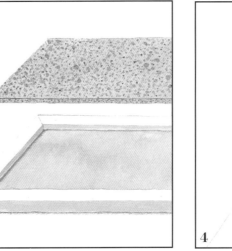

LIVING AND LEISURE

LIVING AND LEISURE

Liberated from the role of "best room," the living room

RIGHT: Two inviting
armchairs placed closed
to French doors create an
intimate sitting area away
from the main living
space, ideal for reading,
contemplating the garden,
or having a quiet chat.
Small clusters of furniture
within a larger living area
create visual interest and
extend the function of a
room. A side table of some
sort, even as small as this
one, is essential in any
furniture grouping.

Now that most people's lifestyles have become fairly hectic,

the concept of the living room as a formal parlor where

visitors are received has been eroded to the point of quaint

historical novelty. With much day-to-day entertaining taking

place in the kitchen, the living room has been liberated from

its traditional function as the "best" room, always formal and

on parade for unexpected visitors. Today's family living room

is a place of vitality and informal interaction – a room where

each generation can relax, read, watch television, listen to

music, and talk to friends, and a place where children play.

LEFT: A combination of slightly battered furniture, plaid fabrics, and practical wooden floorboards softened with a thick rug makes for a relaxing, comfortable environment in which children are bound to feel welcome. A wicker folding screen enables half of the room to be divided off for playing, eating, or working.

LEFT: Elegant furniture can work in a family context. Here, a soft sofa combines with formal armchairs. A batter-proof wooden floor and an indestructible coffee table mean that adults and children can happily coexist. Pictures dotted along one wall provide interest in an otherwise unadorned living room.

has become a place of vitality, informality, and comfort.

Leisure, the buzzword of our sound-bite society, has a double-edged attraction these days. Now that leisure time increasingly consists of bursts of activity squeezed into snatched moments, the opportunity to stop and do absolutely nothing is at once vital and elusive. As a result, home has an increased significance, as the one place where a mobile phone can be switched off, an answering machine switched on, and your refuge from the world begun.

A family living room should therefore be a place of balanced calm – a space where you can draw comfort and reassurance from your own personal style, which can in turn be shared with, rather than paraded to, visitors, friends, and family. It should be welcoming and nurturing as well as a place to make your own decorative mark.

LIVING ROOM PRIORITIES

The room should include casual, comfortable seating, several forms of storage, and space for the television, stereo, and maybe a computer, plus toys, CDs and books. Think comfort, practicality, and versatility.

Setting your own style has to come from within, an expression of your own vitality and interests. Use furniture with which you have a natural empathy and the rest should follow, more or less intuitively. You can be guided by the basics of color theory and advice on which fabric treatments will work for particular windows, but the details should come from you, rather than the pages of the latest decorating magazine.

Think of the family, too. If you have toddlers, you may have to rearrange the furniture for a year or two while they are

going through their seek-and-destroy phase. Coffee tables, low-level music systems, and accessible controls are definitely to be avoided at this stage, as are televisions on tables or stands, since young children trying to climb onto them can pull them onto themselves. Your television may be safer if it is either wall-mounted or turned into a reclusive cupboard-dweller and only pulled out on its drawer for peak-time children's viewing and in the evenings. Floor-to-ceiling houseplants may be better replaced by small potted plants placed out of toddlers' reach.

Similarly, when teenagers gather in numbers, you may wish to put away your precious ornaments and the contents of your liquor cabinet, and also make sure there are plenty of throws to protect the furniture.

LEFT: This timbered home with its lofty ceilings is perfect for dividing up into spacious open-plan rooms. The central island of comfortable chairs and a sofa in a conversation grouping leaves ample room for walking through and around the space. A rug adds comfort to the simple wooden floor and defines the sitting area.

A DEGREE OF FLEXIBILITY

Because the living room has to be such a multifunctional room, a degree of flexibility is always useful. The way a particular family relaxes and each member organizes his or her leisure time is always changing, since a household that includes a mix of ages, partners, pets, offspring, friends, and relations is never static for long; its needs change every couple of years.

This is one reason why self-built and designed homes are becoming more of a popular and attractive option. A home that is planned from the start with flexible spaces for living, studying, and entertaining will evolve naturally through the life cycle of a family, so moving house is not necessary unless the family really wants to uproot and go elsewhere.

Often a living room is the one space in the house that is big enough to serve as a multifunctional space. And even when it isn't large enough, there is sometimes scope for knocking together two rooms or opening up a hallway to widen the space and provide additional alcoves or nooks to enable you to fit in a desk, computer, or extra seating.

In many instances, the living space may double as a playroom, dining room, or work space. Keeping such a room functioning in this many ways demands practical surfaces, low-maintenance furnishings, a flexible furniture layout, and a style of decoration that embraces the room's various roles.

Multipurpose furniture is also a great boon. For example, an ottoman with a lift-up lid will provide storage, a footrest, and seating as well as doubling as a table when needed. Or, if the children have taken over all the spare bedrooms, a sofa bed can allow the living room to moonlight as a perfectly good guest bedroom.

A SENSE OF WELCOME

Comfortable sofas that envelope you as you sink into them, and soft cushions you can fall on to, are as appealing to adults as they are to children. Arranging this seating around a focal point is a good way to draw people into a space, making them want to sit down and stay a while. The obvious focal point is a fireplace, but other possibilities include a window with a fabulous view, a collection of paintings, an antique rug, an interesting bookcase, a "media" wall (housing TV, video recorder, and stereo in one attractive, built-in storage system), or a low table. You could even rearrange the furniture twice a year, so the focal point is the view of the backyard in the summer and the fireplace in the winter.

Scent plays an important part in setting a mood – walking into a room that has a

LEFT: In a converted schoolhouse, dramatic windows frame an abundance of views through to the garden and allow the natural daylight to stream in. A sitting area fits neatly into one corner of the large space, leaving the French doors to the garden easily accessible. There is plenty of room for a long dining table with generous seating around it. The furniture is uncomplicated and sturdy enough to withstand tough treatment by the children.

BELOW: Far from being cramped, compact living can often be comfortable and inviting. Timber boarding, generous sofas, and simple furnishings allow a sense of calm to pervade this small space, where warm colors add to the coziness.

lovely aroma is hard to forget. Lavender produces a calming oil, so – who knows? – you might even manage to quiet over-wrought and overactive children by laying lavender sprigs underneath rugs. You can always dream about the day when they will lie down and roll over in a quiet moment of repose, in the way that cats do when they come across catnip in the garden.

Flowers are life-enhancers, reinforcing our connection with nature and providing color and scent in abundance. For maximum impact include fragrant seasonal flowers such as hyacinths, wintersweet, narcissi, daphne, lily of the valley, and osmanthus in spring; old roses, nicotiana, verbena, lilac, and sweet peas in summer;

and later-flowering honeysuckles or plants with aromatic foliage such as eucalyptus and myrtle in autumn.

REAL FLAMES

Candles, too, provide a heady atmosphere, as well as an evocative flickering light, when scented with sandalwood, citrus fruit, or rose. Flames have always soothed the spirit and relaxed the mind, and a real fire, however minimal, is irrepressibly reassuring. Generous logs are best, of course, but smokeless fuel will do if urban restrictions apply. Sprinkle bay leaves and rosemary sprigs onto recently chopped logs in a basket, or toss rosemary or lavender sprigs straight onto a roaring fire.

ABOVE: An informal mix of textiles on furniture, floor, and windows provides the decoration in this white space. A collection of paintings and other pictures, together with a large mirror and painted fire surround, adds further color and pattern.

FLEXIBLE FURNITURE

An informal approach to family living is a real advantage in living spaces that are host to a clutch of different activities in any one day. By creating a variety of seating and activity zones, you will be able to mix and match furniture and accessories according to mood or time of day.

COMFORT ZONES

Forming specific areas of interest in a living space makes the room more functional and increases the comfort factor. In addition to arranging seating around a focal point (see page 94), try to create one or two other seating areas, grouping the chairs and sofas for conversation. Not only does this make the room more versatile, but it also is much cozier and more inviting. Lightweight chairs that can be moved around easily are more practical than heavy armchairs.

You may want one of these areas to include a large table for playing games or doing homework. Make sure that there is room to draw back the chairs away from the table and to circulate around it. You will also need a couple of small occasional tables – ideally, there should be somewhere to put a drink, no matter where you are

ABOVE RIGHT: Beanbags are flexible furniture in every sense of the phrase. Portable, comfortable, and reassuring, they act as magnets to youngsters, usurping the family sofa as the favorite place to rest while watching television, reading, or ploughing through an unnutritious snack. They also save on upholstery cleaning bills.

RIGHT: A contemporary approach to furniture and storage can be family-friendly and at the same time effortlessly stylish. Low-maintenance and easy to achieve, a pared-down living room will always save you time when it comes to the inevitable clearing and cleaning up.

Maximum versatility

Fit lockable casters to large pieces of furniture so that the individual items can easily be moved around when entertaining, cleaning, or temporarily altering the room layout.

✳

Screens can be used in endless ways. Hardwood frames with fabric inserts, plain hinged plywood or MDF (medium density fiberboard) panels, tongue-and-groove sheets, and glazed panels are all available. Use as room dividers or clutter disguisers. (See the project on pages 128-129 for more ideas.)

✳

Keep a low-level table on lockable casters to use as a discreet coffee table. Fit corner protectors when children are young, so that even if they clamber over the table they won't get hurt.

✳

Fold-up tables and chairs are ideal for small living spaces that often get visitors. Fold-down tables mounted on the wall also conserve space.

✳

Ottomans or generous footstools are very versatile. Use them as side tables, footrests, and additional seating (they are often an ideal height for children). Those with lift-up lids will also provide storage inside.

✳

Toy storage baskets and chests can be placed to the side of a sofa or chair at night for use as a side table.

✳

A drop-leaf table can be used as a side table by day, and then converted into a dining table or a place to do homework in the evening.

RIGHT: When having a lot of space matters, a knocked-through living room is ideal, providing a variety of living zones with seating at one end and eating at the other. None of the furniture is fixed, which means the whole room is a movable feast, ready to transmute whenever family needs dictate a new arrangement.

BELOW: Casters on a movable, folding unit are multifunctional heaven. Bookcase, music store, room divider, or screen – roll the wheels and take your pick. Casters are an essential ingredient in flexible, open-plan living spaces, allowing sofas and chairs, tables and larger pieces like this to be moved about at will.

sitting. When children are young, they want to be around you during the day, so a few small-scale chairs and a tiny table will let them feel that they have their own space within the room.

For evenings, when you wish to reclaim the space for adult conversation, peaceful reflection, or supreme inactivity in front of the television, you will need a corner, cupboard, or deep receptacle where the children's clutter can be put out of sight (see page 111 for ideas).

DIVIDE AND CONQUER

Screens will disguise a corner of detritus while looking sleek and fashionable. Use them, too, for dividing areas of activity, painting them different colors on each side for a pleasing contribution to the decor. If a screen is to be used to separate off a home-office area, you could make it double as a bulletin board by stretching ribbon, braid, or tape across the "office" side of

he screen, trellis fashion, and stapling it in place (also see pages 128-9).

One of the most important aspects of a family living room is to allow for areas of quiet within the general melee. One way of separating out the space is to divide a large knocked-through room into two distinct zones, using folding internal doors; for maximum light the doors could be part-glazed. One end of the room can act as the television room, the other a quieter reading space, music area, or playroom. Having an easy chair or two on casters means you can move some furniture between the spaces, as needed.

Open pigeonhole shelves or industrial fixtures used as a room divider will display large items while allowing the area on each side of it a view through into the other. A console table behind a sofa performs a similar function. A hinged bookcase that snaps together could also serve as an unusual room divider.

If you do want to include a separate area for working or studying, consider a discreet, fold-down desk or one contained within a freestanding cupboard. A built-in shelving system in an alcove could be adapted so that a simple leaf extends out from a middle shelf, with a stool or office chair tucked underneath it. (Storage ideas for this area are covered on pages 108-11.)

COLOR STATEMENTS

ABOVE: A single rectangle of strong color on the double doors in an otherwise muted living room lends definition and creates an element of surprise. Small flashes of primary red and yellow in the chairs and cushions contrast with the vivid blue, for a dramatic effect against the neutral background.

LEFT: A glorious fusion of soft blues and greens evokes the sea and sky in this atmospheric living room, where a sailboat seems to float along a shelf and children's toys and pictures could be mistaken for tropical fish. In a modern setting, color will often soften the hard edges of contemporary furniture and design. Here, differing planes of color emphasize the interesting architectural elements of the room, an approach continued over the furniture.

to a playroom stuffed with board games, building blocks, and riotous primary colors fighting for attention.

When two distinct worlds are created within a house, however, they tend to evoke the nursery-versus-home atmosphere of a repressive Victorian upbringing, totally irrelevant to the integrated family life of today. Surely a middle path is the answer. Children need to feel they are part of the grown-up space if they are to appreciate that sometimes a little care and attention to furniture and fixtures is called for.

ALTERNATIVES TO ALL-WHITE

If you still yearn for a neutral haven, then paint the walls and woodwork a wipable white or off-white. One way of protecting emulsioned walls is to apply a coat of matte acrylic varnish. Color can be used on the items that would be impractical in white – upholstery, soft furnishings, and rugs.

The ultimate opt-out is to leave freshly plastered or exposed-brick walls just as they are. Children provide a perfect excuse for not decorating at all. "We thought we'd wait till they're past the food-throwing stage" is one way of postponing the decision until you have more time or money to concentrate on what you really want.

Wallpaper is available in myriad colors, patterns, and textures, and most of them these days are spongeable (an essential in a family home). Make sure no edges come

In a family home, color is a form of creative camouflage. While you may yearn for a totally white room with crisp white upholstery, cream throws, and white woven window coverings, the reality is that this is totally impractical. Unless you do not mind regular dry-cleaning bills and frequent emergency treatment to deal with even the

most cursory of spills, it is better to forgo the white room and opt instead for color, at least for a few years.

Of course, many people do manage to preserve a pristine all-white living room, but it is generally a place where children fear to tread, a sacrosanct space reserved for grown-ups. The children are banished away, allowing inquisitive youngsters to peel off patches when you are not looking – an all-too-common pastime. Wallpaper is good for hiding wall imperfections, and stripes or subtle patterns will disguise the occasional trailing chocolate-cookie fingerprint better than a flat painted wall.

Similarly, fingerprints and spills are far less noticeable on colorwashed walls. Their broken surface patina also disguises unevenness. Break them up with bands of different colors, or paint on a child-friendly color at dado height. If you keep the walls plain, whether neutral or colorful, pattern can be added in the upholstery, removable covers, curtains or blinds, cushions, and throws.

EXPERIMENTING WITH COLOR

Put together a collection of paint and fabric swatches and inspirational pictures from magazines to create a color dictionary before embarking on large-scale adventures. Experimenting with color is the only way to increase your understanding of it. The

Practical color

In a dark, sunless room use white, off-white, or yellow to warm the atmosphere and make the most of the light.

✳

Colorwash walls to provide a broken patina that won't show fingerprints.

✳

Provide splashes of color on cushions, throws, and curtains or blinds. Vases, flowers, ceramics, and freestanding furniture also offer a chance to bring color into a room.

✳

Try painting the ceiling a darker color than the one used on the walls if you wish to enclose a space. Or, to make the room look larger, use white, which reflects light back into a room. Even just using a lighter tone than is on the walls will make the ceiling appear higher.

✳

Cool colors, such as most shades of blue, create a tranquil, leisurely atmosphere.

✳

A living room that has been created by removing the dividing wall between two small rooms may appear too long and narrow. To make it look wider, paint the walls and ceiling in a pale color. Alternatively, you could paint the walls at the ends in a warm, dark tone to draw them in and use a pale color on the side walls.

✳

To make a small living room look bigger, use pale colors. Also, monochromatic or neutral color schemes will make the room look larger than a scheme involving contrasting colors.

✳

If you want to help a large area look cozy, use rich, warm colors.

✳

To avoid monotony in a color scheme, aim to include a range of light, medium, and dark tones. For example, you could have a very light ceiling, light walls, a mid-tone floor, and some dark upholstery or wood. Without the addition of these dark tones the color scheme will lack "backbone."

accepted wisdom of blue being too cool for a sunless room, for example, can be completely overturned if the correct shade of blue is used with, say, a complementary vibrant orange, or if mixed down to a shade that is as much gray as blue. Colors behave very differently according to their natural bias. A yellow composed of green tones will not feel right against a green dominated by blue tones; sometimes apparently obvious partners do not work together. When you have chosen some possible colors, look at them in the morning, in the early evening, and at night with the lights on to gauge how they look under each set of conditions.

LEFT: Neutral emulsioned walls and a wooden floor are brought to life with a cornflower blue sofa and paintings incorporating primary blues, yellows, and reds. Introducing color into a room in this way means you don't have to redecorate completely if you want to replace the principal shades when you tire of them.

ABOVE: Rooms on either side of an entrance hall are painted in different colors so a view through the aligning open doors creates its own interesting perspective. As you walk from one brightly colored space to another, each room has its own distinct identity, yet the overall approach is harmonious and unified.

99

SOFT FURNISHINGS

Designing your own soft furnishings – whether you make them up yourself or commission someone else to do so – allows you to tailor them to your own tastes and budget. Quick, stylish ideas have super- seded the more elaborate treatments, and the demand for instant soft furnishings is being met by an ever-increasing variety of ingenious window treatments, removable covers, and accessories. Simply choosing a style that suits you can sometimes seem the most complicated task of all.

FABRIC CHOICE

In a family home, fabrics should be chosen with an eye on longevity. Quiet pattern and texture will be less tiresome when, after a couple of years, you decide that burnt orange and lime green look decidedly out of date. Choose an enduring color scheme that can be subtly accented or highlighted in a variety of ways. Ring the changes with unexpected combinations of texture or pattern, such as wool trimmed with calico, or thick, chunky corduroy accented with moiré taffeta.

Removable covers are the practical for sofas and chairs, at least while children are young, when upholstery takes a harsh beating. It is more family-proof if covered with a small-patterned or checked fabric, as plain fabrics will always show stains more readily. Investing in an additional set of covers in a contrasting or patterned fabric

RIGHT: This invigorating blend of ethnic textiles is perfectly at home in a relaxed country cottage, proving that traditional chintz can be successfully swapped for more exotic influences. A loose arrangement of sofas, windowseat, and mismatching armchairs is tied together with a richly patterned collection of throws, cushions, and kilims, creating a comfortable, lived-in look.

Choosing fabric

Sunlight, friction, and dirt all age fabric, including cotton, so try to protect your soft furnishings from these three as much as you can.

*

Cottons are hard-wearing and work well on sofas and chairs in family homes. Simple tickings and checks look especially fresh.

*

For a luxurious finishing touch, add oversized cushions in deep midnight blue velvet, burgundy silk, or camel-colored ultrasuede.

*

A natural selection could include a jute rug, linen cushions, checked curtains, a sofa with loose covers in twill or ticking, and soft woollen throws.

*

Corduroy, a heavy ribbed cotton, is a tough fabric suited to upholstery. It is gradually shrugging off its associations with 1960s and 1970s decor and clothing.

*

Having new upholstery treated with stain-repellent finish such as Scotchguard, either before it leaves the factory or *in situ*, will lengthen the time you have before cleaning becomes essential. The finish will survive much laundering and a few dry-cleanings.

*

Plain fabrics can be dressed up or given a new lease on life by adding throws and cushions. Sofas and chairs will retain their appeal for longer if not covered with a loud pattern, which soon palls. Small patterns, however, do help to camouflage marks.

...

RIGHT: The bigger the sofa, the better, as far as family living is concerned. Dark colors or gentle patterns show fewer marks than light colors. When young children and affectionate pets are around, removable covers are more practical than fitted upholstered covers.

BELOW: Simple soft furnishings are often the most successful, in terms of practicality and style, as this room demonstrates. When a sofa is past its best, throws disguise the shabbiness while adding visual interest. A small butterfly chair with removable cover is useful both indoors and out on the porch. If the view from the windows is good and privacy is not required, sheer curtains filter light without hiding the view.

will provide a bit of seasonal variety, and having a spare set will also encourage you to clean the covers regularly.

CUSHIONS AND THROWS

Complicated pattern can be introduced on a plain sofa by means of cushions and throws, giving the impression of a rich textural mix. Throws both protect and embolden chairs and sofas. Nubbly wool or cotton waffle-weave blankets have the versatility of being decorative by day and functional by night, when family members can wrap themselves up in them to relax. Or make a simple cotton throw to cover a sofa or armchair completely and decorate it with simple, colorful appliquéd felt shapes, such as flowers, using large hand stitches.

Cushions are integral to comfort and relaxation. Use oversized squares covered with textural treats such as ultrasuede, wool, woven tapestry, or velvet. Opulent fabrics

used on a small scale are one way of conjuring up luxury in an otherwise functional setting. Such indulgent cushions can always be whipped off the sofa when a group of toddlers appear for a full-scale wrestle.

WINDOW TREATMENTS

When children are small, luxury fabrics are not a good idea for curtains or blinds. Silk, heavily textured white damask, and velvet are better left for formal rooms or for when the children have stopped playing hide-and-seek behind them. Washable cotton is preferable and in a pattern or color that is easy to live with for a few years. However, if you are keen to dress the windows in a more elegant fabric, velvet or silk can be draped over a pole above a window, out of harm's way. It's always better to work around your offspring than fight against the decorative limitations they impose.

Windows are no longer swathed in yards of heavy fabric to create a focal point. That approach can easily overwhelm a room. Cool, understated, and neatly functional solutions that create a feeling of space and light are more popular today. A venetian

blind, shutters, a roman blind, or a roller blind can be used in isolation, perhaps softened by adding light ticking or calico curtains simply clipped to a thin rail or with a tab or cased heading.

UPHOLSTERY FABRIC STAINS

However careful you are about preserving upholstery, if you share your life with children of any age and pets, there will be spills and stains to contain. Here are some straightforward remedies:

- Remove the food or grease deposit and blot the stain with a white cloth or paper towel. Apply talcum powder and leave until it absorbs the color of the stain. Wipe away with a cloth and repeat the process if the stain remains.

- Always treat milk spills straight away, otherwise you will never get rid of the smell. Sponge with lukewarm water then blot dry using a soft white cloth or paper towels. If the stain persists, use a spot stain remover. Use the same technique for spills on the carpet.

- Dampen a fruit juice spill with water, pour on some table salt, and rub in gently with a soft cloth. Leave for a few minutes, then vacuum off. Repeat until the stain has disappeared.

LEFT: Though strictly coordinated furnishings can stifle the personality of a room, this gentle combination is easy on the eye. Striped cushions are subtly echoed in roman blinds and sofa piping, while the tones of taupe are continued on the coffee table and in the carpet – cautious fabric-combining at its best.

FLOORS

The floor in living areas can take a lot of punishment, particularly when children, their friends, and their pets are tramping back and forth on their way to the backyard or kitchen. Yet at the same time, comfort is a top priority.

THE CARPET QUESTION

For many people, soft landings and a lounging surface are more important than anything, and consequently they choose to carpet their living rooms. Yet carpet does have a few inherent disadvantages for a family home. A supreme dust-attracter, it can make allergy-sufferers extra-sensitive, while completely sealing a floor and not letting air circulate. It is also susceptible to staining. But despite these drawbacks, carpet retains credibility as a soft, comfortable floor covering and is available in many, many colors. Darker shades and a gentle pattern are best for disguising stains. However, a neutral shade of biscuit or taupe will prove more versatile if you decide to redecorate in a different style or color before the carpet has begun to wear out.

For some people carpet is anathema. They move into a home and the first task to be completed is the ritual ripping out of all the carpets, followed by a couple of weeks dedicated to sanding and varnishing floorboards. Only then will they start thinking about decorating and personalizing the space. In some parts of the world,

such as Scandinavia, wood flooring is seen as the only sensible option, and carpet is treated as an unnecessary and unhygienic anachronism.

NATURAL MATTING

Natural floor coverings are a popular compromise and are both elegant and neutral in appearance. They can be used as mats, runners, or wall-to-wall carpeting, and either on their own or as a base for rugs. Sea grass is relatively soft underfoot, resists stains well, and is the least expensive of all the natural matting. Coir has a rougher surface, which children may find painful, but is ideal for heavy-traffic areas such as an open-plan room. Sisal is the most expensive and is available in various weaves, such as herringbone, twill, bouclé, and plaid. You can also buy a sisal-and-wool weave. Colors of these natural floor coverings range from off-white and soft pastels, such as straw and pale green, to russet and strong reds and blues.

LEFT: Unadorned wooden stairs can often seem too monastic when viewed in conjunction with a whole room of stripped floor-boards, so decorating the risers is one easy way of making a statement without investing in stair carpet.

RIGHT: Laid over generous underlay, the more expensive types of matting are surprisingly soft underfoot. Here the matting is made even more comfortable with a fringed woven rug for a modern country look. Rugs tend to look better against matting than they do against carpet, but it is important to anchor the rug in place for safety.

TERRACOTTA AND SLATE

Some country cottages have original slate or terracotta floors, which, while chilly underfoot and deeply unkind to tumbling children, have an inherent beauty that it is sacrilege to disguise. Place a soft rug over the top for warmth, and you will have the best of both worlds – a floor that is easy to maintain but provides a degree of comfort.

WOOD FLOORS

Laid over existing subfloors in modern homes, wood-strip floors are becoming increasingly popular. The warm tones and rich texture look wonderful in a living room, though they can be noisy, especially if your living room is not on the ground floor and people below must listen to footsteps.

Solid wood-strip flooring should really be laid by a professional, but some of the laminated types, particularly the so-called "floating floors" (in which the boards are secured to each other instead of to the subfloor) are fairly easy to install.

Floorboards can be painted in a checkerboard or freehand design as a colorful alternative to carpet. Make sure the design is one you can live with for a while. Use emulsion paint plus several coats of varnish, or gloss paint for a sleeker look.

RUGS

Rugs are perfect for protecting floorboards and for defining seating areas in a living room. Bold Modernist designs in thick wool, traditional dhurries, ikats, and Oriental designs all make dramatic decorations. Low-cost, low-maintenance choices include rag rugs, narrow Scandinavian-style cotton runners, and flat-weave kilims. Select rugs that match your budget and your decorative style, and anchor them to the floor for safety.

Carpet stains

Wherever there is a combination of children (or adults!) and food or drink, it is inevitable that spills will happen. The key to dealing with a stain is to act quickly, before it has time to set.

*

FOOD
Remove any food deposits, then apply carpet shampoo solution, following the manufacturer's instructions. If this dramatically cleans the carpet, you may have to treat the rest of the carpet so that the color remains uniform.

*

GREASE
Cover the stain with a piece of brown paper, then apply the tip of a warm iron to the area until the grease is absorbed. If the grease is still there after you have done this, sponge the area with a dry foam carpet shampoo, rubbing it in gently for a few minutes using the applicator on the can. Wipe off the foam with a clean cloth. The treatment can be repeated from the beginning if necessary. Vacuum the carpet when dry.

*

FRUIT JUICE
Mop up the spilled juice right away. Rub with a stain-removing bar, then use carpet shampoo. When dry, dampen cloth with methylated spirits and dab onto any remaining marks.

*

BEER, SPIRITS, WINE, TEA, AND COFFEE
Drink spills should be mopped up immediately. Sponge the stain with warm water or seltzer and then blot it dry. If the stain is still visible, treat it with carpet shampoo. The classic trick of pouring white wine onto a red wine stain is a quick fix if you don't have time to apply carpet shampoo.

*

CHEWING GUM
Remove chewing gum by scraping off as much as possible, then press a plastic bag containing ice cubes on the remainder. When frozen, chewing gum becomes brittle and is easier to break off the carpet tufts.

LIGHTING

Lighting is often overlooked in favor of the seemingly more adventurous tasks of planning a room's layout and choosing furniture and fabric. Generally undervalued, it is frequently left until too late. In fact, the right lighting will give even the dullest room a certain vibrancy, creating a fundamental air of comfort. Similarly, the wrong lighting will prevent a room from being as attractive or functional as it could be, no matter how good the furnishings.

Whether your natural style is urban chic or rural simplicity, appropriate lighting is not hard to source and implement. A good rule of thumb is to provide at least five different light sources within a living room – more if the room is large. These should ideally be on three or four different electrical circuits so that the lighting level can be adjusted as required.

TASK LIGHTING

Make sure that various activities in the living room – whether reading, writing, studying, or sewing – are well lit. Task lighting here usually takes the form of table lamps, varying from ceramic bases with conical shades of natural fibers to scrupulously contemporary steel constructions resembling arthritic giraffes. Make sure there are no trailing cords that anyone could trip over and ensure lamp bases are stable so young children cannot pull them over.

LEFT: Simple table lamps placed close to a sofa make good task lights, but be sure to avoid trailing cords.

BELOW LEFT: Clip-on lights provide portable pools of illumination and are useful for reading or for tasks that require clear light, such as sewing or writing. Swivel mountings lend extra versatility.

RIGHT: Although by day large windows in this triple-aspect room provide ample light, at night halogen lighting kicks in. Accent lighting is provided by a contemporary track system of swivel halogen spotlights, which also produces background lighting. Halogen floor lamps by the sofa punctuate the space and provide light for reading.

GENERAL LIGHTING

A form of background lighting is also essential. Once again, lamps can provide this. Many living rooms are ruined at night by a harsh central illumination that flattens surfaces and flatters nothing, so if you have a single pendant light, install a dimmer switch if it does not already have one. When set on low, it supplies background light, while setting it on high allows it to serve as a task light.

RIGHT: Three categories of lighting can be seen in this room. Wall sconces on either side of the fireplace provide general lighting, while a stylish table lamp serves as a task light not only for the table but also for the sofa in front of it. Mood lighting is provided in the form of chunky pillar candles placed on the mantelpiece.

Indirect lighting that is set behind cornicing, or uplighters set above picture rails or on top of built-in cupboards, disperses a soft light into the room without being directional. Classic wall sconces are another means of providing pleasant background lighting and are particularly suitable in a traditional or period-style home. Halogen downlighters recessed into the ceiling would work very well in a contemporary decor.

ACCENT LIGHTING

Accent lighting is decorative rather than functional, although it does contribute to the overall level of light in a room. Use it to draw attention to the most interesting aspects of the room, from architecture to furnishings or pictures.

Low-voltage halogen spotlights are perfect for highlighting displays on alcove shelves. Wall-mounted uplighters (which must be mounted above eye level) provide subtle background lighting in a room, bouncing light off a ceiling and back into the central space. Freestanding uplighters placed in corners or between large pieces of furniture or plants punctuate the space and create pleasing pools of light and shadow across a room. These lights, too, must be stable so choose the small, squat type instead of the tall, thin sort, to ensure that children cannot knock them over.

A good way of accenting paintings is to cross-light them using two spotlights, angled so that the beams of light cross on the picture surface.

MOOD LIGHTING

Candles are a good way of marking a transition from the hectic daytime banter and squabble to a serene calm in the evening. A row of nightlights set along a mantelpiece or a favorite candlestick with a scented candle will revive the spirit. Water and light reflected in a glass bowl filled with floating candles is a similar indulgence that can be reserved for the quiet evening hours or when entertaining. Remember never to leave candles unattended, especially if children are around.

STORAGE SOLUTIONS

BELOW: With ingenuity it is possible to create valuable storage space in the unlikeliest places. Here, in a clever variation on the more usual bookcases flanking a chimney breast, floor-to-ceiling shelves have been built into narrow alcoves formed by knocking through into the actual chimney-breast from the sides.

Storage has become something of a spiritual quest in our consumer society. With more and more ingenious and bizarre storage solutions appearing by the day, we are constantly being encouraged to take notice of unnecessary clutter. There is virtue in keeping clutter under control, but the lost souls who have always lived with an element of chaos around them will continue to do so, albeit with a touch of angst.

Nevertheless, now that there are custom-made storage units available for objects as diverse as door keys and photographs, magazines and CDs, there is good reason to take a long, hard look at all your belongings, their storage needs, and your home's storage inadequacies.

REDUCING CLUTTER

A family home is able to generate industrial quantities of clutter in the space of a day, much of which finds its way to the living room. Toddlers and their visitors emptying toy baskets, teenagers leaving clothes and belongings around the place, groceries not put away, unfinished paperwork, a basket or two of ironing waiting to be done in front of the television – these are just a few of the sources of instant clutter.

Our current obsession with neatness helps to account for the recent popularity of Shaker style. The Shakers' classically designed storage systems were elegant, built-in, and entirely practical. Peg rails held chairs out of the way so floors could be cleaned; only essential items were kept in the home, such as sewing equipment or tools; and they were all kept dust-free and out of sight behind beautifully proportioned cupboards and drawers.

Today, however, we have many more belongings than are strictly necessary for everyday living. Tidied away or discreet display are the new maxims for modern

ABOVE: Freestanding storage is good for rooms where the architecture would not benefit from being encroached upon by built-ins. A huge armoire like this will disguise anything, from the TV to stacks of videotapes, while the handsome blanket box probably contains toys and emergency throws for when children invade.

living, yet in order to achieve this harmony and space, a drastic clearing-out must often be the starting point.

YOU AND YOUR NEEDS

First, look at your living space and its architectural qualities. Fitting the storage to the architecture will help achieve a sympathetic balance. In a modern space, freestanding open shelving will add architectural interest in its own right, while a period home with interesting cornicing would benefit more from an antique cupboard or simple built-in shelving. Alcoves on either side of a chimney breast call out for shelves and fitted cupboards, while tall rooms can carry floor-to-ceiling shelves stuffed with books, without stifling the space. In family living spaces you may need to incorporate toys, children's videos, and computer equipment.

The next stage is to take a critical look at your belongings. Does your precious collection of old LPs really need pride of place on your shelves? Are dust-gathering ceramics improving your room and your life? Are you forever nagging the children about leaving their things out? Why are there always newspapers strewn indiscreetly around the room? It can only mean one thing – your storage systems need attention.

LEFT: Pigeonhole shelf arrangements are ideal for both storage and display, not to mention informal lighting. Breakable items are usually safe placed high up, while toys and craft materials can lurk on the lower shelves.

ABOVE RIGHT: Tall rooms fitted with integral ceiling-height cupboards are storage bliss for hoarders. All sorts of unsightly belongings can be concealed in neat boxes, tin trunks, and baskets in a tribute to good organization. Glass doors are more decorative than solid ones but the contents obviously have to be supremely neat if they are in full view.

Look at your available space and, if necessary, measure the places in the room where storage can be installed. Gather together any items of awkward shape or size and calculate exactly where everything can be housed. Try to store objects closest to where they are used, rather than just where they look good. Very often the burden of storage can be displaced to other areas of the home.

Items on display – framed pictures and photographs, collectibles, ceramics, memorabilia, ornaments – will add to the overall sense of clutter if they are simply scattered around the room. Put away (or throw away) all those items you walk past everyday without even noticing, then arrange the ones you do want to keep into several groups to achieve maximum impact. Collections that have a unifying theme, however tenuous, will look far better than completely arbitrary groups.

FITTED OR FREESTANDING?

Which alternative you favor in the fitted-versus-freestanding storage debate depends very much on your circumstances. If you plan to remain in your home for some time, then built-in solutions are probably best. Shelves that are architecturally integrated, appearing to form part of the wall, provide continuity and a neat home for books of all sizes. Those that not only line a wall but also continue above and around doorways and windows are both pleasing and practical, offering a large and continuous storage and display area.

As elsewhere in the home, window seats built into bays are extremely versatile, providing seating and storage simultaneously. Seats that incorporate pull-out drawers make more sense than those with lift-up lids, since you do not need to disturb the seating arrangements in order to get at the contents.

In awkward spaces or in a home you are merely passing through, freestanding units work best. Choose fluid arrangements that can be reorganized or added to when your needs change, whether it is a forged-iron framework lined with oak or pine shelves, a slot-together, adjustable shelving system, or some other type of unit. Wall-mounted glass-fronted cabinets offer a movable feast of storage and display, providing a dust-free setting for ceramics, precious antique books, and nature collections.

STORAGE FOR SMALL ITEMS

In a fluid living space where adults take over from children in the evening, toys should be stored out of sight when the busy day is over. Devote a cupboard, wicker trunk, blanket box, or fabric-lined basket to this purpose. A toy chest set on casters can be quickly converted into a side table for evening, finished off with a table lamp, a vase of flowers, an interesting bowl, or a pile of magazines. Keeping some children's books in a basket that can be moved from room to room is a good idea. It will encourage your children to look at them and you to take a few minutes off with them and read a quiet story.

Dedicate a temporary space to storing books and magazines. A basket on the floor is easily accessed and can be emptied on a weekly basis. Photographs, CDs, and tapes could be stored in fabric-covered or colored cardboard boxes or in steel tins on shelves. Spaces in alcoves covered with a curtain or blind are useful for hiding clutter, especially if the alcoves are fitted with adjustable shelves.

If you are using a portion of your living room as a work space, office paperwork will need to be stored out of sight when the working day is over. The above suggestions for children's toy storage would be suitable, or you could use an ottoman with hanging files hidden inside.

RIGHT: Freestanding furniture on a large scale such as this looks almost built in. Featuring drawers, display space, and open shelves, this storage scheme offers maximum versatility and practicality. As long as there are doors and drawers, there is an opportunity to channel the clutter away from the floor and tabletops. Another attraction of a unit like this is that items behind glass doors are less exposed to dust (and children's inquisitive fingers).

HOME ENTERTAINMENT

ABOVE: A piano or other musical instrument can be at least as entertaining as new computer technology or the latest soap opera on television, and it is a piece of decorative furniture in its own right.

As technology engulfs us in the form of mobile phones, 24-hour news, Internet information, fax machines, and digital, cable, and satellite television, there is a strong temptation to banish the gadgetry from sight in a living room. Whether you view media technology as a necessary evil, a great weekend toy, or a harmful deterrent from the finer things in life, its influence and presence have to be integrated into a family home. Soon, our TVs, videos, stereos, computers, and CD-ROMs will all be inter-linked within a home and probably sited in one place. Designers are already at work on storage systems for housing such a hodge-podge of equipment. In the meantime, there are various ways of tackling the issue.

ABOVE: Young children are more likely to become avid readers if they see their parents and siblings enjoying books. Comfortable, well-lit places for the family to indulge in this simple and important pleasure should always be incorporated into the living space, preferably well away from the TV and computer.

TELEVISIONS AND STEREOS

The great television debate – to hide or not to hide it – rages on. There are those who regard television cabinets as the height of bad taste, believing that televisions are functional pieces of equipment to be used and viewed accordingly. Some people feel it is acceptable to hide the set but it must be in an honest piece of furniture such as an old armoire. Others prefer purpose-made units or set up a home media center behind louvered doors. Whatever your solution, try not to make the television a focal point.

Stereos are best stored near wall sockets. Like TVs, they can be housed in a cup-board, as long as it is ventilated, since the equipment gives off heat. Speakers sound better if they are not left on the ground. Inconspicuous stands in corners work well, as do shelf-mounted versions. Trailing wires on open shelves can be bundled in a plastic wire-management tube. Label each wire to make it easier to move equipment.

ABOVE: Tucking a television neatly away behind closed doors means it does not have to become the focal point of a living space.

RIGHT: In an increasingly competitive world, many children's lives are neatly regimented into one activity after another, with practically every pursuit, from learning to exercise and play, occurring in highly structured environments geared to achievement. More than ever, children need time for being children and just relaxing in a comfortable, unpressurized home.

Ten ways to persuade children to watch less TV

The most drastic step is simply not to own a television in the first place.
If this radical idea is completely out of the question with your family, then try a few of these
suggestions instead. All-out confrontation of the "no, you are not watching television now"
variety usually ends in tears and resentment on both sides. The visual age is with us,
whether we like it or not, so damage limitation is probably the safest bet.

*

1 Take the time to read a book or to play a game with the child, instead of switching
on the TV and diving for the coffeepot and newspaper.

*

2 Use a piano or other musical instruments as a diversion. If children display a talent
for music, consider giving them additional music lessons, but remember
to encourage them to practice.

*

3 Limit viewing hours to a set pattern each day and a little extra on weekends.
Threatening to ban viewing altogether is a good way to produce the worst behavior!

*

4 Allocate one program per week as the family show and sit down together
to watch it. Children will enjoy the communal experience, then be more
inclined to do something different afterwards.

*

5 Make children watch an educational program way above their heads and pretend
that it is all that is on (this only works on children under three years old).

*

6 Insist that you watch a major sporting event to which they will barely relate.
Once protests have diminished they will soon be off to a different game.

*

7 Rather than refusing point-blank to switch on the TV, set a reasonable time limit,
say 15–30 minutes, then mutually agree to turn it off.

*

8 Ask teenagers to make a contribution to the cable TV fees before they are
allowed to spend hours in front of the set.

*

9 If you think a particular program unsuitable, impose a video
alternative in a persuasive manner.

*

10 Get children into the habit of turning on the television only to watch a specific program,
and then switching off as soon as it is finished. Discourage channel-surfing or getting
drawn into the next program. Avoid having the television on in the
background or during mealtimes.

COMPUTERS

Computers were not designed with aesthetics in mind and are often difficult to store. A purpose-built system hidden within an alcove cupboard is often the answer, or you might consider a trolley with a pull-out shelf for the keyboard. You can also get "armoire offices," which are reproduction armoires pre-wired for electronics, with drop-down work surfaces for keyboards and roomy shelves for screens. Where a computer with CD-ROM is needed in a living room, consider housing the complete entertainment system in one space and plan a system around it. What may look like a floor-to-ceiling cupboard will, in fact, house all the technology in a neat, architectural line.

Chrome stacking systems are another way of storing and displaying media equipment. Tall units are designed to house stereo and television, while smaller, interlocking elements are suitable for storage boxes, videos, and CDs. In a system like this everything is visible and therefore accessible. This is excellent when the children are older but not so great with toddlers, who are fascinated by the sight of so many movable objects. Cupboards with doors are best when children are young.

the imries, **relaxed island living**

Richard and Pippa Imrie have five children spanning 20 years, two dogs, and a lifestyle made hectic by the sheer weight of numbers. To relieve the pressure on their Bellport, Long Island, home they regularly downshift to a simpler life at their self-built wooden house in Hawaii.

The island of Maui is casual rather than chic, a place where organic produce, sushi, and sunshine dominate a health-conscious approach to living and eating – a place to relax after the hectic schedules of their New York life. The ocean views from the Imries' home on the peaceful north shore are a long way from the tourist circus further south, and at least half an hour's drive to the nearest carton of milk.

The whole family did live in the house for two years, but being so isolated did not prove to be a practical year-round solution. However, the two eldest boys, Chico, 26, and Max, 18, still spend long periods of time at the house as they are both studying at a college on the island, so the two family homes are well inhabited.

Above: Wash day can be a challenge when the electricity supply is limited. Fortunately, the sun is a very efficient clothes' dryer, and there is something comforting about traditional rows of wash hanging outside.

Above: The dog pretends to stand guard at the front door but is, in reality, enjoying the sun like everyone else.
Right: A swimming pool enables everyone to escape the heat and proves an irresistible magnet for the children when friends and family come to stay.
Below: Retreating to the shade of the verandah for a drink and a chat.

Richard makes frequent trips around the world in connection with his work as a fashion photographer, while Pippa runs a mail-order children's clothing business, Pippers, from an office close to the Bellport house and from home when resident in Maui, but they are both originally from Scotland. Building their own home in Hawaii has proved to be the perfect way of combining living and leisure for such a large family.

This house is definitely a place to escape to with friends, but also works as an extension of their main home on Long Island. As the children grow up, they have another place to hang out, complete with swimming pool, a great climate, and a simple existence, while entertaining friends and putting up extra guests is no hassle in such a relaxed environment. A changing hut by the pool easily doubles as extra sleeping accommodation, and bunkbeds in two of the bedrooms also allow for guests.

Richard oversaw the building work down to the very last detail. For example, hearing about a house being demolished in Bellport, he purchased the window frames, shipped them to Hawaii, and incorporated them into the architectural drawings. Small lions

House Rules

* Mix and match old and new.

* Buy it chipped so you are stress-free from the start.

* Paint old furniture for a brighter outlook.

* Use the children's artwork as decoration.

* Have a dump bin handy for instant
tidy-ups of family clutter.

* Blame the children for any mess.

* Keep the larder well stocked with a few basics
for instant meals.

* Don't turn down any offers of help with cooking
and make sure everyone clears their own plates
at the end of a meal.

Above left: Crowding around huge dishes of freshly prepared salads, the girls consider how quickly they can demolish the contents after a tiring morning of swimming. Big families consume food as soon as it appears on the table, so Pippa always caters in bulk.

Above centre top and bottom, right: Serving lunch to a crowd buffet-style is much easier than setting a table for a more formal sit-down meal. Everyone can help themselves, then take their dirty dishes and glasses straight to the dishwasher. No help, no food!

punched into the wooden shutters are a visual reference to the Imries' cultural roots. Solar panels provide heat and light for the house, although once the pool has been filtered, there is only sufficient power to light and heat one room in the evening. With nothing but the basics in terms of utilities and food supplies, simple living is the sole option. It really does concentrate the mind when all laundry has to be done by hand and line-dried, hot water is strictly limited, and popping out for last-minute provisions is impossible.

To cope with such a large family, through necessity Pippa has over the years developed a decorating ethos that is best described as "clean country." Time is too short for complicated cleaning routines, fitted upholstery, or a strict adherence to only one decorating style, and as a result, a relaxed, low-maintenance approach prevails throughout the house. A large shoe rack placed outside the front door hints that footprints only create more chores. Within, wooden floors are robust, easy to clean, and good to live with. Slightly battered, brightly painted furniture mingles with antique pieces in a happy convergence of styles, more traditional than contemporary.

The kitchen is always at the core of such a people-heavy home. In the Imries' kitchen, open shelves packed with glasses, plates, and cutlery are organized in such a way that everyone can see and grab the contents with ease. Instant meals, quick drinks, and regular snacks can be had by all, at any time. If everything were always cleared away behind doors after each mealtime, the hinges could simply wear out with so much repeat business. Catering-size pots, pans, and dishes are required for even a simple supper. The kitchen also boasts a worktop/breakfast bar as big and as wide as possible.

The home was built very much with leisure in mind, and the swimming pool is indispensable in this climate. The changing pavilion by the pool doubles as a spot for the teenagers and their friends to congregate and get away from the adults. A generous wooden verandah dotted with chairs and hammocks encircles the house, extending the living space enormously. Weather is not an issue here, as it is unreservedly warm, even when it rains, and the house is secluded, so window coverings are not vital. Natural light is in such abundance that often candles and garden flares suffice on a warm evening.

Above left: Relaxed living involves using loose throws over furniture that young children use while preserving other spaces for adults and older children. Videos stored on open shelves mean wet-weather entertainment is always on hand.

Above right: Huge, squishy sofas and a large ottoman mean the whole family can just about squeeze in together if necessary. Alternatively, one person can enjoy serious rest and relaxation with a good book while the others are outside.

With electricity restricted to the main living area, there is no chance of sloping off to watch TV in another quieter part of the house at night. But there is enough space for several different living zones within the one room. When there is work to be done, a small fold-down desk in the entranceway doubles as a work space. And then, of course, there is the verandah, which, in this perfect climate, can be used for most of the year.

Most of the bedrooms nestle under the eaves of the house and are reached via wooden ladders. Simple bunks for the girls' rooms make excellent use of a limited space, with small shelves fitted between the vertical wall struts. A bed ladder topped with carved horses' heads and a large collection of colored rosettes reflect a love of horses and riding.

Living for part of the year on such an unspoiled island provides a very welcome relief from the mad-paced life of New York. Taking time out to restore the spirits, get back to nature, and just spend time with the whole family together is something to be cherished. In a large family, so much of everyday life is devoted to simply getting through the household chores, ferrying small ones to school and other activities, and entertaining after school that sometimes there is no time left to simply BE and catch up with one another. As the Imries have successfully proved, an island retreat is the idyllic answer.

Above: A muslin-draped bed is an instant cooler in a hot climate.

Above left: Simple bunks are neatly built into the wooden framework of the house and finished off with a carved horse-head ladder for equine-loving girls.

Below left: A fold-down desk in the hallway is the perfect place for catching up on domestic paperwork when the need arises.

Right: Swinging on the hammock with not a care in the world. Bliss.

"Living part of the year on an unspoiled island where life is stripped of artifice and modern convenience revives the spirit, restores creativity, and, best of all, completely relaxes all members of the family, including the dog."

PLASTER plaques

These plaster plaques are a good way of recording the tiny hands and feet of toddlers who will grow all too quickly into clumsy teenagers. Children enjoy making the plaques too, not just because they have to get nice and messy but also because they are intrigued by the finished result. You can leave the plaques white, paint or colorwash them, or rub dark boot polish over the surface and then burnish with a cloth. To further personalize the plaques, get children to write their names in the semi-wet plaster just after removing their hands or feet. The finished plaques make lovely keepsakes and ideal gifts for doting grandparents.

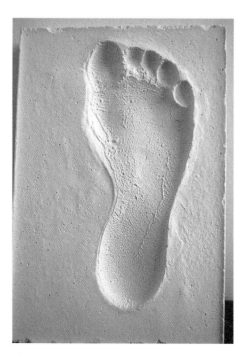

YOU *will need*

* 2 x 1in (50 x 25mm) PAR softwood:
  2 boards approximately 8in (200mm) long
  2 boards approximately 7in (180mm) long
  (see step 1)
* Masking tape
* ¼in- (6mm-) thick hardboard:
  1 piece 10 x 10in (25 x 25cm)
* 4in (10cm) length of plastic-coated
  garden wire
* Modeling clay
* Plaster of Paris
* Bowl or jug
* Sandpaper
* Acrylic or emulsion paint and
  flat artist's brush (optional)
* Dark boot polish and soft cloth (optional)

1 Measure the length and width of your child's hand or foot in order to decide on the finished size of the plaque, then have the wood cut to length accordingly. Join the pieces of wood together to form a rectangle with sides about 2in (5cm) high; secure the corners with masking tape. Place the box shape on top of the piece of hardboard. There is no need to join the two together, but make sure that there are no gaps, otherwise the plaster might seep out. Plaster hardens quickly along fine joints so the box will quickly adhere to the board.

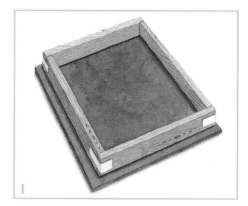

2 For hanging the finished plaque on the wall, you need to create an integral hook by fixing a wire loop in the mold before you pour in the plaster. Twist a 4in (10cm) length of plastic-coated wire into a loop, leaving the two ends spread apart and pointing upwards slightly. Cover the loop with a small lump of modeling clay and stick it to the hardboard base of the box near what will be the top end. Be sure to leave the two ends of the wire pointing upward so that they will be secured when the plaster is poured in.

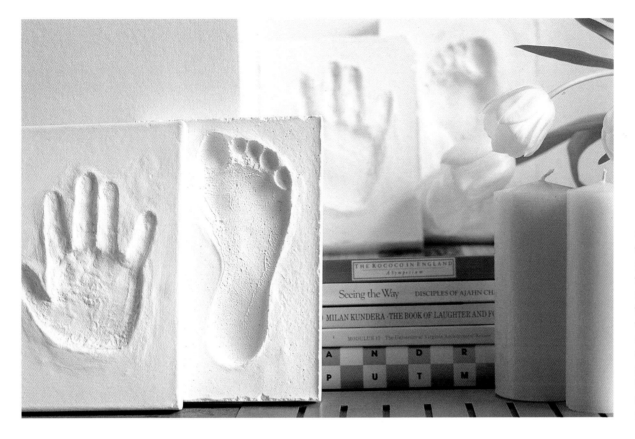

LEFT: Plaster molds of tiny hands and feet are a precious memento of a time that quickly becomes nostalgic. As huge teenagers descend on a well-stocked fridge to consume its entire contents, you will be grateful for a reminder of how sweet, innocent, and appealing these large people once were.

Following the manufacturer's instructions, add the plaster of Paris to an old mixing bowl or jug of water (never add the water to plaster of Paris) until it makes a thick, creamy consistency. (The plaster will start to set immediately, so make sure your child is close at hand.) Quickly pour the mixture into the mold to a depth of approximately 1in (2.5cm). (Do not dispose of any excess plaster down the sink, as it will harden in the drain and cause damage.)

3 When the plaster is slightly firm to the touch, place the child's hand or foot gently into it (avoiding the wires of the hanging loop) so that the plaster comes about halfway up the fingers or toes. Try to hold the hand or foot as steady as possible to allow the plaster to set and form the shape. As it begins to set, it will become warm. Carefully and gently remove the child's hand or foot from the cast so as not to disturb the shape and immediately wash the hand or foot thoroughly.

Leave the plaster to set completely (this will take about 45 minutes) before removing the tape and the wood box.

4 Pry the plaque away from the hardboard base and leave to dry out completely. The modeling clay will come away to reveal the hanging hook embedded in the plaster. If you wish, any rough edges can be gently rubbed with sandpaper. The plaque can now be painted, colorwashed, or coated with boot polish and burnished if required.

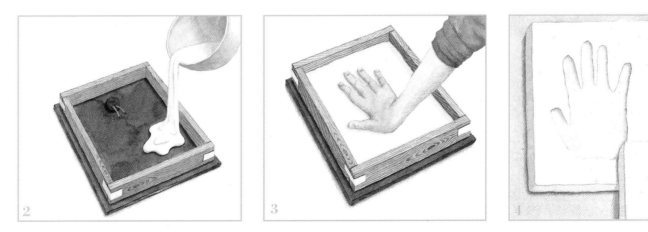

BLUE DAISY throw

Throws are endlessly useful, whether you want decorative additions to beds and sofas, quick feet-warmers, or family heirlooms. This throw in blanket fabric is decorated with appliquéd flowers, simple embroidery, and buttons for a folksy feel. If you wish to match a particular shade, you could dye the fabric. Most 100-percent wool cream-colored blanket fabric can be dyed using multipurpose or machine dyes, but the dye can make the wool slightly felted. Dye the blankets before cutting them to size, as dyeing, especially in the washing machine, can shrink them by up to 25 percent. The throw measures 68 x 80in (173 x 203cm).

ABOVE: There is something very comforting about wrapping yourself in a favorite throw and snuggling up on the sofa – especially when teddy is in on the fun.

RIGHT AND FAR RIGHT: This warm throw is made from a large-scale patchwork of woollen blanket fabric, decorated with simple flowers and buttons for extra detail.

YOU will need

* Blanket fabric in teal, cream, royal blue, and pale blue (see Preparation for quantities)
* Fabric remnants of 4 different cottons
* Fusible interfacing and an iron
* Polyester sewing thread in teal, cream, royal blue, and pale blue
* Small amount of worsted-weight knitting yarn in dark blue and royal blue
* Selection of buttons in blue and cream
* Sewing machine with needle suitable for heavy fabrics
* Tapestry or darning needle

Preparation: Cut the blanket fabric as follows: *teal*: 2 rectangles, each 24 x 30in (61 x 76cm); *cream*: 2 rectangles, each 24 x 30in (61 x 76cm); *royal blue*: 4 squares, each 12 x 12in (30.5 x 30.5cm); *pale blue*: 2 strips, each 12 x 47in (30.5 x 119cm), and 2 strips, each 12 x 59in (30.5 x 150cm). Using matching thread, make parallel lines of stitching on the teal rectangles to create a striped pattern. Do the same on the cream rectangles, then stitch parallel lines at right angles to the first ones to create a checked pattern.

1 Cut four squares of fusible interfacing, each slightly larger than the complete flower. Iron one to the wrong side of each of the four fabric remnants, following the manufacturer's instructions. Draw six petals on each square and cut them out. Position the petals, interfacing-side down, on the right side of the four royal blue squares, and iron in place. If desired, secure them

1

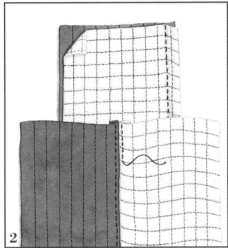

1

4

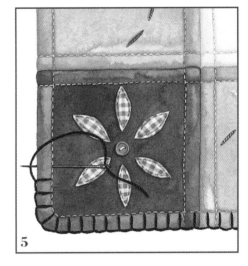

5

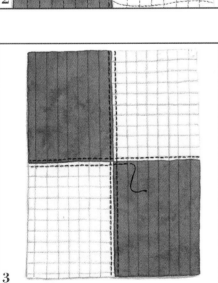

3

further by machine stitching (either straight stitch or zigzag) around the edges.

2 With right sides together, pin, tack, and stitch a cream rectangle to a teal rectangle down their long edges, making a ½in (1.2cm) seam. Press the seam open then topstitch ⅜in (1cm) from the seamline on both rectangles, using thread to match each color. Join the other pair of cream/teal rectangles in the same way but with the colors in reverse order. Remove the tacking.

3 In the same way, join one pair of cream/teal rectangles to the other pair, forming one large panel with a checkerboard pattern.

4 Use the same method to join the two longest pale blue strips to the long edges of the center and to join a royal blue daisy square to each short edge of the two remaining pale blue strips. Join these top and bottom borders to the short edges.

5 Turn under and press a single ½in (1.2cm) hem all around the edges of the throw; machine stitch. Work blanket stitch, as shown, around the hemmed edge, using worsted-weight knitting yarn and a tapestry or darning needle. Use the same yarn to decorate the borders with wavy lines of running stitch. Sew a button in the center of each daisy, and add more at random around the border.

STAMPED and appliquéd curtain

Muslin is inexpensive and is easily made into a decorative curtain for doors or windows where an element of disguise, rather than complete privacy, is required. Either stick to natural tones of cream, string, and biscuit for a subtle backdrop or buy a bright shade and decorate it with other colors for a stronger visual statement. The stamp used for the leaf motif is made from a thick synthetic sponge, but you could create an equally effective stamp from a halved potato. Three-dimensional objects such as small curtain hooks or matchsticks arranged in a pattern and glued onto thick cardboard also work well. The stamp needs to be sturdy enough to use over the whole curtain; if in doubt, make a couple.

YOU *will need*

* Thick synthetic sponge
* Felt-tipped pen and craft knife
* Muslin to make the curtain, with enough extra fabric for the printed patches
* Matching sewing thread
* Sewing machine and iron
* Fabric paint
* Small roller
* Narrow curtain pole
* Café-curtain clips

1 To make the stamp, draw a motif on the sponge using a felt-tipped pen. Cut around the shape to a depth of roughly ½in (1.2cm) with a craft knife.
2 Make the curtain by turning under and pressing a double hem on all four sides of the fabric; pin and machine stitch. Cut separate pieces of muslin for the printed patches, large enough to accommodate the stamped motif comfortably and allowing for a narrow hem. Put some fabric paint in a dish and run the roller through it, then apply the roller to the stamp to cover its surface with paint. Practice on scrap fabric to get used to the technique before printing on the fabric patches.
3 Once you are happy printing, stamp the motif onto the patches. Leave to dry, then iron to fix the paint, following the instructions on the paint.
4 Turn under and press a narrow hem on all four edges of each patch. Pin and tack the patches in place on the curtain, roughly spacing them out. Machine-stitch each patch to the curtain, then remove the tacking. Hang the curtain from the pole using evenly spaced metal café-curtain clips.

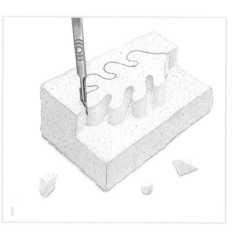

FOLDING screen

Screens are endlessly useful in a family home for dividing up space and hiding clutter. This screen is designed to give visual peace on one side and on the other side act as a vital accompaniment to a home office, with its hook-on storage system. It is simply made from a softwood framework forming four hinged panels that are faced with fabric on one side and hardboard on the other. This screen is 6ft (1.8m) high, but the height can easily be adjusted. The casters lend extra flexibility, while the strong hinges mean the screen will fold into a flat-pack when not in use. Choose a fabric that is sturdy, otherwise you will need to line it.

YOU *will need*

* 2 x 1in (50 x 25mm) softwood: 8 boards 6ft (1.8m) long and 12 boards 2ft (600mm) long
* 24 angle brackets
* Drill
* Screwdriver and screws
* Hardboard: 4 sheets, 6 x 2ft (1800 x 600mm)
* 4⅓yd (4m) of 60in- (150cm-) wide fabric or 8⅔yd (8m) of narrower fabric (plus the same amount of lining if you will be lining thin fabric); allow extra fabric if you are matching a pattern
* Staple gun and staples
* Emulsion paint and brush
* 6 brass butt hinges, 3in (7.5cm) long
* 8 casters
* Hooks

1 Cut the boards to form the long, vertical sides of the panels. For each panel, fix three short boards between two long boards using an angle bracket and screws at each end of each cross-piece. Make sure all pieces are attached at 90-degree angles – this will ensure the panels all fit together properly. For the central crosspiece, the angle brackets should be attached on opposite sides for added strength, as shown in the illustration.

2 Cut out a 78 x 30in (195 x 75cm) piece of fabric for each frame, making sure that the corners of each piece are square. For each frame, place a piece of fabric wrong side up on the floor and lay the frame centrally on top. Stretch the fabric around to the reverse side of the frame and staple it to the back with a staple gun at intervals of about 3in (7.5cm), stapling the top and bottom first before the sides. If using a striped fabric, ensure that the fabric is evenly stretched so the stripes all run in exactly the same direction on each panel. Miter the corners at the back and staple them in place.

3 Drill rows of holes in the hardboard backing panels at the required height for the hanging hooks. Make sure the holes are not drilled where the central crosspiece will be. Paint the panels with emulsion paint (you may need to apply two coats). When completely dry, fix them to the reverse side of the framework with screws at about 6in (15cm) intervals. Paint over the screw heads to hide them.

4 Join the four panels together by fixing the butt hinges near the tops and bottoms of the panels

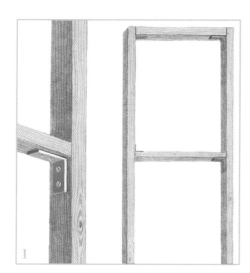

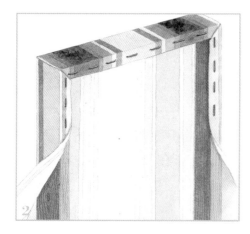

so they fit snugly on the edge of the frame. The pair of hinges that join the two middle panels should be on the opposite edge to all the other hinges, so that the screen can be folded up concertina-fashion. To finish off, fit two casters into the bottom corners of each panel, and insert the hanging hooks in the drilled holes. You may need to open up the metal hooks slightly in order to fit them into the holes.

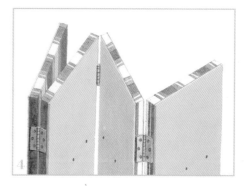

ESCAPE ROUTES

ESCAPE ROUTES

Anyone who looks after a family requires space and

ABOVE: A comfortable
armchair and an ottoman
placed in a quiet corner
close to a view of the
outdoors beg to be
occupied. An arm's reach
away from reading matter,
this is an ideal spot for
taking time out to read,
think, or even sleep.

The daily routine of family life can be incredibly demanding.

The relentless cycle of cooking, cleaning, doing laundry,

carpooling, planning, and shopping threatens to strain the

nerves, scramble the brain, and wear out the body. To

prevent things overwhelming you, it is essential to build

escape routes into your life. When the chores start to

outweigh the high points of family life, it is pure joy to know

that a prearranged treat, a snatched hour of complete

leisure, or a personal sanctuary is within reach – a place or

a pleasure that will soothe tired nerves and nourish the spirit.

BELOW LEFT: Work spaces make remarkably good retreats from the demands of family life, since getting down to some single-minded concentration provides as good a break as any. Filled with natural daylight, this mezzanine workroom is far enough away from the main part of the home to be a peaceful place to work.

LEFT: There is nothing like a long, luxurious bath for soothing frayed nerves. When the need for calm consumes you, retire to the bathroom, lock the door, hide the bath toys, and rejuvenate the spirit with a deep bath and absorbing reading matter. Add candles and music for the complete experience.

time for relaxation and a spot of pure self-indulgence.

Anywhere or anything that allows you to be yourself, unwind, and switch your mind into a different gear is an escape route. It might be an actual spot, such as a window seat overlooking the garden, a potting shed, or a workroom. Or it could be some sort of treat – perhaps relaxing with a favorite book or having lunch with friends.

Work or self-improvement can be another means of escaping the daily grind. Despite replacing one routine with another, it is a good way of turning the mind away from purely domestic concerns. A day in the study or workroom will often strengthen and refresh you in preparation for another strong dose of family life.

Learning a new skill is always energizing, whether it is a stained-glass evening class or a correspondence course, a series of daytime lectures or a decorating workshop. Sport and exercise are great revivers too, increasing your energy levels and sense of well-being while keeping your body in good condition. You may feel completely exhausted at the end of the day, but forcing yourself to take some exercise really is guaranteed to revitalize you.

MAKING TIME

Even if it is taking the dog for a walk, a quick ten-minute workout on exercise equipment, or simply a self-indulgent half hour of doing absolutely nothing, make sure your escape route becomes just as much a permanent feature of your life as the daily chores. It can be invaluable when you need a tonic to revive you quickly, but building it into your daily routine will help to prevent things from getting you down in the first place.

If there never seems to be time left over for these pursuits, then sit down and rearrange the timetable. Schedule everyone's leisure pursuits and "escape route" time. Be sure to give them advance notice of *your* escape route time, too.

Good time management is as vital in the home as in business, since looking after a family is all about controlling the demands on your time, patience, creativity, and bank balance. Homemakers often have to juggle activities, people, and emotions faster than even the busiest workplace manager. Therefore, prioritize everything that needs doing, whether it is getting a leaking roof fixed, writing letters, stocking the freezer, or tracking down a good ballet class.

Routine breakers

Take the children out for lunch occasionally. For added interest, combine it with a trip to the local library, a visit to the park, or a simple wander around a store. Even a car wash can be fascinating to a toddler and you will be able to sit still for ten precious minutes.

*

On the weekend take off for a whole day with the family. Leave early in the morning, eat meals out, and return tired but happy.

*

Write a letter you have been putting off for too long or phone a neglected friend to catch up on all the news.

*

Start a decorating project – stripping paintwork, painting shelves, making curtains – but make sure you follow it through to the end or you will be surrounded by half-finished work.

*

Sort through the family keepsakes and decide which ones can go and which need preserving and displaying.

*

Sort out all your piles of photos and put them into albums.

*

Weed the garden, then sit back with a drink and admire your work.

*

Arrange a children-swap with a friend and use the time solely for yourself – to read, exercise, go to a health club, visit a museum, play the piano, or whatever else you never have time to do on a normal day.

LEFT: A bedroom retreat can afford to be a completely child-free zone, if used as a regular escape route. Decorated and furnished in calm, neutral colors, this room offers the perfect spot to keep bedtime reading matter close at hand: shelves built into a narrow alcove. A balcony with a rocking chair provides an additional retreat.

RIGHT: A draped bed, four-poster, or carved head-board adds a romantic element to a bedroom retreat. This delicately carved French headboard is painted white to blend with the paneled walls, muslin canopy, and pale bed linen. Unlike the rest of the home, white can be used in an adult bedroom, which is less exposed to marauding youngsters.

Resolve to undertake at least one of these jobs per week and let the family know if it will involve their help or cooperation.

SUITABLE SPOTS

The bedroom is an obvious retreat. Not only is it one of the few rooms where adult belongings predominate over children's toys and family clutter, but the decoration can be as self-indulgent as you like. Here, more than anywhere, practicality can take second place to aesthetics. If, in addition to a family bathroom, you also have an en-suite bathroom attached to the main bedroom, this offers a further opportunity to indulge yourself. A foamy hot bath and a facial in a serene bathroom free of squeaky toys and teenage acne remedies will restore not just your pH values but also your sense of calm.

Other places within the home offer potential escape routes, too. A study or guest room furnished with books and a sofa or sofa bed makes a good private space. A converted loft could also be furnished in this way – or it could house a Ping-Pong or pool table for more active relaxation.

PLANNING PARENTS' BEDROOMS

The bedroom is sometimes the only room in the house that can truly be labeled an escape route. Here is the ultimate refuge, offering private space and a chance to express yourself with a style of decoration unimpeded by the practical demands and restrictions of family life.

PRIORITIES

The important components for a grown-ups' bedroom are the bed (see page 140), storage for clothing, good lighting, a dressing table or mirror, and maybe some form of seating. It may also double as a second sitting room, a workroom, or an exercise room. But whatever the purposes to which it is put, the bedroom is a primary escape route and should be furnished with that in mind.

The parents' bedroom is often the largest, yet, ironically, the parents spend much less time in the bedroom than their children do, going to bed later and waking earlier to prepare for work or to make sure offspring, particularly teenagers, begin the day on time. For these reasons and to make the best use of space, some parents may temporarily assign the largest bedroom to a teenager, or to two siblings who are sharing. One of the main attributes of a successful family home is flexibility. Never think of a home as a static structure confined to a sole purpose. A fluid approach will yield more creative results.

NATURAL AND ARTIFICIAL LIGHT

Main bedrooms have traditionally been east-facing, so they receive the early-morning sunlight. However, this is less important today than in the days when natural light was more significant than the lightbulb.

Soft romantic lighting is an essential element and can be achieved in a number of ways. Dimmable hinged bracket lamps mounted on the wall at either side of the headboard will provide understated illumination as well as excellent reading light. Having lamps on both sides enables one person to read while the other is asleep. Table lamps on bedside tables are an alternative, but they are not as good for reading by. The ideal system allows you to turn the lights on and off from either the doorway or the bed.

ABOVE LEFT: An elegant daybed strikes a note of glamour against informal blinds and a polished wooden floor. Keeping a favored, valuable piece of furniture in the bedroom is a good way of preserving it from children's attention.

RIGHT: A wall of windows surmounting bookshelves makes this ground-floor bedroom cum library a calm spot for reading and relaxing. French doors open directly onto lush woodland in case a sudden need for a quick walk interrupts the thought process.

RIGHT: Light and airy, a bedroom tucked under the eaves in a converted barn is an ideal retreat at the end of a long day. The white-painted walls and ceiling, neutral-toned furnishings, and use of wood promote a sense of calm, as does the pleasing view.

You will also need lamps around the dressing table and dressing area. Make sure that they are placed at the edges of a dressing table mirror rather than above, where they will cast unflattering shadows, making you feel more Addams family than adequate. Lighting built into wardrobes, in the form of small strip lights or halogen spots, is handy when scrambling around in the morning half-light for two matching socks.

Task lighting may be necessary for specific areas such as a writing desk, sewing table, or computer workstation, while good general lighting, from overhead lights or wall lights, is useful on entering the room – fit a dimmer so you can vary the intensity. Candlelight is always romantic, but don't fall asleep before extinguishing the flame; nightlights in suitable containers are safer than conventional candles.

PERSONAL STYLE

The decorative style of the bedroom is very much a personal thing, but make sure that both parties are in agreement before you set off on your voyage into country roses or strict minimalism. A good night's sleep in an environment that is nurturing for all is the best escape route.

People often long for at least one room they can decorate purely for personal pleasure, choosing the colors and materials they adore without being castigated by the rest of the family. Colors for inducing relaxation include soft greens, gentle ochres and, of course, warm neutral tints. Strong red is to be avoided unless you favor an in-your-face bordello or dining parlor atmosphere, while a very dark green or blue could look too severe and unemotional in a room where sensual pleasure and coziness should be priorities.

SIMPLICITY AND CALM

In our eco-oriented times, many people have turned to the all-white bedroom, with its pure and healthy associations, as an antidote to the chaotic, polluted daily grind. Such a clean and neutral canvas encourages us to expunge stress and fatigue in an atmosphere of monastic calm – and this is the one room in a family home where an all-white decor is not tempting fate.

The trend for simple decor goes hand-in-hand with this ethos of making the bedroom a calm, fresh place, with an abundance of pure air, restorative scent, and gentle light – a sensory oasis within the noise and bustle of a family home. Simple blinds or curtains are now often preferred to heavy swags-and-tails or fussy festoon blinds. The treatment should allow in plenty of natural light during the day but be able to block it out when necessary. If one of you is a naturally light sleeper, you may wish to use thick fabric or blackout lining.

TACTILE QUALITIES

Thick pile carpet is lovely to walk on barefoot, but many people these days prefer simple matting such as sisal, sea grass, or coir, or bare floorboards either stripped and varnished or painted. Hard floors can be softened beside beds and on main traffic areas with soft sheepskin throws, woven cotton rugs, and kilims or floor runners, Scandinavian style. For more comfort you could consider a wall-to-wall 100-percent wool, or wool-and-sisal, flatweave carpet, which resembles matting but is soft.

Even in the most pristine, private bedroom, your children may arrive for reassurance and a cuddle at any time of the night when they are distressed or ill. Allowing space for them in your bed and providing a basketful of books and toys will show that although this is your special space, they are not totally excluded.

RIGHT: In a spacious open-plan sleeping and bathing space, a platform and low storage unit help to set the bath area apart. The large bed with its simple duvet makes the room seem bigger. One huge painting of a teddy above the bed is a nod to family life, but the pristine air of the room lends itself to quiet contemplation.

The versatile bedroom

If you have sufficient space, create a small sitting area in one corner or near a fireplace. Include a couple of easy chairs, a small table or chest, and a reading lamp.

*

Once you have the main furnishings – a good bed and ample storage – consider which extras will allow you to use the room fully. If your bedroom is relatively cool and there is sufficient space, it could be a good place to install some fitness apparatus, such as a skiing machine, treadmill, or exercise bike.

*

If you have young children who are in the habit of coming into the bedroom before you get up, keep a basket of toys close at hand. Choose quiet toys to try to encourage a more peaceful start to the day!

*

Include a bookcase for your favorite bedtime reading. The most convenient spot is within easy reach of the bed, or you could create a reading corner at the other end of the bedroom.

*

Preserve the bedroom as a chore-free room. Keep ironing boards, domestic paperwork, and piles of unsorted clutter somewhere else.

*

If you have an en-suite bathroom, keep it as a child- and toy-free zone where you can indulge in long, scented baths.

CHOOSING BEDS AND BED LINEN

RIGHT: An iron bedstead is at once rustic and romantic. Here it provides a classic country element in an otherwise modern setting. White bed linen is timeless and luxurious.

BELOW RIGHT: Bright checked soft furnishings introduce vivid color into a neutral bedroom. When the throw is cast off at night, the room reverts to a cool, white haven.

The bed is the main comfort factor and focal point in a bedroom – in fact, it is the most important piece of furniture in the entire home – so go for the best you can afford. Choose the biggest one that you have room for: not only is a king-sized bed more comfortable to sleep in, but it is also far less cramped when young children pay an early-morning visit.

BED TYPE AND POSITION

The width of the bed is not the only important factor – the sizes of the people who are sleeping in it matter too. Tall people will find sleeping in a bedstead with a footboard constricting; for them an extra-long bed base is more suitable. The heavier you are, the firmer the bed needs to be. This also applies to people troubled with back pain. Anyone who is prone to dust-induced allergies will benefit from a bed with wooden slats, to provide breathing space between the mattress and the floor.

There is a superb choice of styles of bed available today, from elegant antique or reproduction sleigh beds to streamlined pallet bases for futons, and from space-saving platform beds to elaborate antique brass bedsteads. If you buy an antique bed, check that you will not have a problem finding a mattress to fit; the size you need may be different from modern ones. Also, antique bedsteads are often quite high off the ground and it can require some agility to climb up into them.

Four-posters are one big statement but bed curtains and drapery are not to every-one's liking, although children will delight in making an instant den in them. Sleek modern four-posters are designed to look good with hardly any hangings.

Wrought-iron bedsteads are available in enduring classic styles or streamlined modern designs (although the natural-home lobby claims that if the iron becomes magnetized, it can redirect the earth's natural magnetic field and, over a long period, produce disturbed sleep).

The position of the bed is also thought to have a bearing on the quality of sleep. Feng shui, the Chinese art of placement, suggests that beds should be diagonally opposite the door, so that anyone in bed will be able to see people entering and leaving. If this is impossible, then you could place a mirror between the bed and door for a better view.

PILLOWS AND MATTRESSES

Use one pillow that is neither too thin nor too bulky. It should support the nape of the neck without flexing it too much. A neck-case pillow used in conjunction with a normal pillow is useful if you are prone to neck strain.

A good mattress should provide support for the spine but have enough give to allow hips and shoulders to slip into their natural position. Some couples, especially those in which one person has back trouble, or one person is much heavier than the other, find

LEFT: A muslin canopy and traditional patchwork quilt lend homespun charm to a cool room with a terracotta tiled floor. A canopy is a good way of creating a feeling of coziness and making an otherwise ordinary bed seem special, and the filmy muslin prevents a heavy appearance or claustrophobic feel. Generous pillows in blue checks decorate this bed and add further touches of color.

that two separate mattresses on one base, or two completely separate single beds zipped together, can be a good solution, since each mattress can be chosen to suit the individual's own needs. This solution is also helpful in couples where one person is a restless, light sleeper.

A mattress with pocket springing, in which each spring moves independently of the others, is preferable to, and more expensive than, one with open springing, in which

the springs are interlinked. (Another type, posture springing, is a deluxe version of open springing.) A third alternative is a high-quality foam, which is recommended if you are prone to dust-induced allergies.

Make sure that the mattress is made from natural materials and contains non-magnetic springs. Polyurethane foam is sometimes used as a stuffing but it is both flammable and an irritant. A good alternative is latex foam, which is hygienic and non-allergenic. Some natural materials such as wool and feathers are equally irritating to the allergy-prone, so check all materials when you buy.

BED LINEN

Bedding can make the difference between indifferent sleep and deep, luxurious slumber. There is nothing like the feel of slipping between pure linen or Egyptian cotton sheets. They are not as easy to care for as poly-cotton, since they do need ironing, but the pleasure they give more than compensates. They provide the perfect prelude to the best escape route of all – uninterrupted, rejuvenating, quality sleep.

BEDROOM STORAGE

Good storage is essential if your bedroom and bathroom are to function effectively as escape routes. A closed cupboard door, a lidded storage box lid, or a basket tucked underneath a shelf is a metaphorical lid on the clutter that continually threatens to escape into our quiet spaces.

SEASONAL CLEAR-OUTS

Storage in the bedroom has to be ample and versatile if the room is to be an oasis of calm. The best starting point is to go through all your clothes, shoes, and accessories at the end of each season. Remove any items that are worn out or unloved or have not made it out of the closet or drawer for two years. Ignore any sentimental second

ABOVE: Purpose-built footwear storage is the solution to that heap of shoes at the bottom of the wardrobe. Behind sleek and colorful doors each pair of shoes is kept dust-free and in full view for easy selection.

RIGHT: Tented wardrobes are endlessly versatile. Stack boxes on the shelves inside, pile them high with sweaters, or dispense with shelves and suspend clothes from the hanging rail. Another advantage is these wardrobes can be transported from room to room.

thoughts and set them aside for a thrift shop, a yard sale, or the recycling bin, depending on the condition.

Next, literally pile up everything you need to store, from shoes and scarves to sports clothes. Group the items by type or size, as well as when they will be needed and whether they will be used frequently. Calculate how much clothes-hanging and drawer space you are likely to need, allowing extra space for purchases, acquisitions, and seasonal variations.

STORAGE IDEAS

If your home has limited closet space, you might need to create your own storage solutions. Investing in whole walls of built-in cupboards does not make sense if you are planning to stay in a house only short-term. Also, you may not like the look of neat lines

ABOVE: A small room adjoining a main bedroom is perfect for a dressing room. In this neat annex, purpose-built shelves containing clothes, baskets of accessories, and shoes make choosing what you are going to wear a positive pleasure.

RIGHT: An antique, glass-fronted armoire houses a neat collection of lidded baskets and folded towels and linen in an elegant wood-floored bedroom.

of cupboards but prefer a more eclectic approach, incorporating attractive containers like baskets, neat cardboard boxes, antique leather suitcases, or blanket boxes. Take a look at the many small-scale storage solutions that are available, such as tie racks, shoe holders, and underbed drawers, then decide which would be suitable for your storage requirements.

Shoes can be stored in open pigeonholes that double as a low bench, on shelves or racks, or in narrow canvas bags that hang in the closet. Tall, narrow cupboards are good for housing sports rackets, golf clubs, or surfboards, as well as small items hung on the inside of the door. A shelf at the top can be used to slip in sneakers, tennis balls, and tracksuits for easy access.

FAVORITE THINGS

Keep some space free for your favorite luxuries, well-loved books, scrapbooks of inspiring images to charge your imagination, or keepsakes to help you remember special events or people. A battered trunk, metal chest, or time-worn box full of these good things will lift your spirits when daily trivia starts weighing you down.

BATHROOMS

The bathroom has always been a place of retreat and indulgence to some extent, but these days, when domestic and working lives are so rushed, the opportunity to soak in a tub of hot, scented water is all the more beneficial. En-suite bathrooms are increasingly popular, offering both privacy and the chance to take your time, but there is still a place for the family bathroom, where siblings tussle for the toothpaste and dispute the ownership of various bath toys. (For advice relating specifically to children's bathrooms, see page 196.)

BATHROOM PLANNING

Planning a bathroom involves working around the hard, cold fixed elements – toilet, sink, bath, and possibly shower – to introduce as much comfort and style as the available space will allow. Whether you are planning a bathroom completely from scratch or merely updating it, draw up a room plan with scale drawings of the various fixtures. Moving plumbing can be very expensive, so talk to a plumber in detail about all your requirements right at the beginning. Decide on the best configuration, bearing in mind you will also need working space – for example, alongside a bath where you would need to kneel when bathing young children. If you have sufficient room for an extra basin, it will certainly prove useful, even in an en-suite bathroom occupied only by two adults.

SHOWERS AND BATHS

The ideal bathroom has both a bath and a shower, or at least a shower attachment in the bath, with a screen or shower curtain, but a small en-suite shower room squeezed into the main bedroom is also useful.

In both a bath and a shower, a grab rail and a non-slip surface are recommended,

ABOVE LEFT: Steps up to a tiled bath area double as display and storage space in a bathroom in which natural materials and textures offset the hard white surfaces.

RIGHT: This color scheme is the reverse of that in the bathroom above left; here, natural wood predominates and white is used as an accent. The curtain with its unusual scalloped edges softens the straight lines of the wood.

LEFT: A separate walk-in shower eases congestion in a family bathroom.

RIGHT: In this spacious bathroom there is plenty of room for a large, tank-like bath – great for long soaks. Opposite it, a line of cupboards houses a pair of basins, with capacious storage underneath. A long mirror on the wall above allows two (or even more) people to use the mirror and basins without having to jostle for space. Ample lighting can be dimmed whenever atmosphere is more important than visibility.

and are essential if young children or the elderly will be using the bath or shower. Make sure the shower has a thermostatic control to prevent anyone, especially children, from being scalded.

Showers use considerably less water than baths – unless you are comparing a shallow bath with a power shower. Though wonderfully energizing, a power shower can quickly empty the hot-water tank, particularly if family members are showering in rapid succession.

BATHROOM STORAGE

However small the room, you will also need some storage space. The traditional spots are in a cupboard under the basin, in built-in units, or in a bathroom cabinet. These are all useful, of course, but less conventional storage can work just as well. If there is space, an old armoire or chest of drawers holds a lot and looks good. Even the space behind a bath panel can be utilized with a pull-out unit. Whatever form of storage you have, medicines and cleaning materials should be kept in a locked cupboard or well out of reach of young children.

Open shelves – perhaps serving as a room divider to separate the toilet area from the rest of the bathroom – are versatile and also provide a good place to display the attractive bottles, bars of soap, and candles that help to give the bathroom a truly sybaritic feel. Square glass tanks stacked on their sides also provide attractive storage and display.

WALLS, FLOORS, AND WINDOWS

Surfaces need to be practical in any bathroom. On the walls, tongue-and-groove paneling and ceramic tiles are timeless, comfortable to live with, and easy to clean. Vinyl papers and anti-condensation paint are also suitable for bathrooms.

Flooring must be waterproof, non-slip and ideally warm underfoot. This rules out ceramic tiles, but well-sealed cork tiles are suitable, as are linoleum, vinyl, and rubber-stud flooring. Sanded floorboards, if heavily varnished (preferably with yacht varnish), can be appropriate but are not as practical. Carpet is not a good idea in a bathroom.

Window treatments are best kept simple. Roman, roller or venetian blinds, shutters, or bare windows with frosted, etched, or textured glass are all practical options.

LIGHTING

Mirrors ideally need to be lit from the side if you want to be able to see what you are doing. For practicality plus atmosphere, combine light from recessed overhead halogen downlighters with candles. Lights should be sealed to make them resistant to splashes. Ensure that all lighting and shaver sockets conform to electrical regulations.

WORK SPACES

Though very different from the leisurely and luxurious treats that provide such enjoyable escape routes, work is an effective way of getting away from the domestic routine. Being able to work from home is an enormous boon to any parent coping with raising a family at the same time. However, making the space used for an office or studio as inviting and efficient as possible, quite often on a limited budget, can be a challenge.

SETTING UP THE OFFICE

Now that working from home has become an increasingly common part of family life, there is a whole new industry devoted to creating unobtrusive office equipment, storage solutions, and mini offices for the home, or a corner of it. The age of the professional-looking home office is upon us, although the self-employed are very often, by definition, more concerned with their solitary occupations than with creating a space inviting to visitors. Yet those home-workers whose clients or customers do need to visit them at home often live in horror of anyone actually wanting to see their work space, such as it is – an amalgamation of cast-off filing cabinets, chipped tables with coffee rings, and myriad stacks of books and papers. Creativity may be flowing, but slowly, through a mountain of unfiled chaos.

The basic components of a work space – desk, technology, lighting, and possibly the chair – can often be squeezed into a deep

alcove and closed off with a sliding or concertina door. Choose the location carefully, as a living room or bedroom may be occupied at the very time you want to pour over some document or other. An under-utilized space such as a landing or the area under the stairs makes a good home for a work space that does not have to become a

LEFT: Idle space tucked behind one wall of a landing is put to good use as an airy studio, complete with drawing board, natural light, and storage. A small meeting area, including a table and directors' chairs, makes good use of the open space at the top of the stairs.

RIGHT: Sometimes a work area has to be located wherever there is space. The contents of a garden shed can often be shifted to a garage or other outdoor storage area to make way for a self-contained office or studio, providing all the peace and solitude one could possibly want.

self-contained office. Even a shed or garage can be converted for this purpose. Work spaces for creative activities such as pottery, sculpting, textiles, or graphic arts are often successfully contained in sheds or roomy lofts.

Planning a work space involves deciding what furniture and equipment you need

RIGHT: Creative pursuits can require quite a bit of space, so the work area has to be dealt with imaginatively. In this textile designer's studio, an old linen cupboard provides tailor-made storage, while the work surface makes the most of the natural light. Colorful cushions create a spot where creative thinking can be pursued in comfort.

and finding a place where everything can be accommodated. In a bedroom, for instance, a pile of shiny technology lodged in between pieces of period furniture will not look right. Similarly, a battered antique desk and classic pieces of study paraphernalia may not bring space and light to a minimal corner. As far as possible, let your work space blend into your surroundings without allowing it to be swallowed up. Make sure that there are enough sockets to connect all the technology you need and that all your storage requirements can be met (see box at right).

STORAGE SOLUTIONS

Storage can be simple and practical, or decorative to suit you and the room. Paperwork builds up quickly in a home office, where there often isn't the space for several filing cabinets or cupboards. Computer disks, stationery, and reference material all need to be close at hand, while large-scale items such as looms or painting equipment and materials obviously need a bit more thought and space.

A wide range of inexpensive but stylish corrugated cardboard storage boxes is available, in whatever configuration of drawers, shelves, or files you need. Other types of boxes and also baskets make good individual containers. Small office trolleys with shelves or suspension files are ideal for storing equipment and papers that need to be transported from place to place. Computer workstations that are built into a large cupboard also provide useful storage.

CHILDREN IN THE OFFICE

In a family home where one parent works part-time, it is a good idea not to make the

work space too interesting. Computers with fascinating colored screen-savers and with enticing games attract children at all hours. One way around this is to make it clear that during certain hours the computer is for your use only. Another solution is to pretend not to be able to work the games – cruel but convenient. Yet another approach, albeit a more expensive one, is to have more than one computer. (You can at least justify it on the grounds that it will be useful when the other is being repaired.)

Make sure the work space is purely functional rather than littered with interesting nooks, bulletin boards, or gadgets that will engage the attention of a visiting toddler or teenager. Decorate it accordingly, in one or two colors, not an elaborate scheme.

Label the space as "workroom" and always refer to it as such, even if it doubles as a guest room or dining room. Remember to put important papers away before children are tempted to cover them with their own creative masterpieces.

Planning a work space

Check that there are enough sockets for the technology to be contained in one place. Allow for lighting, computer, printer, modem, phone, fax, kettle, radio or mini stereo, heater for winter, electric fan for summer.

✳

If space is tight, choose a desk that can also double as a storage unit and computer workstation. Make sure it is the right height for working comfortably: work surfaces should be 25-30in (63–76cm) from the floor. The computer screen should be at eye level and the keyboard at a height that allows your forearms to be parallel to the floor and your elbows at your side. Adjusting the height of your chair may be necessary.

✳

A comfortable and ergonomic chair is probably the most important investment of all if you will be spending much time in it. Make sure it supports your back well and allows your feet to rest on the floor. The height should be easily adjustable.

✳

Lighting is particularly important. Light the desk with a directional task light such as an anglepoise lamp and provide sufficient general light elsewhere in the work area. Avoid positioning the computer or lighting so that there is glare on the screen.

✳

Storage should suit your particular situation, but make a list of the main items you will need close at hand, such as stationery, pens and pencils, diskettes, reference books, telephone directories, calendar, bulletin board, work samples. Don't forget a trash can and a paper recycling bin.

✳

In a small space an ionizer will help to improve the atmosphere. Certain houseplants, such as the Boston fern, rubber plant, English ivy, bamboo palm, and dwarf date palm, will also improve the air quality by absorbing chemical vapors from common pollutants like formaldehyde.

QUIET CORNERS

Creating a "quiet corner" in an unlikely spot adds an intriguing element to a home as well as providing a cozy place to enjoy some peace and quiet. Spots like this are good for retiring to when children are busy with toys or television and you feel a break coming on. Do some deep breathing and a quick three-minute relaxation routine – you may even fit in a short nap.

Whether the resting area is in a traffic thoroughfare within the home or in a limited, enclosed space, it could require some ingenuity. Setting it up may be very simple or it could prove to be a larger undertaking, but it will certainly be worth the creative thinking required. For example,

a pair of chairs flanking a small table provides a natural spot for two people to sit and chat. An armchair with a pile of books and magazines adds enormously to the comfort of a spacious bathroom.

SPACE EXPLORATION

Consider the potential of every nook and cranny and find underused areas in your home. The quirkier the space you utilize, the more appealing it will be. You might be able to open up the space under the stairs and install a freestanding bookcase, a trunk for storage with a lamp and scented flowers on top, or a small sofa or armchair. Visitors as well as family will be instantly drawn to the space.

ABOVE RIGHT: It takes very little to turn a small, plain table or desk under a window into an ideal place for writing letters or simply daydreaming.

RIGHT: Comfortable chairs tucked into a quiet corner of the house will always find willing occupants. They may be piled with clean laundry half the time, but at least they look inviting.

LEFT: Well-worn leather armchairs are ceaselessly reassuring and welcoming, rather like a favorite sweater that has seen better days. A checked throw draped over an old sofa, with a dog draped over that, adds to the relaxed informality of this cozy room under the eaves.

Landings are often underexploited. A large painting, a squishy chair, and a bowl of fruit will provide a comfortable stop-off point when you find yourself returning laundered clothes, discarded toys, and empty cups to their homes.

COZY CORNERS

A corner of a room could be devoted to a piano or other musical instruments, a music stand, and sheet music, forming an ideal setting for relaxation, if not actual quiet. Or install floor-to-ceiling bookshelves on both walls in a corner, and add a comfortable chair or two and a reading light to draw in the bookworms. Similarly, a writing desk or table, however nondescript, will become a

natural focal point when accompanied by a chair and some subtle task lighting.

A conservatory, sun lounge, deep alcove, bay window, or any other space that is an annex to a larger room also provides an opportunity for a quick escape. All it needs is some sort of seating to make it as comfortable as possible.

Children also like quiet spaces, so consider converting a storage room into a reading den, a space devoted to children's hobbies such as model-making, or a haven given over to a particular collection or obsession, be it natural seashore treasures or action figures. Ban a television in this room, but encourage the children to listen to music or play instruments here.

COMING AND GOING

Hallways and entrances are good resting points when they are spacious enough for wooden benches or chairs. Flowers always provide a welcome, while a mirror and table will add to a sense of quiet in a space where people can pause on their way in and out of the home. Fold-down tables are particularly versatile in narrow hallways where traffic is regular. They make good instant work surfaces for writing checks or searching through your handbag for your keys.

A porch furnished with a rocking chair, swinging seat, hammock, or elegant steamer chairs cannot fail to relax the mind, providing a quick escape from noise and clutter inside the house.

REST AND RELAXATION

head-and-shoulders or complete body massage or an aromatherapy massage can make you feel like a new person.

Sometimes a quiet half-hour with a magazine, a cup of good coffee, and a piece of chocolate cake will bring more comfort than a week at a health spa. Life is for living, so don't feel guilty about a little hedonism now and again.

Owning pets has been proven to help relaxation. Cats and dogs are obviously the most domesticated, but simple pleasure can also be taken from such child-oriented additions to the family as guinea pigs and rabbits.

Hobbies can be relaxers too, whether it is a penchant for miniature railways, wine-making, sewing, or making pottery.

Of the more active forms of relaxation, Ping-Pong, pool, and working out on exercise equipment are all activities that can be enjoyed by the whole family in the home. Physical activity usually ends with a feeling of well-being and achievement, even if your 11-year-old has just proved that agility can overcome strategy at Ping-Pong.

Gardening is a good means of escaping the house. Cutting back plants in the autumn and spring, weeding, digging, and mowing the lawn are all good jobs for relaxing the mind and exercising the body. Armed with a sharp pair of pruning shears and a couple of hours, you are guaranteed a sense of purpose and renewal.

Proper relaxation, whether it comes through quiet rest or active leisure, allows the senses time to rejuvenate in preparation for another day, another pile of laundry, or even a different approach to the regular routine.

One of the simplest relaxation methods is simply to fill a bath with hot water and aromatic oils, place a scented candle nearby, and then lie back for a blissful half-hour soak. Hot tubs, Jacuzzis, and whirlpool baths with their gentle micro-massage will also help you to unwind. A

LEFT: Dogs certainly know how to relax, so although putting your own feet up may be a rare occurrence, the dog will always have time to join in.

RIGHT: A conservatory is not only an extension of the living space, it also brings the garden into the home, particularly when French doors maximize the light and the view. Here, an improvised bent-wire curtain pole and loosely tied gauzy drapes float tantalizingly between the two spaces, bringing a cool breeze into this tranquil spot.

OVERLEAF: An improvised bedroom set up on a cool verandah, close to lush vegetation but a safe distance from the local wildlife, is a perfect solution on hot nights in the tropics. Peace and solitude among thriving plants, translucent drapes, and a soft metal-framed bed conjure images of vacation-style relaxation.

Parents' escapes

When you feel that the walls of the home are starting to close in on you, the most effective antidote is a complete escape from family life.

*

Get someone to look after the children for a weekend and escape with your partner to a favorite place, even out of the country. You will return with a renewed enthusiasm for family life (even if you are exhausted all over again by the time you have been back with the children for a few hours). Remember, though, that you will have to reciprocate the favor if it is a friend who takes the children off your hands.

*

Arrange a regular children-swap with a friend on a fortnightly or monthly basis and use the available time to get out somewhere on your own. Start lessons on a musical instrument, visit museums, or simply explore the nearest city. Join a health club – the initiation fee alone will compel you to go regularly.

*

Go to the sea, a lake, or a river and have a picnic and a long, peaceful stroll along the water's edge. Water always seems to have a soothing effect on jagged nerves.

*

During school vacations, arrange some full-day excursions to places none of you have ever seen before. Visit places where the whole family can gain something from the experience. Try teaming up with other families – you may find that your own children are less fractious with others around.

151

the doreys, **a place by the sea**

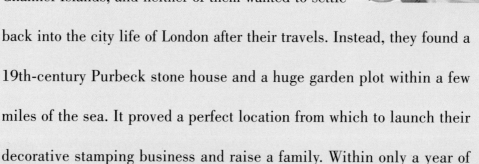

The rolling hills of England's Dorset coastline were where Sasha Dorey grew up, so escaping back to her roots seemed an apt move after traveling around the world for a year with her husband and business partner, Jon. He too grew up near the sea, on Guernsey in the Channel Islands, and neither of them wanted to settle back into the city life of London after their travels. Instead, they found a 19th-century Purbeck stone house and a huge garden plot within a few miles of the sea. It proved a perfect location from which to launch their decorative stamping business and raise a family. Within only a year of moving in, the house was enlarged and transformed, the business was established, and their first child, William, was born – a fast schedule by anyone's standards.

Above: Children love food that allows them to fiddle and make a mess. Scooping out mussels and dipping bread in the juices is just great. *Below left and right:* A summerhouse is the perfect backdrop for eating outdoors when the weather is good. Used for storing fold-up tables and chairs, it also doubles up as a peaceful spot in which to read, think, or simply escape from the family when everything gets to be too much.

The idea for the stamp business came out of Sasha's ruminations about how to decorate their newly

acquired home. Having picked up an antique stamp during their travels in India, she decided to use it for decorating the walls. The idea for the business emerged and Jon, an engineer, addressed the technical necessities for producing a range of decorative stamps that worked on a variety of surfaces and materials. Today their line of stamps sells in numerous countries around the world, through shops and by mail order.

Sasha is involved in creating the designs, while Jon runs the business side of things. Their children have also been known to provide design suggestions for their line of children's stamps. The Doreys have also branched out into paint, and their antique paint-finish kit, which gives interior walls the look of old plaster or stone, has been used in their own living room. Trying out their decorative ideas in the house has always helped in the development of different products, and Sasha often experiments with new colors, stamps, and techniques in small areas of their home, such as the front porch.

The original stone farmhouse was in fact a series of small cottages that had been knocked into one big home with eight poky bedrooms, but Sasha and Jon liked the atmosphere and so decided to open up the space in order to allow more light to sweep through the house. In addition, they added a seamless extension that has almost doubled the size of the home. This provided a large family kitchen and separate utility room on the ground floor, plus two more rooms upstairs. A large conservatory gave them more ground-floor living space and a relaxed seating area. Even the staircase was moved to make more sense of the new room layout. The entire building program, including the major structural changes, was carried out while William was a tiny baby. Although this was probably the worst time possible to experience such upheaval, it did mean that the entire family benefited from the transformation virtually from day one.

During that first year in the new house, the stamp company was born in a garage outbuilding. When the business outgrew the available space, the workshop and office moved to premises just down the road, allowing the house to become more of a refuge away from the company. Since the Doreys spend their working days engulfed in color and pattern, the chance to escape at the end of

Above left and centre: A purpose-built conservatory with glazed walls and ceiling leads off the kitchen and provides a quiet area for adults, away from the frantic activities of the cooking and eating areas.

Above right, top and bottom: In the kitchen, Sasha's beloved colors of blue and white provide the decorative scheme. A lobby off the kitchen has been converted to a utility room and includes a cupboard for cleaning equipment and a deep butler's sink.

House Rules

* *Live where you feel happiest rather than where*

is most convenient.

* *Decorate one bedroom in white for visual peace.*

* *Drape sofas by day to protect them.*

* *Use practical, safe flooring in the kitchen so children*

can tear about.

* *Add a conservatory, if possible, for additional living space.*

* *Transform an outside shed into a summerhouse.*

* *If possible, involve your children in your working life*

for extra inspiration.

* *Punctuate different living spaces by laying*

different flooring in each one.

each manic day to a home of calm neutral palettes became a top priority. The only rooms where stamps are in evidence are William's bedroom, where crocodiles and mice creep around the tops of the walls and a variety of stamps adorn the chest of drawers, and his sister Bella's room, transformed by pink roses into a floral haven. Otherwise, the decoration is informed by an enduring appreciation of a natural palette: calm schemes tempered with coastal blues, gentle seascapes, and nautical motifs, inspired by the paintings of Sasha's parents, who are both artists.

In the kitchen and adjoining utility room, Sasha's love of blue and white is captured in the checkerboard-patterned vinyl floor and the tiled splashback. The simple farmhouse-style solid-wood units painted in blue or white are complemented by well-worn natural-wood work surfaces and tabletop, and a limed-wood dresser. Beautiful yet functional, this is a space that the children can career through on tricycles without fear of ruining the decoration.

Although the Doreys prefer a simple approach to decoration, an abundance of paintings throughout the house lends it a definite warmth. Everyday clutter is dispatched to large cupboards, which

Above left: **The living room has delicate, colorwashed walls in a soft plaster pink, a paint from the Doreys' decorative stamping business. White loose covers are protected with arm covers, but otherwise it is a relaxing space, simply styled.**

Above right: **Sasha's parents are artists and their sea-inspired paintings make a handsome display on the stairs and landing. The whole house has a slightly nautical atmosphere with white walls, tongue-and-groove cupboards, and splashes of blue.**

"Escaping the pressures of London life for a simpler existence in the country meant finding a home with a large garden and plenty of space to start up the business."

Sasha believes are vital when you have small children. Much of the furniture was bought by Sasha at auction or local junk shops. She loves spending time searching out simple, interesting pieces to restore, paint, and age, and this relaxed approach to furniture means that the children and Arthur, the much-loved chocolate labrador retriever, can do no great harm to any one piece. In the living room, they have even dared install white sofas and chairs, but the loose covers can be whipped off and cleaned relatively easily. Generous corner protectors and throws cover the parts of furniture that receive the most wear.

When Sasha and Jon feel the need for time out or a quiet read of the newspaper, the conservatory is their favorite "grown-up space" within the house. Placed off the kitchen, it's also a good spot to keep an eye on what is happening in the kitchen.

Another retreat is the main bedroom of the house, decorated in cool white. White on walls, woodwork, furniture, and bed linen is quiet to live with and provides a clean break from the rigors of children, work, and color. A chaise longue reupholstered in pure white is an element of sheer indulgence at one end of the room. Generous white wardrobes built along the walls of the connecting dressing room are in keeping with the rustic architecture. Steps lead down to an *en-suite* bathroom where sinks are fitted into units that provide additional storage space.

In the children's rooms, Sasha has created comfortable, welcoming spaces that include toys, storage, and sturdy furniture that will not age before the children.

Above and top left: A guest room feels as though it could be in the middle of the Aegean sea, with its fretwork radiator cover, simple blue and white furnishings, and a pale blue, colorwashed bathroom *en-suite*.
Left: Bedtime stories are extra-special in a cabin bed.

Everyone, especially the children and Arthur, the labrador, adores the space and freedom in the garden. It includes a large wooden jungle gym, and lots of nooks and crannies for games of hide-and-seek, so for half the year the children do much of their playing outside. One of the beguiling features of the garden is a summerhouse painted and stamped by Sasha for the enjoyment of children and adults alike.

Above: The main bedroom is painted and furnished in pure white for a calm, peaceful atmosphere, and decorated with some of the one-of-a-kind antique pieces that Sasha enjoys collecting.
Below left: An elegant chaise longue upholstered in white fabric provides the ultimate clothes-dumping area and also acts as a quiet reading corner.
Below right: His and her sinks in a symmetrical *en-suite* bathroom leading off the dressing room.

BATHROOM shelf

RIGHT AND FAR RIGHT:
This neat shelf, displaying
luxurious, pampering
lotions and oils, is
suspended from wall
hooks with leather thongs.
The advantage of this
hanging method is that the
shelf can be raised out of
young children's reach.
The base and back of the
shelf are painted with a
subtle harlequin pattern.

BELOW: The bathroom is
the perfect place to
display seashells collected
on trips to exotic places.

Bathrooms are often short of storage space, so this shelf conserves space while giving a substantial collection of toiletries an attractive home. In fact, the shelf is versatile enough to be used in any room. It could hold stationery in a workroom, diaper-changing paraphernalia in a nursery, a favorite collection in a child's room, or spices in the kitchen. The decoration of the shelf could be altered to suit the room, and the dimensions could also be adjusted; the one shown here is 21½in (550mm) wide, 7¾in (195mm) high, and 6in (150mm) deep. Made from MDF (medium-density fiberboard), which is inexpensive and easier than wood to decorate, this project requires neither carpentry skills nor a major time commitment.

YOU *will need*

* ⅜in- (9mm-) thick MDF (medium-density fiber-
  board): 2 end pieces, 7¾ x 6in (195 x 150mm),
  cut into a curve at one corner (see step 1);
  1 bottom piece, 21½ x 6in (550 x 150mm);
  1 back piece, 21½ x 7¾in (550 x 195mm)
* Drill
* Wood glue
* Hammer and nails
* Emulsion paint in white and cream
* Flat artists' and small round artists' brushes
* Ruler and low-tack masking tape
* Leather thong, 39in (1m) long
* 2 hanging brackets

1 The end pieces curve from the top back to the bottom front, so make a paper template for this and ask the lumberyard to cut them for you. Drill ¼in (6mm) holes in the end pieces, as shown, a little way in from the top and back edges. Glue the end pieces in place on top of the shelf and secure by nailing up through the base. Glue and nail the back piece in place.

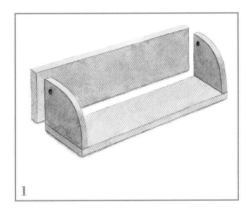

2 Paint the shelf with a white undercoat and then with a topcoat of cream. When completely dry, measure and draw the diamonds on the bottom and back pieces with a pencil and ruler. Mask around the white diamonds with low-tack masking tape, and paint them in, then remove the tape before the paint has completely dried. (Or, for a softer edge, paint the the diamonds freehand, without masking.)

3 Cut the leather thong in half, and attach a length at each end by threading it through the hole. Knot the ends then knot it again near the shelf. Fix brackets to the wall and hang the shelf from them using the thongs.

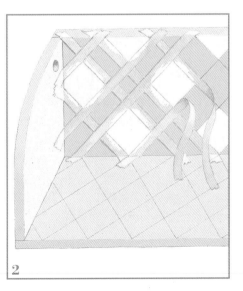

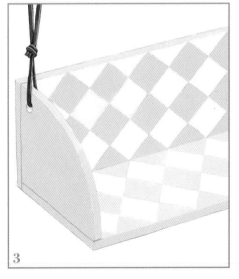

BOTANICAL PRINTS wall decoration

This ingenious idea makes a pleasing change from paint or wallpaper, and the botanical prints look good in even the most elegant of rooms. Black-and-white or color photocopies of out-of-copyright prints are simply pasted onto the wall with wallpaper paste and then varnished to protect them. White paper often looks too harsh, but it can be quickly "antiqued" using a tinted varnish after it has been stuck to the wall; alternatively you could use parchment-colored paper.

As an alternative to botanical prints, you could use photocopies of architectural or classical engravings, of antique maps or fashion plates, of newspaper cuttings, even of luxury chocolate wrappers or bank notes. Other possibilities include modern maps; sheet music; and family memorabilia such as certificates or school reports. The treatment works best on a limited area: on a single wall, above a dado rail, enclosed in an alcove, or in a small room such as a bathroom, landing, or study. Or the idea could easily be adapted for use on a screen, headboard, or trunk.

BELOW AND RIGHT: Lining walls with botanical prints gives a room a unique and stylish look. this technique could easily be adapted for use in children's rooms, perhaps using some of their own artwork.

YOU *will need*

* Photocopies of prints in color or black-and-white
* Scissors
* Reusable adhesive
* Wallpaper paste
* Pasting brush
* Spirit level or plumb line
* Paper-hanging brush or cloth
* Seam roller or cloth
* Damp sponge
* Flat acrylic varnish (plain or tinted)
* Varnishing brush

1 Before you apply wallpaper paste to the sheets, stick them temporarily in position with reusable adhesive, to check that you are happy with the overall scheme. To help you position the sheets, lightly mark out a system of grid lines in pencil, using a spirit level or plumb line. If necessary, trim any sheets to fit. Now mix up some wallpaper paste according to the package instructions and brush it onto a few sheets using a pasting brush. Be sure to brush the paste right to the edges. Do not paste all the sheets at once – just work on a few at a time.

2 Place one sheet in position on the wall, brushing from the center outward to the edges with a paper-hanging brush or soft cloth. Place the next sheet so that it butts up to the first and brush it in place in the same way.

3 You may need to add a little extra wallpaper paste along the seams. Wipe off excess paste with a damp sponge, then run a seam roller or cloth

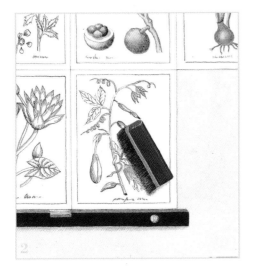

along the seamline to ensure the edges are stuck down well. From time to time, use the spirit level to check that the sheets are still being pasted on horizontally. When you reach the ceiling, baseboard, a corner, a door, or a window, position the pasted sheet on the wall and mark a crease line where the sheet has to finish. Now remove the sheet, cut along the crease with scissors, then put it back on the wall and continue as before.

4 When all the sheets are completely dry, brush on a couple of coats of varnish using a varnishing brush, allowing it to dry thoroughly between coats. This will help to prevent sheets lifting at the edges.

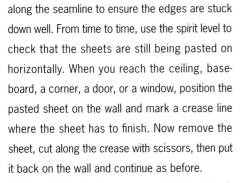

PAPER lamp shades

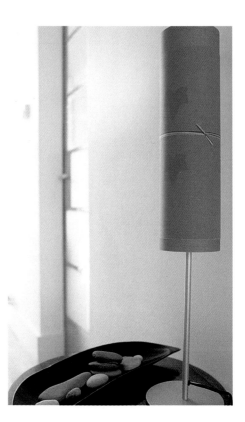

It can often be difficult to find just the right lampshade for a room. Sometimes a color is difficult to match, while at other times the shape or the lamp base is right but the shade itself is uninteresting. Yet it is a simple process to make your own from heavy paper using the framework of an old lamp shade as the starting point and then adding small decorations between layers of thin paper. For safety reasons, be sure not to exceed the recommended bulb wattage of the original lamp shade.

BELOW AND RIGHT:
Taking an old lamp shade apart and making a custom-designed replacement is a good way to ensure the shade matches your furnishings. Small, flat, decorative items sandwiched between the layers of paper produce pleasing patterns and shadows when the light is switched on.

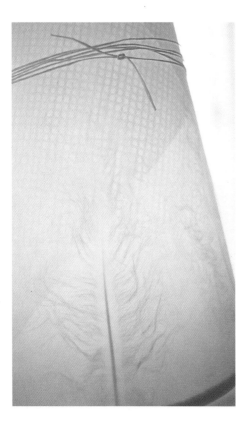

YOU *will need*

* Old conical or cylindrical lamp shade
* Heavy paper and scissors
* General-purpose adhesive
* Masking tape
* Tracing paper or thin colored paper
* PVA glue and brush
* Flat decorative items such as leaves, feathers, stamps, scraps of handmade paper or graph paper, colored candy wrappers, shapes cut from colored paper, motifs cut from wrapping paper
* String or ribbon

1 Carefully take an old shade apart, removing the covering from the frame. Lay the covering flat and use as a template to cut out a new shade in paper.
2 Glue the shade to the base ring of the frame, holding it in place with pieces of masking tape until the glue dries.

3 Insert the top part of the frame into the shade and glue it to the edge of the card. Glue the two edges of the shade together and leave to dry.
4 Using the template, cut out a layer of tracing paper or thin colored paper; stick it in place with diluted PVA glue. Stick your decorations on top with diluted PVA glue, then add another layer of thin paper, gluing it in place with diluted PVA. Tie string or ribbon around the middle of the shade.

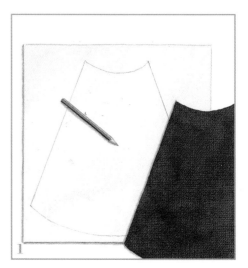

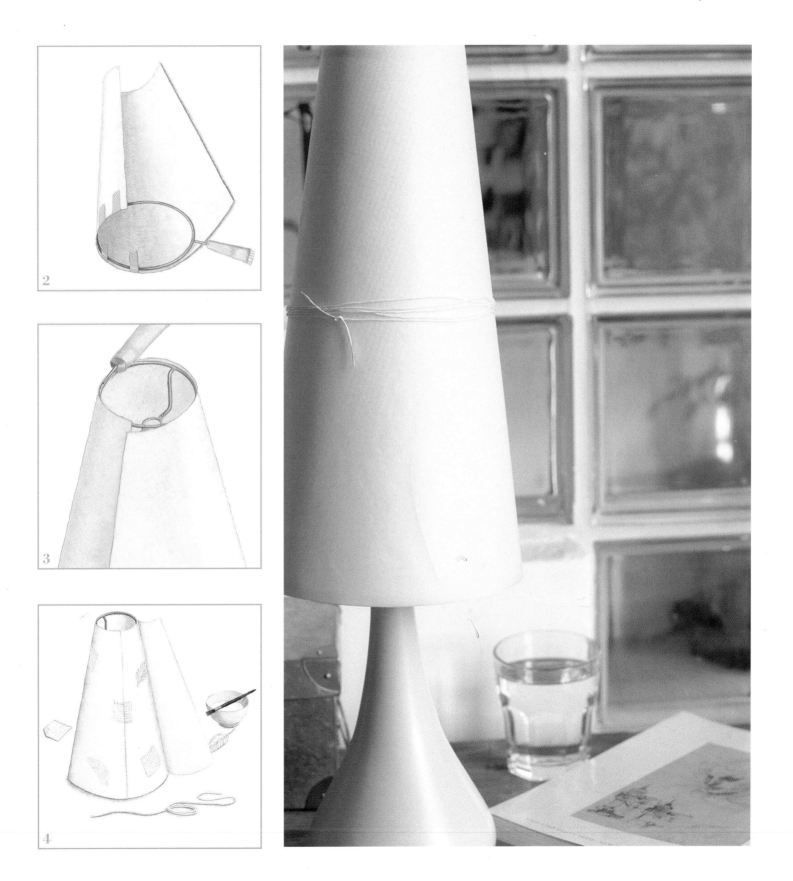

EMBROIDERED bed linen

Embroidery transforms cotton or linen sheets and pillow-cases into bed linen that is distinctive and personal. Even young children can learn simple embroidery, providing a lifelong opportunity for creating keepsakes such as samplers and cushions as well as bed and table linen. This border design is worked in just two stitches – chain stitch and running stitch – which progress quickly. Embroider either onto a sheet and pillowcase you have bought or onto bed linen you have made from plain cotton sheeting.

ABOVE: Children adore bed linen that has been customized with familiar motifs or images.

ABOVE RIGHT: A treasure chest of old embroidered linen, to be handed down through the family.

RIGHT AND FAR RIGHT: An embroidered edging of floral motifs along a sheet and pillowcase is both delicate and appealing.

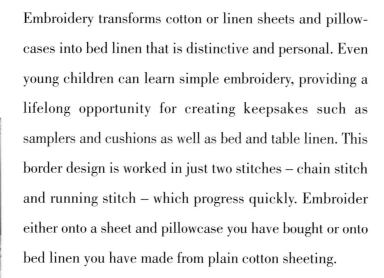

YOU will need

* Single cotton or linen sheet and pillowcase
* Contrasting sewing thread and sewing needle
* Dressmaker's carbon paper and tracing wheel
* Embroidery hoop
* DMC stranded cotton in lilac 210: 3 skeins for a single sheet, 1 skein for a pillowcase
* Crewel (embroidery) needle, size 6

Preparation: Sew a line of tacking stitches in contrasting thread 2in (5cm) from the edge of the sheet or pillowcase to form a guide line. Enlarge the template to your chosen size on a photocopier. Using dressmaker's carbon paper and a tracing wheel, transfer the template onto the sheet or pillowcase edge, positioning the main stem so it begins and ends on the guide line. Repeat until the pattern runs the whole width of the sheet or pillow-case border, matching the end of one repeat with the beginning of the next (indicated by the lines on the template). Place the fabric in the embroi-dery hoop. (You will need to move the hoop along the fabric as the stitching progresses.)

1 Work from right to left, using three strands of thread. At the beginning, knot the embroidery thread and insert the needle from the right side, about 2in (5cm) from where the first stitch will be and in the path of the subsequent stitches. Start

stitching, working all the stems and leaf outlines in chain stitch as shown here. Once the tail of the thread has been covered by stitches, snip off the knot. Continue until all the stems and leaf outlines have been worked.

2 In the center of some of the leaves, work one or two lines of running stitch. It is important not to carry any thread across the back of the fabric, because long strands are likely to get caught, thus damaging the embroidery. Instead, start and stop frequently, securing the thread by using the needle to weave the tail of the thread into several existing stitches on the wrong side. Remove the tacking threads when the embroidery is complete,

CHILDREN'S SPACES

CHILDREN'S SPACES

The impact of children on a house or apartment

RIGHT: Storing toys in an aesthetic but accessible manner is one of the major challenges in children's rooms. The only way to keep a system going is for adults and children to know the natural homes of each set of toys, from tiny figures to plastic tea sets, building blocks to doll clothes. Once everything has a designated home – be it a box, underbed drawer, shelf, or cupboard – putting it all away at the end of the day is much easier.

Children change you. Not only are previously ordered lives turned upside down, but the demands on space, furniture, and time mean that you and your home must adapt, virtually overnight, and look at everything from a different perspective. The idea of a stylish, well-defined home may quickly recede in the face of busy children who make heavy demands on you and your resources. Decorating budgets can be decimated as family needs usurp the "new curtains" fund and the "dream kitchen" nest egg. More than ever, you need to become efficient, inventive, and economical.

LEFT: Decorating a baby's room need not mean throwing good taste out with the bathwater. A considered approach to making a room cheerful but not gaudy is the key. Here, a combination of natural wood and wicker mix well with the lime green walls and navy paintwork to create a look that will endure for several years. The large crib easily converts into a small bed when the slatted side rails are removed.

LEFT: This compact bedroom doubles as a playroom with the addition of pigeonhole shelves, bench, table, and painting easel. The brightly painted wooden floor, thoroughly varnished, withstands spills and hard wear, while the wooden bed is both secure and enduring. The fireplace has been cheerfully decorated using colors that tie in with the alcove cupboard and the open shelving.

changes your views on design and decoration dramatically.

New babies, especially the firstborn, bring with them pure joy – as well as many belongings, much equipment, and plenty of work. Adapting your house to cope over the next two decades with a succession of toys, noisy preschoolers, fighting siblings, school-friends for sleepovers, and emotional teenagers playing loud music is a major challenge, one best tackled with flexibility, humor, and creativity.

VARIED DEMANDS

A family home is a place where family members at various times will want to gather together, relax in comfort, work in peace and solitude, watch TV, listen to music, play with toys, enjoy craft activities, play instruments, not to mention eat and sleep – demands enough for any household.

And whereas children were once banished to a nursery at the top of the house, young-sters these days tend to colonize the entire home, taking up every available spot for toys and clutter, and assuming that all the space is at their disposal. Yet adults need a quiet area or two of their own, and chil-dren's spaces need to be demarcated. This can be done in a number of ways.

The bedroom is the most obvious place for children's belongings once they are beyond the early years, although sometimes a shared bedroom may not be large enough to take the paraphernalia of more than one child. Playrooms can be created in quite small rooms if floor-to-ceiling space is used to good effect. A family room off a kitchen or a designated portion of a living or dining room can be a good space for older children

to use as an informal study area, with maybe a communal computer and desk or table. This is a good spot for a piano, too. Children need their space as much as adults, so try to contrive an area they can call their own but where friends and other members of the family will be welcome (and able to fit in).

Everyone has memories of their bedroom as a child. It may have been the cozy bed and bedspread, the pattern of the wallpaper, or the way shadows danced across a wall as cars or people passed by outside. Children need to feel secure in their own rooms, so providing the right kind of furniture, together with furnishings that reflect your child's tastes as much as your own, is an important element of a happy family home. Environment is just as central as love to a child's developing personality.

Child safety

Set up at least one smoke alarm and check the batteries regularly. Always keep a supply of spare batteries.

＊

Make sure loose rugs are fitted with nonslip mats underneath or, better yet, are anchored to the floor with tape, to prevent children from sliding and skidding into furniture or falling down.

＊

Avoid trailing cords from lights. While children are young, put safety covers on electrical sockets that are not in use.

＊

Never leave medicines in a child's room. This is surprisingly easy to forget if you are administering medicine at bedtime or in the middle of the night when you are half-asleep.

＊

Make sure windows are fitted with locks (with the key handy in case of fire). Do not place any furniture under a window, since toddlers will probably be tempted to climb onto it.

＊

Check that all paints and varnishes in the home are water-based rather than oil-based. Oil-based gloss paints can sometimes cause allergic reactions.

＊

Redecorate if it hasn't been done for a long time, since old paint may contain lead, which can be toxic. Make sure young children are kept out of the way when old paint is being removed.

＊

Attach freestanding bookcases or cupboards to the wall with brackets to prevent them from becoming unsteady or being pulled over.

＊

Cover sharp corners on furniture with soft or padded corner protectors while children are little.

＊

Fit automatic doorstops onto the tops of door frames so that the doors will not slam shut and trap a child's fingers.

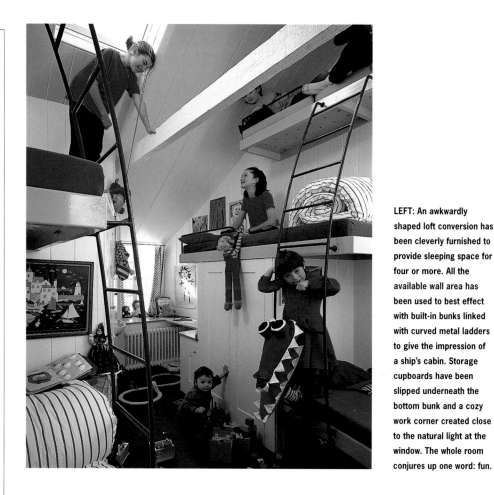

LEFT: An awkwardly shaped loft conversion has been cleverly furnished to provide sleeping space for four or more. All the available wall area has been used to best effect with built-in bunks linked with curved metal ladders to give the impression of a ship's cabin. Storage cupboards have been slipped underneath the bottom bunk and a cozy work corner created close to the natural light at the window. The whole room conjures up one word: fun.

Besides, this is one area of the home where parents usually feel they can take a more adventurous approach to decoration. Borders, painted or decoupaged motifs, and bright colors are all more stimulating and fun than scrupulously stylish plain walls.

ESTABLISHING PRIORITIES

Since many children's bedrooms also double as play area, refuge, workroom, and personal space, and since they need to house toys and games, hobby equipment, clothes, a bed, seating, and a desk, plus perhaps a TV, computer, and music equipment, the word multifunctional is nowhere more apt than here. It is the one room where versatile or multipurpose furniture will genuinely be used for a variety of purposes. The starting point in planning a child's room is to ask yourself a series of questions:

- If this is your first child, how many more are there likely to be?
- Is the child going to be in the same room for at least the next five to six years?
- Is the room going to double as a play area or a shared room?
- Is the room big enough to adapt to more furniture within a couple of years?
- Is the flooring suitable for children to play on without worrying about spills?
- How can sleeping, playing, working, and storing best be incorporated?

Put yourself in the child's place and establish what the priorities should be.

LEFT: In a high-ceilinged room, good use has been made of the available space by building a platform bed on top of the storage area, to use for guests and sleepovers. Fitted with elegant metal safety rails and a sliding, library-style ladder, it is functional yet gently sophisticated.

THE NURSERY YEARS

The arrival of your first baby induces a combination of joy, fear of the unknown, and a suspicion that life will never be the same again. Preparing a nursery for the new arrival is part of the waiting process and an exciting opportunity to plan and decorate a room from scratch.

ADVANCE PLANNING

The temptation to effect a complete transformation, so that your precious newborn is cocooned in an aesthetic overload of stenciled motifs, frills, and bold primaries, can be difficult to resist. But two years down the line, when your discreet bundle has turned into a whirlwind of energy and destruction, your enthusiasm for pretty bows or chunky tractor designs may have diminished, in tandem with your bank balance. To prevent the decorative flourishes from getting out of hand, always keep in the back of your mind the idea that the nursery has to be flexible enough for a newborn baby, a toddler, and a preschooler to feel at ease, all within a span of five years.

Decorating a nursery with an eye on the future will help prevent you from making extravagant choices that will quickly become inappropriate. Think too about the potential size of your family. If you are planning to have four children and you have the space to keep one room as a permanent nursery, then do a really thorough job so that each infant will enjoy the same splendor for its first 18 months.

Think too about how long you are likely to live in this home, since quite often people move house after the arrival of a second child. Advance planning may well have a bearing on how you use your present home. If you will be staying where you are, take a flexible look at your existing space. Two siblings may be better off in a larger bedroom while parents move to a smaller one for a few years. You might knock

Nursery necessities

Moses basket or rockable cradle, plus crib (not sited too near a window or a heat source such as a radiator) and natural-fiber sheets and blankets.

*

Low-wattage bulb in a bedside lamp, or dimmer switch on overhead light, for use while feeding and diaper-changing at night.

*

Changing mat and possibly a changing table, such as one with a rim around the edge and drawers for diapers and toiletries (never leave the baby on it unattended). Because of the risk of a baby rolling off a table, the floor is usually the safest place for a changing mat.

*

Hygienic lidded bucket or bin for dirty diapers.

*

Small chest of drawers or cupboard for clothes storage.

*

Basket or box on casters for toys.

*

Posters or framed pictures, mobiles, and an attachable musical crib toy.

*

Thermometer for checking that the room temperature stays in the range of 65–73°F (19–22°C), the recommended range for newborn babies.

*

Baby alarm.

*

Comfortable chair with cushions for nighttime feeding.

*

Baby bath or bath insert.

FAR LEFT: A neat, portable wicker Moses basket, suspended as a rocking cradle, is echoed by a chest of drawers consisting of small wicker baskets for pull-out efficiency. Though ideal for a baby's needs, this versatile piece of furniture will also work well when the child grows older and storage needs change.

LEFT: A painted chest of drawers sits happily against a plain wall decorated with wave shapes. Stenciled yachts dance across the sea for entertainment at diaper-changing time.

LEFT: This understated parents' room is proof that you do not always have to sacrifice style just because you are sharing the room with a young baby. Here, the crib is perfectly at home and easily accessible at the bottom of the bed. The crib cover and cushion echo the checked fabric used elsewhere in the room.

BELOW: Painting the headboard of a crib or bed lifts the decoration in a room. This underwater scene will provide a welcome distraction for any baby not in the mood for a nap.

through a small boxlike nursery room into another bedroom so you will have a nursery "annex" that will be useful once the baby is sleeping through the night. Children enjoy the reassurance of each other's company at night, at least until the issue of personal space becomes important.

DECORATING THE NURSERY

Once the necessities are dealt with, you can have fun adding decoration and color to a nursery. The predictable colors of blue and pink can be dispensed with in favor of a more generic approach that is neither overtly masculine nor particularly feminine. Research has proven that very small babies perceive only strong primary colors, so even if you hate such vivid tones, incorporate a colorful mobile or some posters.

Painted walls are sensible options since they last a long time and are easy to touch up when scuff marks appear. You can always liven them up with stenciled or block-printed motifs or borders. However, patterned wallpaper with a wipeable finish or vinyl wall covering will probably look good for a long time, since the pattern will camouflage any marks you cannot wipe off.

FURNISHING BASICS

Confine furniture to the basics and add more as your child grows and his or her demands change. The basics of crib, diaper-changing space, a comfortable chair for feeding, and storage for toys and clothes can really be quite minimal. Choose furniture that would not look out of place in an adult's room; special nursery furniture is very tempting but soon becomes redundant.

For the first three months, a baby will be happy in a Moses basket or rockable cradle. After that, you will need a sturdy crib,

preferably one with adjustable sides, and a new mattress that conforms to the latest national safety regulations.

Use cotton sheets and wool or cotton blankets in the crib. Comforters and pillows should not be introduced before a child is one year old.

THE PRESCHOOL YEARS

RIGHT: Young girls enjoy a touch of luxury and an excuse to indulge in prettiness, and they usually adore a bed with curtains around it. While this red-and-white checked canopy appears to be quite lavish, when it is no longer required it could easily be made into curtains, cushion covers, a throw, or part of a quilt. Combined with the painted metal-framed bed and simple chandelier, the ensemble has a Scandinavian look.

Preschool essentials

*
Bed with a good mattress and a temporary guardrail.
*
Bedside table, and a lamp with stable base and a switch that the child can reach easily.
*
Underbed storage or stacking crates, baskets, blanket box, or toy chest for larger toys.
*
Low table and chairs for activities.
*
Bulletin board for paintings.
*
Closet wardrobe or a simple hanging rail for clothes.
*
Chest of drawers or shelving system for nonhanging clothing.
*
Bookcase or extendable shelving for a growing collection of books and also for games and toys.
*
Curtains made from a thick fabric or with a dark lining to encourage young children not to get up at the crack of dawn on sunny summer mornings.

Toddlers can seem to become small, independent people almost overnight. The maturing process is generally very sudden and dramatic, as stumbling toddlers are transformed into feisty, opinionated preschoolers who want to do everything for themselves without any adult help. Battles over inconsequential issues such as the color of today's socks or a choice of soft drink can assume exaggerated importance in the mind of a small child.

ENCOURAGING INDEPENDENCE

Although accepted wisdom purports that it is two-year-olds who have temper tantrums and become inconsolable over minor matters, any parent will tell you that a three- or four-year-old is capable of much more concentrated, intense emotion. Encourage independence and appreciate how difficult it is for newly liberated three-year-olds to stand up for themselves (literally), learn to get their clothes on, and make what to them are difficult decisions over which games to play. Praise rather than prevention makes these years easier to manage.

During this time children are likely to begin playing in their own bedrooms or in a playroom away from their parent or caretaker. Therefore, making their rooms both inviting and functional becomes all the more important. Toys and games should be visible and within reach, so a child can select them easily. Storage should be interesting enough to make children actually want to help with cleaning up. (For more ideas see page 194.)

Take into account the gender of your child, as the interests of boys and girls do start to diverge around the age of five. However much you encourage girls to play with train sets and boys to appreciate dolls, there comes a point at which they start to follow a predictable course.

Toys and games accumulate quickly, making it worthwhile to sort through them regularly. Pass them on to younger siblings or relations, bag them up for the attic or get rid of them via a garage sale or secondhand shop. There is always a busy market in good-quality secondhand toys and clothes.

LEAVING THE CRIB BEHIND

The move from a crib to a full-sized bed occurs at the age of about two years. If you are thinking of moving an older child from the crib to a bed to allow a new baby to have the crib, remember that young children can be very possessive about their beds. Try to

leave a reasonable time between the child moving out of the crib and the baby moving into it, so that the child will not feel that the baby is pushing him or her out.

Don't forget that for a while a guardrail will be necessary to stop the child from

rolling out during the night. Not only is it safer, but it also makes the child feel more secure. Bunkbeds are not suitable just yet, but you could buy the type that can be used as two separate beds until all the children in the family are old enough to be able to play on the higher bunk safely.

ART GALLERY

Space for display is absolutely essential. A giant bulletin board or cork-covered wall will hold the latest splotchy masterpieces from nursery school or play group plus a few family photographs and treasured postcards. If you want to avoid using thumbtacks, cover a board with felt, then stretch lengths of ribbon across the felt in both directions, stapling the ends at the back. The child can then simply tuck items for display under the ribbons. You will also need flat surfaces for displaying treasured cereal-box creations and other indeterminate models involving discarded paper towel rolls and a lot of paint and glue.

ABOVE: A daybed and an indestructible wooden floor with plenty of space for playing on make this airy bedroom the perfect multifunctional child's space.

LEFT: On the wall next to these rustic bunkbeds built under the beams, a trompe-l'oeil dormouse and mole are tucked under patchwork quilts. Bunkbeds have an irresistible appeal to children, and although a preschool child is too young to sleep in the upper bunk, an older sibling could use it provided it was fitted with a guardrail.

THE IN-BETWEEN YEARS

THE FIRST DESK

As a child becomes an independent reader and writer, a desk, a good chair with a straight back, lamps, and bookshelves become important features of the room. Old school desks, which are readily available in junk shops, provide storage space too. A desk that folds down from the wall or is part of a platform-bed system is useful where space is limited. If space is really tight, you could buy a corner desk or create one yourself by simply fitting a triangular piece of wood across a corner.

POSITIVE CONTRIBUTIONS

Decoration is a subject for discussion and cooperation now. This is a good time to change furnishings such as curtains and bed linen to reflect your growing child's taste and interests. If you kept pelmets and upholstery plain in the nursery and pre-school room, you can extend the color scheme with cushions and different colored or patterned curtains or blinds.

Five- to ten-year-olds have solid opinions on color and pattern, often based on cartoon heroes and peer-group fashions they have admired in their friends' rooms. Resolve to incorporate their ideas, at least where practicable. Encourage children to have their say on colors, even if you end up with a pretty pink girly room or a lurid blue boy's room; remember, these colors can easily be painted over in the future.

When children start school and are gone from the house for most of the day, their lives, as well as yours, enter a phase that can best be described as busy, lively, and rewarding. Parents may suddenly find themselves with more free time, or at least less of a juggling act. Yet this new phase, with afterschool activities, friends coming over to play, and the odd sleepover, will ensure that another close look at the way the family home functions is in order.

The child's bedroom starts to become a place of refuge and reassurance. It is a room to retreat to for quiet playing, reading, and thinking away from the hurly-burly of the rest of the home.

ABOVE LEFT: As children get older, the furnishings and decoration of their bedrooms still have to be practical – and robust enough to survive friendly battles and games between siblings.

RIGHT: This child's bedroom exudes cool and calm. A built-in single bed with neat underbed storage extends around the corner and turns into a desk with drawers tucked underneath. The structure has been painted to tone with the walls, making the small room seem more spacious.

LEFT: Children enjoy creating their own decorative schemes. Here, patterns and motifs have been painted on the wall in a similar yellow to that used on the lampshade and headboard.

RIGHT: Even the nursery-rhyme set of coat hooks and the period dollhouse are in keeping with the traditional decoration of this bedroom.

OVERLEAF: Plain walls are enlivened by stamps of mice and crocodiles marching in single file. The matching wooden bedsteads are a decorative feature in their own right, while old pine furniture is a good choice for the in-between years as it makes for an easy transition from child to teenager.

Get them to join in with simple stenciling and painting, and by arranging bulletin boards with favorite images, certificates, and badges, drawings donated by friends, mysterious club documentation, and time-tables of events. A calendar, a clock, and an ever-changing arrangement of posters will be educational and creative.

Hobbies become obsessions now, so leave room for accumulations of acorns, seashells, gaudy stickers, and soccer cards or baseball memorabilia. Collections are fiercely protected so make sure they are housed out of reach of inquisitive toddlers who could wreck months of careful hoarding in a stroke.

Toys get small and fiddly at this stage. Construction sets, miniature dollhouse accessories and clothes, and pieces of board games too easily find their way between floorboards, and inside vacuum cleaners, and junk drawers, never to be seen again. Cardboard boxes, drawers, baskets, and boxes on casters will solve a clutter crisis. (For more ideas, see Storage, page 194.)

FRIENDS COMING TO STAY

A low platform bed with play space and a storage area beneath provides an economical use of space in a small room and can be used safely from about the age of six. Alternatively, as sleepovers become a regular feature of life at this age, a divan bed with a trundle bed makes sense, as does a bunkbed. Or you could resort to a fold-up bed stored elsewhere, a second mattress kept underneath the child's bed, or an inflatable mattress. Sleeping bags are also always useful.

SHARED BEDROOMS

Bedrooms shared by two children need even more careful planning, particularly the sleeping arrangements. Bunkbeds are good solutions for children over about six years old. They often incorporate underbed drawers or at least space for storing baskets of toys underneath the lower bed. A small corner shelf mounted on the wall above the upper bunk will be useful for the child sleeping up there, as it will provide a place to keep a clock and a drink of water. (If there are younger siblings around, a bunk-bed is not advisable yet – see page 177.)

Two single beds, placed parallel, could be separated with a small chest of drawers, making bedside tables unnecessary. Or they could be placed at right angles to each other, with a purpose-built cupboard in the corner between them; however, the bottom of the cupboard door would have to be above the top of the bed.

To prevent arguments, include two of everything – two bedside lights, two wardrobes, two chests of drawers, two bulletin boards and two boxes or baskets of special things.

Allow enough communal floor space, maybe with floor cushions, for both children to play, ideally with room to lay out train tracks, board games, or dolls' tea parties.

Consider splitting part of the room using bookshelves or a curtain in order to allow each child to have his or her own space and privacy. If the children are of different ages, you could separate the older child's work space from the younger one's play area.

THE TEENAGE YEARS

Now is the time to take a romantic weekend break, become nostalgic for the exhausting, chaotic preschool years, and remember how cute your enormous, uncooperative, grumpy, unkempt teenager once was. Abandon any notion of having much say in the style of a teenager's room – but be prepared to pour your bank balance into certain requirements that were once luxuries but are now almost essential for any seriously hip teenager. Computers, stereos, CDs, backpacks, and designer-label sneakers and clothes are but a few of the status symbols that the teenager's room is expected to accommodate. Be grateful for any communication your offspring does favor you with, but be careful not to appear too pathetically appreciative of the teenager's occasional urges to rejoin society.

INFORMALITY AND FLEXIBILITY

Not surprisingly, home design magazines, as well as books, often gloss over these years, since so many teenagers' rooms resemble ragged patchworks of pop-star posters and pictures of sporting heroes whose celebrity rarely outlives the lifetime of a book – or even a magazine article. Heroes come and go but the necessities of a teenage den endure. The space has to be informal, welcoming (at least to peers), flexible, and easy to keep reasonably clean and neat (this is best achieved while the teenager is out).

RIGHT: Using painted wood throughout a room looks informal yet stylish. This teenager's den comprises a low sleigh bed and a good-sized work corner, all painted one color to make the space seem bigger. Even the striped rug and cushions echo the graphic lines of the floorboards, wood-clad walls, beams, and banister.

LEFT: Flexible furniture in the form of a drawer unit set on large casters and a lightweight plastic easy chair is a good solution in a bedroom where teenagers gather in numbers. A simple metal-framed bed looks less bulky and cumbersome than a wooden bedstead. The large, uncurtained window and translucent canopy over the bed add to the light, airy feel, while strong colors have been used to tie the whole space together.

If a teenager has a specific interest or obsession such as sports, music, or books, this will very often provide the decorative basis of a room. Where once teenage rooms were all dark purple walls finished off with deep black baseboards, the new millennium's "green" preoccupations have brought a welcome return to neutral colors and natural materials. If it threatens to look too bland, introduce a few funky elements, such as a fake-fur-covered wardrobe, or a tabletop with a bold decoupage design.

Dump bins are handy as receptacles for teenagers' dirty (or clean) clothes, sports equipment, school reference books, magazines, CDs, and tapes. Metal wastebaskets, laundry baskets, filing cabinets on casters, colorful mobile magazine holders, or mere fruit crates or painted cardboard boxes will all perform much the same function of clutter control. (For more ideas, see Storage, page 194.)

ESSENTIAL FURNISHINGS

To create additional space, think in terms of three dimensions, not just two. A high platform bed provides plenty of space underneath for a chest of drawers, a desk, and lounging space. Some adult-looking versions have a desk underneath, with an armchair next to it that can unfold to become a second bed. A hammock or other seat can be suspended from sturdy ceiling joists with chains, or a fisherman's net can be slung from huge metal hooks to house footballs, sports equipment, or backpacks and other outdoor gear. Shelves, too, can be suspended from tension wire to provide contemporary open storage and a place to display sports trophies, personal mementos, and enduring toys.

If there is room, an armchair with a good reading light nearby provides a comfortable place to study or relax. A specific entertaining space can be created with a low table on casters, floor cushions, or a daybed furnished with squashy cushions and bolsters. A small TV set will provide additional independence, although this may mean that you never catch a glimpse of anyone for hours on end.

A desk of some sort is essential. If the one used in childhood is too young-looking, consider a secondhand office desk. Alternatively, one or two filing cabinets on casters slipped underneath a table or counter provide storage as well as lots of room to work. Another idea is to build in a counter along one wall, providing space for a computer and other equipment as well as a versatile and spacious work surface. It is important that if there is a computer, the screen and keyboard are at the right heights (see page 147), so you might want to consider a computer workstation to house it. Some of these have built-in desk and storage space as well.

FINDING EXTRA SPACE

Additional teenage spaces can sometimes be found on a spacious landing or in a converted attic, or in an adjoining garage. The area could, for example, be turned into a mini music studio, mirrored practice space for aspiring dancers, workout area for fitness enthusiasts – or just a sitting area for friends to gather.

PLAYROOMS

LEFT: The color red – featured on the walls, in the painted furniture, and in the checked upholstery – makes a bold backdrop for play.

RIGHT: Large, soft play cubes and a thick exercise mat transform this landing into a delightful play area suitable for even the most energetic of toddlers.

For larger families, a playroom can be almost a necessity, but even small families and tiny houses will benefit from devoting one room exclusively to toys and children's paraphernalia. It can be as little as a storage room or sun lounge, as makeshift as a corner of a shed or garage, or as gloriously practical as a room off the kitchen that leads, in turn, to the backyard.

SITING THE PLAYROOM

Although most often sited on the ground floor, a playroom can also be created in a redundant loft space, a spare bedroom, or a basement. However, when children are very young they will want to be close to you, which means on the same level.

There is never a time when a playroom becomes redundant. It will effortlessly metamorphose into a study, TV room, game room, guest room, teenage den, or hobby space according to family need.

If you do not have anywhere at all that could be devoted exclusively to a playroom, you could perhaps make a dining room, family room, or guest room do double-duty. Plan the storage and furniture ingeniously so that the room can quickly be converted back to the original purpose when necessary. If you have turned the dining room into a playroom, when you have a dinner party you won't want to spend half the day cleaning up the room. For activities and storage, use existing furniture (table, chairs, dresser, sideboard), protecting it all as necessary. Make sure all the toys, games, and other clutter has a home. Try to avoid having to move anything out of the room – that way you can save your time and energy for preparing the meal.

SUITABLE FURNISHINGS

How you furnish a playroom obviously depends on what other purpose it will be used for, if any. How old the children are is another crucial factor. Certain practical considerations are worth taking into account. Flooring (see pages 190-1) should

LEFT: An old industrial building finds new life as a playroom of generous proportions. Simply furnished with a corner bench and plenty of checked cushions, the space is defined with a blue painted border around the window and a collection of objects hanging from the ceiling. Not devoted exclusively to juvenile furnishings, the space also boasts a grandfather clock and "grown-up" table with chairs, ensuring comfort for any adults who join the children.

BELOW LEFT: A battered junk-shop table finds good use as a work surface for small children. Painted chairs match the striped walls, contrasting with the vivid green door and baseboard. The limed floorboards and broken patina of the table provide an effective foil for the strong colors.

be tough and durable so that train sets, car tracks, glue, poster paint, and food spills will not spoil the surface.

A discarded adult sofa, covered with a throw, is ideal in a playroom, while a sofa bed, futon, or daybed is highly suitable too. Combine it with a couple of squishy easy chairs, beanbags, or floor cushions, plus good overhead and task lighting.

You will also need ample shelving systems or cupboards. Battered junk-shop cupboards can be renewed by sanding and varnishing or painting. Children will enjoy dictating colors and motifs and helping to apply them – after all, it is their room. Any

freestanding bookcases should be anchored to the wall to prevent children from pulling them over. Chests, blanket boxes, and deep baskets with lids make good dump bins for small toys at the end of each day, while giant-sized versions can house ride-on toys and foldaway slides and tents when you want to clear the space.

Other essential components of a successful playroom include a blackboard and easel, a large bulletin board, and a generous worktable and chairs. If you want to use your dining table, protect the surface with a felt undercloth and PVC tablecloth. Dining chairs can also be protected with

slipcovers or throws. A miniature set of chairs and a table are a good idea if there are toddlers or preschool children about. Not only can they use them for various craft activities, but you may also want them to eat in this room when their friends come over to play. A small television, a stereo, a children's tape recorder, and a box of simple musical instruments would also be very popular.

As with other children's spaces, you will need to make flexibility a priority when decorating. Multigenerational soft furnishings will give you greater scope to use the room for different purposes.

CREATIVE ACTIVITIES

Keeping preschool children entertained and stimulated while you catch up with chores and household tasks is a major challenge in a busy family home. Quite often you can set up your child with an activity at the kitchen table, spend some time explaining or playing together, then get on with loading the dishwasher, doing some cooking, or making a quick phone call. (Prepare to be interrupted, however.)

The following decorating activities work well for entertaining, educating, and keeping boredom at bay, especially on rainy days. If you really can't stand the mess that painting, pasting, and dough can cause, then do not attempt them at all. Children presented with enticing materials and then told not to make a mess with them will quickly feel crushed, not creative. As long as you are prepared to cover all delicate surfaces with large sheets (save old ones – they are invaluable) or plastic coverings, any mess can quickly be disposed of.

PAINTING AND PRINTING

Use rolls of cheap lining paper or discarded computer paper for painting. An easel with paper clipped to it allows children to stand up while painting so they are less likely to dip their elbows in the paint or knock the jar of water over. Improvise paint palettes with old egg boxes, margarine tubs, and ice-cream containers. To personalize each child's bedroom, draw around the child while they lie on a strip of lining paper, then get them to paint in the details.

Allow the children to experiment with printing techniques. Make printing blocks from sponge, potatoes, or polystyrene sheets or cardboard stuck onto empty thread spools, or use rubber stamps; choose simple motifs such as boats, animals, or flowers. Small-scale decoration can be used for wrapping paper or posters that can then be framed. Or print on aprons, napkins, place mats, and tablecloths with fabric paints.

COLORING, CUTTING, AND PASTING

Create a coloring template by photocopying simple outlines of houses, people, and nature, then getting children to color them.

Paste wide strips of paper onto walls as decorative borders and protect them with a coat of matte acrylic varnish.

Children love making decorations for specific celebrations such as Halloween, Thanksgiving, Hanukkah, Christmas, and Easter, so keep them busy creating paper snowflakes, pumpkin masks, and Easter bunnies when the time approaches. If they decorate sheets of paper, you could get them laminated at your local print shop, to make seasonal place mats. Children also enjoy producing their own greeting cards and party invitations, so keep a permanent supply of colored and patterned paper, glue, and stickers on hand.

RAINY-DAY BOX

A rainy-day box is invaluable when new entertainment is suddenly demanded, when children who come to play are at loose ends, or when a child is home ill. Include in it a soft foam ball, a flashlight and batteries for playing chase with shadows on the ceiling, story tapes, and puzzle books or a new reading book. You might also add stickers, old greetings cards, and scrapbooks,

ABOVE: Children's paintings have been saved, trimmed, and carefully pasted onto this wall to make a striking wallpaper collage that positively sings with color.

LEFT: A craft corner slips into the space underneath a wall-mounted plate rack. Round tables are good for collaborative efforts with children and their friends, and the lack of a carpet is a positive bonus.

FAR LEFT: Children adore painting, so try to set up a place where they can work without having to worry about making a mess.

together with glue and cellophane tape for those craft moments. Older children could sort out holiday photos and then compile a record of the vacation or of the whole year in words and pictures.

When boredom overcomes youngsters or it is just too wet and cold to step outside, get out the rainy-day box and make some books or greeting cards. Sheets of colored paper can be folded in half and secured with staples or string to make a book. Make a cover by sticking on a picture or decoration. Children can make up their own stories and do their own drawings, though for younger children you could provide a few words and outlines for them to color in. Or they could make a book about something that interests them, such as food, cars, trees, flowers, or animals. They could cut out pictures from old magazines (which you have saved with this purpose in mind) and combine these with their own words and hand-drawn images.

THEATRICALS

Dressing up is another simple activity all children adore. Keep a supply of boys' and girls' outfits and periodically add any discarded accessories such as jewelry, hats, scarves, gloves, and shoes to the dressing-up box, along with scraps of luxury fabric such as velvet, brocade, or shimmery gold and silver Lurex. Face paint is a good way of adding to the fun – tigers, fairies, princesses, and pirates are all popular.

Also keep a supply of old sheets and blankets on hand for making dens on rainy days. Drape them over chairs or tables and supply pretend or real food and drink to the inhabitants within.

Puppet theaters also provide a good opportunity for children of different ages to cooperate in creating and staging a "show." The simplest theater can be made from large discarded cardboard boxes or a roll of corrugated cardboard cut into shapes and

glued together. Decorated with poster paint, curtained with fabric scraps, and detailed using gold and silver markers, designs can range from a candy-striped Punch and Judy theater to an ornate deep red-and-gilt music hall. For a sturdier alternative, hinge three panels of plywood or MDF (medium-density fiberboard) together to form a triptych. (Be sure to position it where it cannot be pushed over by young children.)

Older children will also enjoy making their own puppets. Tape or glue papier-mâché heads to wooden spoons; or stuff fabric with heavy curtain interlining or kapok, and tie or sew these heads onto lengths of thin doweling.

SOWING AND GROWING

Growing things always delights children, particularly when they can see results in just a few days. Mustard-and-cress is marvelous for children's first attempts at this. Cut the top off a baking potato and make a small hollow. Line it with damp cotton wool and sprinkle on a few cress seeds. Decorate the potato with eyes, a nose, and ears and place it in a paper cup. Within a few days the potato will sprout green hair.

When children are learning the alphabet, plant cress seeds in the shape of the initial letter of their name on damp blotting paper and leave in a warm dark cupboard to encourage the seeds to grow. (Do not allow the blotting paper to dry out.)

At Christmas time, hyacinth bulbs and cacti provide color and a chance to appreciate nature. If children paint some pots to house the bulbs, they can give them as gifts. In the summer, fava beans, nasturtiums, and sunflowers all provide instant gratification for fledgling gardeners.

LEFT: Making masks is always a popular activity at parties or when children want to put on a show. Make the masks three-dimensional by adding egg-box cups and yogurt containers for noses, plus yarn and string for hair.

FAR LEFT: Dressing up never goes out of fashion, even if Granny's old evening dresses do. Give a basket or box over to discarded clothes, hats, beads, and handbags for makeover sessions.

RIGHT: Two generations working together can often produce a professional-looking result, as on this fire surround that frames the storage area within the unused fireplace.

Help, it's still raining!

Children can suddenly become very boisterous when they know they can't go outside. Put on a lively music tape and instigate an on-the-spot exercise routine to burn off some energy. It's good exercise for you, too!

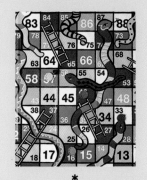

*

Divert bored children by suggesting a craft activity such as making books, painting boxes for collections, or making greeting cards. Start a rainy-day box and ask the children for their suggestions. Provide the basics of scissors, glue, tape, and glitter, then add new items to the box every so often. Keep a few surprises in reserve, such as shiny stickers, new stamps and an ink pad, or special scraps of fabric or paper.

*

Get out the dress-up clothes and suggest the children devise a themed game or play.

*

Make a den with upturned chairs and tables, blankets, and sheets. Provide flashlights for lighting and paper and pens for making signs. When everything is prepared, serve sandwiches, drinks, and potato chips or cookies to the inhabitants. Good for an hour's worth of entertainment.

*

Resort to the traditional standby and bake a cake. These days this is more of a novelty than a routine, and most children love the process of greasing the tins, weighing out and mixing the ingredients, decorating the finished cake, and rapidly devouring the result.

JUNIOR DECORATORS

Children often have strong views on how their rooms should be decorated. With a little tact and a strong push in one direction, you can make the decision-making process a satisfying family event, and perhaps even inspire the kids to help with the work.

Applying stencils to walls is an activity that children will enjoy. Instant results are always popular, as are the processes of making the stencils themselves or selecting them from the store. Alternatively, use stamping (see page 186) on the walls, floor, or curtains; it is even easier than stenciling. Choosing colors is one way of allowing children to experiment, and incorporating their favorite flowers, animals, and patterns into their rooms will make them feel more involved in the home.

If you cannot face the thought of the children getting involved in a total revamp of their room, you could mark out a specific area for their experiments. This could be a dado-height border around the room or a large square in the middle of one wall.

Start off on a small-scale item, then experiment on large pieces of paper before graduating to a bigger surface such as a door, a piece of furniture, or fireplace. Be really bold in your choice of project, creating overall patterns or decorative borders on walls, and games areas or painted "rugs" on floors.

FLOORING

Flooring in children's spaces has to be, initially at least, durable and stain-resistant. While the most practical, and often cheapest, solutions include stripped or painted wooden floorboards and "resilient" floorings (cork, rubber, vinyl, and linoleum), these surfaces are never as forgiving of scraped knees and tumbles as carpet. To get the best of both worlds, combine a hard or resilient flooring with large rugs.

FLOORBOARDS

If you are exposing existing floorboards in a young child's room, make sure that the boards do not have too many gaps between them, since small toys have a tendency to disappear down any "interesting" gulleys. If they are not too prevalent, you can close them up with wood fillets or flexible wood filler. Less-than-perfect floorboards can be painted in zingy colors and designs, as simple or as complicated as your talents dictate. For a tough finish, use water-based paint topped with several layers of polyurethane or yacht varnish.

RESILIENT FLOORINGS

The "resilient" floorings are all versatile, tough, and attractive. Cork flooring is warm and quiet underfoot, which makes it ideal in children's rooms. It is inexpensive and comes in easy-to-lay tile form or as sheets. There is only a limited range of colors available but it can be livened up with the addition of a few colorful rugs dotted around the room. Or you could paint unsealed tiles in strong colors and then lay them in a jazzy geometric pattern.

Less commonly available than cork, rubber flooring is nevertheless useful in children's spaces that receive a lot of wear and tear, since it is warm, relatively soft, tough yet easy to clean, and it provides a smooth surface for toy traffic (unless you choose the studded type). More colors are available now than ever before, including bright primaries that look great in children's rooms. It has to be fitted by a professional.

Linoleum has also regained popularity as it is natural, tough, antibacterial, and now available in exciting colors and effects. Tiles are easy to lay, but sheet lino needs to be professionally laid.

Vinyl is a practical option too. Solid, or rigid, vinyl tiles are the most hard-wearing and, generally, expensive. "Flexible" vinyl is more resilient underfoot but less hard-wearing than other resilient floorings. Resilient vinyl comes in sheet form, as either flexible, "lay-flat" vinyl, or cushioned vinyl. Some vinyls must be laid by a professional fitter, while others can be installed by an amateur.

LEFT: Carpet tiles are ideal for areas receiving heavy wear. In a playroom, tiles ruined by paint can easily be replaced. Use several colors for interest.

RIGHT: For sheer comfort nothing beats the softness of carpet. Here, solid blue carpet is broken up and protected by a rug. Spills on a patterned rug are also less obvious.

CARPETS AND RUGS

There is little point investing in thick-pile luxury carpet, since the amount of foodstuffs and crayons to which it will fall prey makes it unsuitable. Its biggest disadvantage as far as children are concerned is that it is not flat enough to accommodate building blocks or toy cars. For the early years, a heavy-duty flatweave carpet such as cord or a wool/synthetic mix should suffice. If your child is asthmatic, carpets should be avoided, and rugs need to be washable.

ABOVE: The rubber floor in this rooftop playroom is subtly patterned, yet remains smooth enough for heavy-duty toy traffic. Rubber flooring is tough, easy to wipe clean, and available in many colors.

LEFT: Economical vinyl tiles are jazzed up with white stencils randomly applied. PVA varnish seals and protects the designs.

FURNISHINGS AND LIGHTING

RIGHT: Beds offer a good opportunity for a keen needleworker to create heirlooms for the whole family. Patchwork quilts, appliquéd cushions, and soft toys all offer plenty of scope.

ABOVE RIGHT: Combine a simple, scallop-edged check pelmet with a plain white roller blind for a calm, uncluttered look that is not only highly practical but also very up to date.

Planning furnishings in children's rooms is one of the pleasures of parenthood. These are rooms where indulgence does not seem extravagant, nor wackiness over the top. Children gain a great deal of pleasure and stimulation from a well thought out and creatively decorated room.

From the age of three or four, they will have definite opinions on what they like and do not like about their rooms. Some of their ideas, such as turning a room into a cartoon-character theme park or a pink and fluffy heaven, can be subtly toned down or tactfully ignored, but allowing children a degree of autonomy will encourage them to believe in their own ideas.

USING FABRICS

To be practical, window treatments should not be too frilly. A decorative pelmet can be added to otherwise plain curtains, or a roller blind to provide color interest or echo a short-lived theme such as pink floral or comic-strip hero. Roller blinds and Venetian blinds that can be easily pulled halfway or all the way up at different times of the day are very versatile.

Children become obsessed with certain colors in the same way that adults do, so you can indulge your child's passion for, say, orange with a couple of cushions or a bedspread in the chosen color instead of replacing an entire window treatment and chair cover. Keep fabrics in plain colors or simple stripes or checks, then add colors by accessorizing beds, chairs, and floors with bolsters and cushions, throws, rugs, and kilims.

It is a good idea to use blackout lining with curtains or blinds in young children's rooms, especially in spring and summer when they may otherwise wake at sunrise. It will also block out glare from a street lamp outside a child's window. However, it can make the room gloomy when the curtains or blinds are closed.

Children of all ages gravitate to bean-bags, especially those in bold fabrics. Toddlers love wrestling on them and jumping onto them, while teenagers simply like to sprawl on them. Futons, possibly covered with throws, are also good for the horizontally inclined.

ACCESSORIES

If you like a coordinated look, then accessories such as drawstring bags, diaper bags, toy bags, canvas sacks to hang on the walls, baskets with fabric lining, and coat hangers in a chosen fabric can be used to unify a scheme.

A patchwork wall hanging, quilt, or cushion made with scraps of fabric from children's favorite outgrown clothes makes a lasting memento. Devise a design that incorporates family memories, such as the outline of the first family home.

Fabric can be repeated in a dollhouse and on a puppet theater and puppets, while leftover scraps can be turned into animal and flower motifs appliquéd onto accessories. Encourage children to help with the sewing so they can learn the basics or ask for their help in choosing the colors for the

RIGHT: When the architecture allows, built-in bunkbeds can work wonders with a space. Here, it leaves a bigger play area for the children, makes a pleasing addition to the room, and provides shelving within, for tucking away the soft toys that children love to have nearby when they themselves are tucked in at night.

BELOW: Older children need a bedside light within easy reach that they can switch on and off themselves if they are to become keen bedtime readers. A low, wall-mounted light provides better light for reading than a lamp on a bedside table.

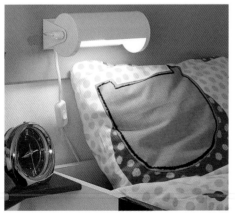

oversized blanket stitches, cross stitches, or slip stitches used to sew the motif on.

LIGHTING

Good lighting is very important in children's rooms. An overhead light with a dimmer switch is useful for checking on sleeping children. Good task lighting for desks is absolutely vital, as are suitable reading lights by the bed and by any armchairs. Make sure that any clip-on lights are safely secured; as they tend to get extremely hot, keep them out of reach of young children.

Novelty lampshades are a good way of allowing children to indulge in passing obsessions. Lots of different designs are available, or you can make your own with the help of your child. Buy a plain white cardboard shade, then add letters, stripes, polka dots, smiley faces, or some other design using felt-tipped pens. Protect your handiwork with matte acrylic varnish.

STORAGE

RIGHT: Deep baskets are ideal for housing large toys such as plastic dump trucks, tractors, and activity centers. Later they can be used as laundry baskets or log baskets, or as storage for young people's equally cumbersome paraphernalia.

RIGHT BELOW: Drawstring pouches are good places for favorite toys so they don't get discarded in the general melee. Use them, too, for bedtime reading or to keep a comfort blanket safe. Don't leave a very small child alone with one, however, as the drawstring could be dangerous.

Containing the clutter of childhood in one room is a dream every parent aspires to, but seldom achieves. Part of the problem is that many children's bedrooms have to be workroom, play space, and clothes store all rolled into one. Nevertheless, adequate, interesting storage can help.

CLOTHING STORAGE

A newborn baby's clothing needs are relatively minimal. A small chest of drawers or cupboard will suffice for at least 18 months. As the child grows up and eventually becomes a teenager, the need for a single small wardrobe graduates to a wall of cupboards and a hanging rail.

One way of tackling this situation is to keep a constant eye on the future. For example, a child-sized wardrobe can be sold or passed on when the child's clothing will no longer fit in it. A tented wardrobe is a good idea for a child, since the interior can be fitted with hanging fabric pockets and shelves to match the covering. It is ideal for diapers and nursery items initially, then as the child's belongings expand, the wardrobe can be either supplemented or relegated to the guest room.

Even with a wardrobe, some drawers are vital. A wooden chest of drawers can be painted several times for different phases of childhood, ending up in the guest bedroom when a child leaves home. A combination armoire that includes drawers and limited hanging space makes perfect sense for the in-between years, and can later be used for hanging shirts and skirts.

SHELVING

As well as storage for clothing, teenagers need some form of cupboard or shelving system for school books, sports equipment, magazines, and other belongings. Wall shelves can be added to – fortunately, since they seem to fill up with alarming rapidity. Placed above a desk, they keep reference books close at hand.

In younger children's rooms, bookcases can double as display shelves while a book collection is small. Bookshelves of any sort are useful long before a child can read, holding diapers, teddies, toys and games, or just about anything. Board games, puzzles, and larger toys crammed into alcove shelves can be further cleared away with a fabric or cane blind that covers the scene at night.

A shelf mounted right around the room at picture-rail height is good for storing soft toys that children can't bear to be parted from, medals and certificates, or delicate collections of shells, fossils, and more dubious flora and fauna, though children will not be able to see the items very well.

BOXES, BASKETS, AND BINS

Pull-out drawers or long, shallow boxes with recessed casters are ideal under the bed, while big crates on casters, wicker trunks, and large baskets are both movable and versatile. Colorful sisal baskets come in all sizes; the smaller ones can be used on desks for holding pencils, rubber bands, and other clutter. Baskets or stacking crates that slot into bookcases or shelving systems are invaluable for sorting and storing the small, fiddly items that young children always accumulate, like building blocks, miniature people, and doll accessories.

An inexpensive unpainted wooden mini-chest with small drawers is also ideal for storing small items and can be used later for school supplies or hair accessories and makeup. Make a feature of it by painting each drawer a different color and then decorating the drawers with a variety of painted motifs. When the child outgrows the motifs, just repaint the drawers.

HAMMOCKS AND PEG RAILS

A miniature hammock slung across an underused corner will also embrace clutter such as teddies, soft shoes, dress up clothes, or hats. Make sure that it is high enough that young children will not attempt to climb into it.

FAR LEFT: Swap dull drawer handles for painted wooden motifs, initials, or colorful baubles to give chests of drawers a fun look. The bedroom's occupant might even be inspired to put away his or her own clothes as a result.

LEFT: Adapt old school fittings or industrial cupboards as chic storage in teenagers' rooms. They will enjoy customizing them to suit their own requirements.

BELOW: Funky storage units and a painted cupboard on casters are ideal for style-conscious teenagers who have an image to maintain.

Peg rails are useful for all ages. Place them low down so children can hang up their own coats, ballet clothes, dressing gowns, and gym clothes. In a nursery, fix them at medium height to store and display special outfits, and in an older child's room, mount them high up to hold everything from sports rackets to hats.

CHILDREN'S BATHROOMS

Whether everyone in the home shares one bathroom, or the children have taken over the main bathroom because the parents have their own en-suite bathroom or shower room, it is not difficult to make the room child-friendly.

FUN AND FANTASY

Themed bathrooms are great fun and can actually look quite elegant. Think of a theme that interests your children and then let your imagination, and the children's, run wild. A nautical theme, for example, could be created by combining wide blue painted stripes on the walls with a red or red-striped roller blind, shower curtain, towels, and bathmat. You could appliqué fish or boat shapes onto the towels, and hang them on a "rope ladder" made from a length of chandler's rope and varnished doweling. Add a

few well-chosen accessories like boats, anchors, string bags, shells, natural sponges, a porthole-like mirror, and a height chart painted to look like a lighthouse. You could even make a plywood splashback for the bath, cutting the top into a wavy outline. Paint it sea blue, with colorful fish and maybe some deep-sea treasure – or get the children to paint it – then varnish it thoroughly before attaching it to the wall with screws. An unpainted wooden or MDF (medium-density fiberboard) bathroom cabinet could be decorated in the same way.

While teenagers may be too sophisticated for a themed bathroom, they might love something wild and colorful. You could try painting walls a bright color and then stenciling, stamping, or block-printing a

Bathroom safety

The bathroom is one of the most common places for accidents in the home to occur, so take special care with safety measures.

*

Keep all medicines and cleaning fluids locked in a wall-mounted cupboard and the key out of reach. Do make sure, though, that all adults know where to find the key in an emergency.

*

The bathroom cabinet should not be within reach even if the toddler climbs onto the toilet, bath, or sink.

*

Make sure razors and scissors are out of reach of children.

*

Always use a nonslip mat in the bath or shower when the children are young. Fit a grab rail onto the wall if there isn't one already.

*

Provide a step or nonslip box to enable young children to reach the basin and toilet easily and safely.

*

Make sure that a glass shower screen is made from safety glass.

*

Check that light switches and light fixtures meet with safety regulations. If you have electrical sockets in a bathroom, take great care when children splash water around.

*

Showers used by children should have a thermostatic control to prevent them from being scalded or chilled.

*

Wooden slatted bath mats (see left) provide a safe, non-slip surface.

really simple, bold border. Or paint some psychedelic wavy shapes on the walls in, say, three colors.

PRACTICALITIES

A sense of novelty in a bathroom always makes youngsters more enthusiastic about bathtime. Greater enthusiasm usually equates with more water being splashed around, so tough, wipeable surfaces work best (see page 145 for advice on the best materials). An integral shower in a bathtub is obviously very useful but it will also ensure that your floor suffers a regular soaking unless you are there to supervise bathtime proceedings.

Storage for bath toys can be tricky in a small bathroom when you also have towels and toiletries, cosmetics, and medicines to keep under control. A stackable crate slotted into a deep cupboard, or drawstring bags hung from hooks on the back of the door or from a peg rail, are possible solutions. Other ideas include a floor basket, a chrome shelving system, and wall-mounted

cupboards. As an alternative to tiles, a tongue-and-groove dado all around the bathroom walls provides a small ledge that is useful for bath toys and accessories. A shelf running all around the room at picture-rail height creates another storage-and-display area.

While a large mirror may seem like a good idea, bear in mind that small children cannot resist the temptation to go up close, usually before a bath, to smear the remains of their dinner over the surface. While children are very young, small, out of reach mirrors are more practical, if less fun. A teenager, however, will appreciate a floor-to-ceiling cantilevered version, preferably in their own bathroom with a do-not-disturb sign pasted permanently on the door.

EXPANDING THE SPACE

To prevent the morning rush for sink and mirror space reaching farcical heights, it is possible to extend the facilities without having to add an extra bathroom. Building vanity units in children's or parents' rooms, or even just adding an extra sink in a large bathroom, can make a huge difference. Another option is to install a shower somewhere else – in the corner of a bedroom, under the stairs, or in a utility room. Adding an extra toilet and sink at ground-floor level is yet another option. When toddlers are being toilet-trained or children pile in from the garden, an extra lavatory downstairs is invaluable. Any of these measures will ease congestion and free up space to allow it to be more child-oriented.

FAR LEFT: Hand-painted tiles make a cheerful backdrop to a plain bath. Use them for a simple splashback or extend them right up one wall for a definite statement.

ABOVE LEFT: Multi-colored rubber suckers with hooks attached are fun, temporary storage solutions in children's bathrooms where towels and net bags full of bath toys always need securing before bathtime.

LEFT: Plenty of bubbles will entice even the most reluctant and grubby of children into the bathtub.

BELOW LEFT: Plastic letters are fun and educational at the same time. Store them in an open net bag to allow water to drip through.

the van der heijdens, **canal living**

Pauline van der Heijden and her husband, Goos Drenth, have lived on a barge in central Amsterdam for over eight years. They find it much less stifling to live on a boat in the center of the city than in a small apartment block where you can always hear the neighbors and see the street life.

Most of the large windows in the barge are fitted into the ceiling, so the view is of the sky, the atmosphere is one of light and air, and the noise of the city is seemingly a million miles away. To make up for the lack of conventional views, Pauline has painted a country scene on one wall of the children's room and flanked it with blue gingham curtains to give the impression of a real window.

A past graduate of the Rietveld Academy, The Netherlands' best-known art school, Pauline studied fashion design at college, then went on to work as a clothes and theater-costume designer. But designing clothes gradually lost its appeal and she began to experiment with papier-mâché, mosaic, and painted furniture after a trip to Indonesia. There she soaked up

Above: A hand-painted fresco provides an instant view at a false window, bringing the country to the canal.
Left: Bathtime al fresco seems fitting when you are surrounded by water on a daily basis.
Right: The gentle lapping of water rocks the barge, making a quiet rest with the newspaper even more soothing. Fringed sun umbrellas provide shade when needed.

the culture of the islands and cities and was completely inspired by the vibrant colors she encountered.

During her first pregnancy Pauline spent a lot of time on the barge, where she found the constant lapping motion of the boat a comfortable distraction. Tiring of the pure white that surrounded her, she decided to paint a chair for fun. Looking at the barge now, it's hard to believe that it was once a clear white space, the sure sign of a designer's home.

By the time her daughter, Guusje, was born, Pauline had transformed the entire space with orchestrated color and pattern on every conceivable surface and material. Curtains were compiled from several different fabrics in many colors, some with appliquéd motifs. Walls were painted deep red, blue, green, or yellow, or a combination of all four in one room. Accessories, down to the last spoon, were splashed with color, creating a finished effect of gypsy chic meets Eastern opulence, tempered with 1950s kitsch – in other words, a gloriously unique and eclectic decorating style .

Goos loved the finished barge, and friends who gathered in the boat urged Pauline to start a new career as an interior decorator.

Several of them commissioned her to create rooms for their own children. She has been busy ever since designing and decorating other people's rooms as a result of her experiments on the barge – a testament to the fact that starting a family often allows a woman to take a different route in her working life.

Pauline likes the fact that often when she is painting and drawing, the movement of the water or bad weather causes the boat to rock or jerk. She may well be in the middle of creating a complicated motif or design, so the resulting wobbles are often incorporated into the work. Straight lines are not always possible with such a shifting backdrop.

Despite being a very contained space, the boat still manages to house six small rooms. At one end is the Atelier, Pauline's studio, where she stores fabrics, paints, and all manner of bits and pieces to do with color. Vivid plastic stacking boxes have wooden labels tied on for identification; even these labels are painted, embellished, or covered in fake fur.

Next to the studio, the bathroom has a mosaic wall that can be seen from the kitchen, where every surface is painted a different

Above left: Simple plastic stacking crates en masse make an excellent storage system for fabric samples and painting accessories. Paper labels tied to the handles identify the contents at a glance.

Above center and right: Pauline experiments constantly in her studio with color, shape, and texture until compelled to apply her designs to the walls in the other rooms of the barge.

color. Indifferent cupboards have been bedecked in an irregular black-and-white harlequin design to jazz them up, while storage shelves and the insides of cupboards are painted with surprising color combinations.

In a small space, storage is important, so the children's room includes painted cupboards, and trunks as well as a curtained alcove for clothes, toys, and bedding. Similarly, Pauline and Goos's bed is literally squeezed into a cabin, with storage space underneath it. Climbing into bed is a simple matter of ascending some steps at the end of a narrow corridor, into a sensory red palace of gingham bed covers, furry red cushions, and a glitzy Buddha under the fluorescent stick-on stars.

In the family space at the center of the barge, a large table for eating is divided from the kitchen area by a piano. Painted chests provide storage, and a vivid sofa adds comfort. The walls are a mixture of yellow, black and white stripes, and pink splashed with red petals, while the chairs at the table are a mishmash of painted wood and leopard-skin upholstery. But sunglasses are unnecessary – the overall effect is not disorganized riot but pleasing madness.

House Rules

* *Live on a boat to experience complete freedom and gentle movement all day long.*

* *Experiment with wild color in children's rooms – they love it.*

* *Study nature for decorating inspiration.*

* *Don't throw away old furniture: strip it down and decorate it for a new look.*

* *Think up motifs relating to your own family and apply them to chairs and doors.*

* *Store creative paraphernalia in unexpected containers such as plastic crates, curtained alcoves, and stacking baskets.*

Above left: Curtained storage in the children's bedroom opens to reveal baskets of organized belongings stacked on recessed shelves. For easy access, the curtains are looped back with a string of Indian fabric birds.

Above center: Laying in bed and looking at the canal through portholes is an experience unique to barge life.

Above right: Appliquéd and fringed curtains are a hallmark of Pauline's talents.

201

> *"Living on a barge has a soothing effect on babies and toddlers. The constant gentle lapping of the canal is calming and mesmerizing."*

Recently the van der Heijdens' second child, a boy named Jan, was born. With only a 13-month gap between Jan and Guusje, and a feeling that toddlers and boats do not always make for the most relaxing combination, the van der Heijdens have reluctantly decided to sell their boat and move to the countryside, where views of the sky and a sense of freedom will still form a major part of their daily life. Of course, they do know many people who manage to live successfully on barges throughout their children's early years. Decks can be made sufficiently childproof and extra care taken when getting on and off the boats. For the van der Heijden family, though, the call of the countryside has become too great to ignore.

Pauline spent her own childhood in a tiny village in Southern Holland where nature was the only raw material available to feed her growing creativity. She spent much of her time playing and experimenting with pieces of wood taken from old furniture in a makeshift workshop in the garden. From this experience grew her appreciation of color and her desire to work with paint. She and her husband want their own two children to know the same freedom that only a generous rural space and a simple life can give, before they in turn discover the pleasures of a vibrant and exciting city such as Amsterdam.

Now that Goos has experienced the color transformation that Pauline undertook on the barge, he is fairly convinced that the new house will stay completely white for a time, while Pauline assesses the potential of the place. They lived against a very neutral backdrop for several years when they first moved to the barge. However, now that color is such an important part of their lives, he doesn't think it will take another pregnancy for Pauline to begin working her magic on the new home. Her sense and use of color is just too inspiring to revert to a pristine white space. And it's guaranteed that the children will love it too.

Left: **Busy decoration and a collection of kitsch ephemera turn the otherwise unremarkable kitchen area into a riot of color and humor.**
Above left: **A funky flowered sixties' chair is more like a mini playpen to Guusje.**
Above right: **Eastern color meets European eclecticism in a room where most surfaces are decorated with Pauline's fine paintwork.**

PAINTED game table

RIGHT: Decorating a rug with hopscotch numbers provides an instant source of fun in a child's bedroom. Ensure the rug is securely fastened to the floor to prevent it slipping during boisterous games.

FAR RIGHT: You can easily adapt the design of this tabletop to include your child's name, date of birth, or favorite animals.

Decorating children's furniture with colors and designs of your own choosing is fun. Let your children help decide what animals and other motifs you include. Instead of the alphabet, you could incorporate the child's name. Don't worry if you can't draw well – the naïveté of the designs is part of their charm. The painting should be neat but loose, with straight lines painted freehand. For bright colors, apply two coats, allowing the paint to dry between coats. The table is made from MDF, which stands up to rough treatment from children better than softwood. It is possible to buy ready-made "blanks" for decorating yourself.

YOU *will need*

* Table in MDF (medium-density fiberboard), plywood, or a softwood such as pine
* Acrylic undercoat and acrylic paints in gold, dark blue, medium blue, red, green, yellow, off-white, and black (or colors of your choice)
* Round artists' brushes in a range of sizes
* Cracking medium and flat brush
* Gloss acrylic varnish, brush, and steel wool

1 Apply acrylic undercoat and leave to dry. Lightly draw the design, using the template as a guide. Paint the checkerboard in the center. Paint the gold areas: the uneven stripes at the outer edges and on the table's sides, the band inside these, and the border around the checkerboard. Paint just beyond the outlines for the adjacent colors so the next colors overlap. Paint dark blue between the gold stripes, overlapping onto the gold.

2 Paint the letters at each end in medium blue, red, and green, again going slightly over the outline. Paint the yellow panels behind the alphabet, overlapping the yellow onto the letters by the same thickness as before.

3 Paint the animals next, again going slightly over the outlines, and starting with the smallest areas. For example, paint the spots and udders of the cows, then paint around them with the main off-white color. Add the eyes last, painting the black pupils then the whites. Now paint the red background around the animals.

4 Paint the dark blue border around the inside of the gold band freehand. Also paint a dark blue border between each yellow alphabet panel and the red portion. Using the rounded (non-bristle) end of a brush, add the gold dots on top of the outer border (but not on the borders between the yellow panels and the red section). Draw the fish on the gold band then add the eyes, pupils first. Apply cracking solution over this gold band and leave to dry. Now apply a medium-to-thick coat of off-white paint to the area within the gold band around the fish; the fish will remain gold. Paint the underside of the table dark blue, and paint two legs red and two yellow. Finally, apply several coats of varnish, sanding lightly with fine steel wool between coats. Also varnish the underside.

CEILING mobile

Very small babies are happily diverted by colorful mobiles that shimmer and sway. For maximum entertainment value, hang mobiles above the crib, bathtub, stroller, car seat and anywhere else the baby spends any time. This plywood mobile is easy to make and even simpler to customize with favorite bits and pieces like shells, pictures, or jewelry, which you can change often so that the mobile does not lose its novelty value. Older children enjoy mobiles too, so get a big brother or sister to help make this project.

BELOW AND RIGHT:
Children love treasure-hunting on the beach but it can be difficult to find a convenient way to display their collection. Turn their favorite items into decorations for a ceiling mobile, where they can be admired without cluttering up surfaces.

YOU *will need*

* Thin plywood
* Pencil, string, and thumbtack
* Protractor (optional) and straightedge
* Jigsaw
* Drill
* Emulsion paint in white and a contrasting color
* Flat paintbrush and artist's brush
* Colored cord
* Decorative clothespins with a hole at the top
* Ceiling hook

1 On the plywood mark out three concentric circles using a pencil, string, and thumbtack to act as a large compass. The circles shown here have diameters of 3in (8cm), 11in (28cm), and 19in (48cm), but you could easily make them larger or smaller.

2 Divide the three circles into eight equal portions; to make them precise, you could use a protractor to make each angle exactly 45 degrees. Draw all the lines with a straightedge, then mark points on the lines 1in (2.5cm) inside the circles at the positions shown in the illustration. Cut out the rings with a jigsaw, discarding the 3in (8cm) circle in the center. Neatly drill through the marked holes so they are just barely big enough for the colored cord to pass through.

3 Paint the rings white on both sides and leave to dry – you may need to paint one side, leave to dry, then turn over and paint the other. Paint the edges in a contrasting color. Allow to dry.

4 Measure and cut the four outer and four inner cords. The lengths will vary according to which items are to be hung from each ring (and therefore how far apart they need to be) and at what height you will hang the mobile. You will also need to allow for the four outer cords forming a hanging loop at the top. Thread the cords through the holes as shown, fastening each with a small knot at either side of the ring to keep the circles level. Knot the four outside cords together at the top to form the hanging loop. Trim the cords to the required lengths at the ends and tie a clothespin to the end of each cord. Clip on your chosen decorative elements before suspending the mobile from a hook in the ceiling.

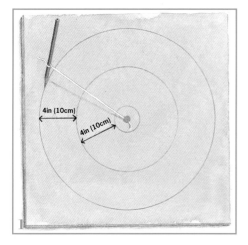

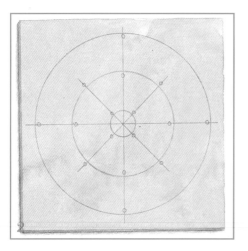

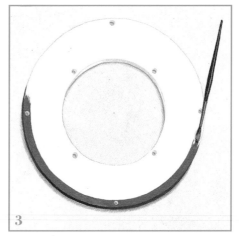

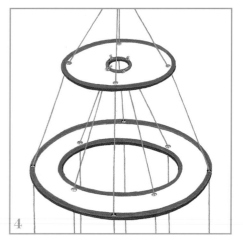

CHILDREN'S blackboard

Children of all ages love messing around with a blackboard, whether it is creating a special picture or playing school, taking pleasure in erasing all their work, or experimenting with colored chalk. Adults, too, can't resist a quick doodle when confronted with an empty black space and a pristine stick of chalk. This is no ordinary blackboard, however. Fixed safely to the wall, it holds a roll of lining paper at the top and contains useful holders for jars of water, paint, or chalk. A generous trough mounted on the wall beneath it catches drips and chalk dust and holds essential but messy paraphernalia. Made from the simplest of materials, including PVC guttering, this is an easy weekend job that will provide hours of entertainment.

YOU *will need*

* ⅜in- (1cm-) thick plywood or formaldehyde-free MDF (medium-density fiberboard), cut to size at lumberyard
* Blackboard paint and paintbrush
* 2 large cup hooks
* Length of 1in (2.5cm) doweling
* 2 aluminum pipe clips with cross-head screws
* 2 fascia brackets
* Screws and rawl plugs
* 6ft 6in (2m) length of standard grey PVC guttering
* 2 internal stop ends
* Roll of lining paper
* 2 glass jars or plastic tumblers
* Bradawl, screwdriver, spirit level, drill, and hacksaw
* Sandpaper

RIGHT: Wherever there is a blackboard, children will be irresistibly drawn toward it. This version has been designed to try to contain the inevitable mess that accompanies an enthusiastic art session.

1 Ask the lumberyard to cut a piece of plywood or MDF (medium-density fiberboard) to your required size, roughly 51 x 39in (1.3 x 1m). Apply a couple of coats of blackboard paint, allowing each coat to dry thoroughly.

2 Insert two large cup hooks about 3in (7.5cm) down from the top edge and 5in (13cm) in from the side edges. Cut a piece of doweling to slot comfortably through the hooks, allowing extra length at either end beyond the hooks. Attach two aluminum pipe clips with cross-head screws at either side of the board, about 7in (18cm) from the bottom, making sure there is enough space in between for the lining paper to hang.

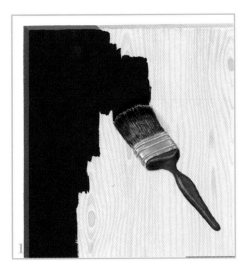

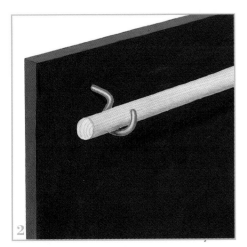

3 The plastic trough is mounted on the wall beneath the blackboard and is supported by two fascia brackets. Decide on the height required and use a spirit level to mark a line for the positions of the brackets. Attach the brackets to the wall with screws.

4 Cut the PVC guttering to length with a hacksaw and smooth the edges by sanding. Clip it into place between the brackets and snap-fit the stop ends in place. Fix the blackboard securely to the wall just above the trough, using screws. Thread a roll of lining paper onto the length of doweling and slot the doweling into the cup hooks. Fit jars or tumblers into the pipe clips.

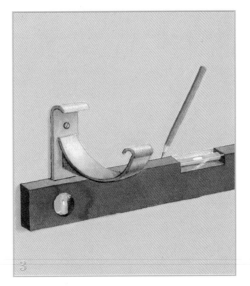

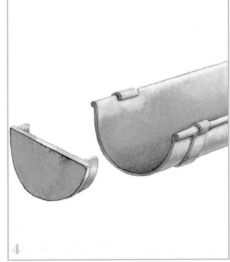

209

FABRIC pockets

Children's rooms seem to breed unspecified clutter, lost pieces of board games, and small, awkwardly shaped toys from nowhere – maybe it multiplies while the family sleeps. This is one room where you can never have enough storage. Alcoves, drawers, boxes, cupboards – you can usually fill all of them and still find plenty to occupy fabric pockets hanging from pegs or hooks on the wall. Stencil, paint, or appliqué the alphabet to the pockets, or use letters, numbers, or words to code the contents, and you will be adding an educational element. These pockets are 6in (15cm) square and the whole hanging is 45¼ x 26½in (113 x 66cm), but you could easily adjust the size to suit your needs.

YOU will need

* 47¾ x 27⅛in (119 x 68cm) piece of calico or canvas, strengthened with fabric stiffener
* Fabric remnants for pockets
* Embroidery thread and embroidery needle
* Sheet of plastic and alphabet stencils
* Fabric paint and stencil brush
* 5 grommets
* Ribbon (if using peg rail)
* Iron and sewing machine
* Masking tape and yardstick

1 From the fabric remnants, cut out 28 squares, each measuring 6¾ x 6¾in (17 x 17cm). Turn under and press ⅜in (1cm) hems on all edges of the squares, taking care to make all the pocket pieces exactly the same size and square; pin and machine-stitch. Turn under and press ⅜in (1cm)

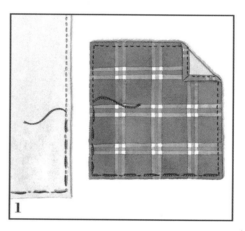

hems on the side and bottom edges of the canvas, and a 2in (5cm) hem on the top edge; pin and machine-stitch. Using embroidery thread and an embroidery needle, work running stitch by hand along the stitching lines on the squares and also on the canvas.

2 Protect your work surface with a sheet of plastic. Stretch the fabric squares so they are taut, and tape the corners to the plastic. Tape a stencil to the fabric square, positioning it centrally. Load a barely damp stencil brush with paint and wipe off the excess on a scrap of paper or fabric, then apply the paint using a circular, swirling action. Fix the colors with an iron, following the paint manufacturer's instructions.

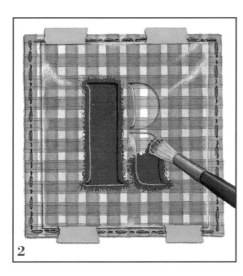

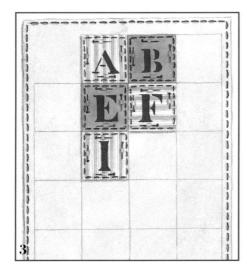

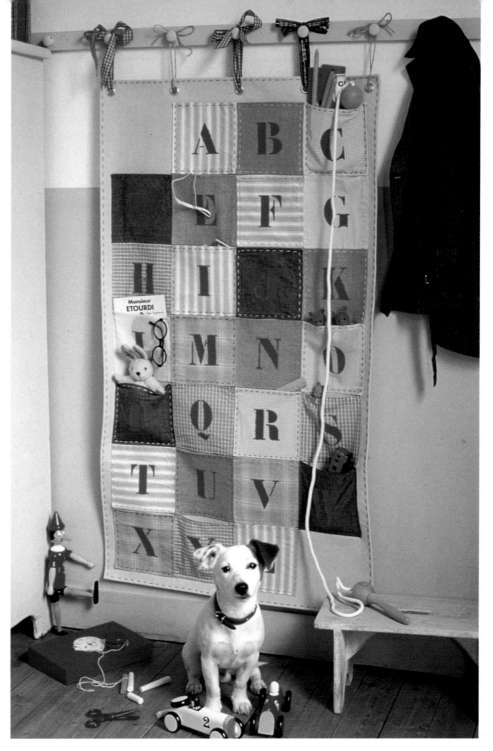

3 When all the pockets have been stenciled, mark out a grid on the canvas using a yardstick and pencil. Allow a border of 1¼in (3cm) at the sides and bottom and a 2in (5cm) border at the top. Position the squares and pin and tack them in place on the grid, one by one.

4 Machine-stitch near the edges, stitching an entire row of squares as one long line. Stitch all the squares' side edges, then turn the hanging and stitch all the squares' bottom edges in the same way, a row at a time. Be sure to leave the top edges open. Remove the tacking threads. Insert the grommets along the top edge, following the manufacturer's instructions and spacing them to line up with the pegs on a peg rail, if using. Tie to the peg rail with lengths of ribbon through the grommets, or simply hang from cup hooks attached to the wall.

FAMILY GARDENS

FAMILY GARDENS

Whatever its size, a garden works as an extension

RIGHT: A tree of any size is the perfect centerpiece for a game of Follow the Leader, even in a small back yard. Children do not need a lot of space to invent their own entertainment. Stepping stones sunk into the grass make a good path, ideal for an imaginary game of Avoid the Crocodile.

The garden of a family home should be functional and child-friendly, whether the children are toddlers or teenagers. For a family with young children, the garden probably also needs to be low-maintenance. Although that obviously precludes a plethora of beds filled with delicate flowers, it does not have to mean a garden reduced to a lurid-colored climbing frame sitting on a worn patch of grass. Steering a sensible middle course between these two extremes is perfectly possible, whether you are adapting an existing garden or designing a brand-new one.

LEFT: The verandah of this wooden house provides a vast outdoor seating area. Adirondack chairs arranged along the house wall allow all family members to commune or divide into natural generational groups. Plenty of floor space allows for serious coloring, communal board games, or solitary reading, even when the weather is wet. An overhead lantern provides muted light in the evenings.

LEFT: In a large garden you have the opportunity to create specific areas of interest. Here, a patio area close to the house has become an outdoor dining area, while the children have colonized a nearby tree with sturdy climbing ropes and a swing. Elsewhere, the large lawn is punctuated with a number of good-sized shrubs – but not so many that the children cannot run around to their hearts' content.

of the home, where a family can be at its most relaxed.

The task of creating a garden that is attractive yet also practical is relatively easy in a large garden that already has mature trees and shrubs separating play zones from decorative borders. By contrast, designing a garden around a simple expanse of grass or paving, or even planning and creating it completely from scratch, is a much longer operation, calling for patience and some imagination. However, the evolution process is itself enjoyable, as each successive year brings new elements and perspectives to the planting.

CONTRASTING APPROACHES

For some busy families, the outdoors is merely a space used for eating and entertaining during summer weekends, a paved area you walk across to reach the shed that holds the outdoor chairs. A few containers stuffed with plants during the summer provide a nod to serious gardening, but the area principally serves as a living space. For other families, however, the yard is simply a place for children to play – pushed out of the back door at first light by parents desirous of fresh air, nature, and exercise for their offspring (and the consequent peace and quiet for themselves).

Still others, no matter how small their plot, are able to lavish care and attention on considered planting schemes in which color, texture, and form merge into a pleasing year-round display. Containers are planted with seasonal bulbs, annuals, and herbs in strict rotation – here there are no sad pots filled only with redundant earth, as seen on so many busy families' patios.

REALISM AND VISUAL SENSE

Planning a family garden from scratch is akin to planning and building part of a home; indeed, garden design employs similar principles to those used in the interior. You have to be realistic about your needs – for example, if you are laying a new lawn, you will need to use a robust "utility" grass mixture, that tolerates hard wear and neglect rather than a "fine" grade. At the same time, you must plan with an eye on the future, building in as much flexibility as possible.

The need for a practical approach does not mean that aesthetics are not important too. A garden should be a natural extension of the house, with the two elements making visual sense when they are viewed together. A house whose rooms are painted in vivid

215

Mediterranean colors calls for a bolder garden than a mere scrap of grass and bare trelliswork. Similarly, a contemporary home that boasts white walls and clean lines inside and out would look incongruous with a country-style garden, all rustic poles and climbing roses.

ESTABLISHING PRIORITIES

It is easy to forget that the garden is not just for gardening. It is a communal space that can, if planned with a growing family in mind, become an outdoor room for eating, entertaining, playing, exercising, and pure pleasure, in many ways a place more versatile than the indoors. So decide what your priorities are and identify your basic parameters. Here are the kinds of questions to ask yourself:

- Do you need additional living space outdoors for alfresco meals?
- Do you have young children who will need sufficient space for running off excess energy?
- How much play equipment do you want to include?
- Do you want to leave a large expanse of lawn that can be used for soccer, badminton, croquet, or other games?
- Do you need to preserve an area for cultivating favorite plants?
- How much space – if any – do you want to devote to growing vegetables or fruits?
- Is a pond an option, or are your children too young for it to be safe?
- Would you like to have any other water feature?
- Will there be a shed and/or greenhouse and, if so, do they need to be hidden by climbing plants?
- Is there anything that needs to be screened from view, such as trash cans or an oil tank?
- Will the garden contain any architectural features such as a gazebo, summerhouse, pergola, or arbor?

PLANNING THE SPACE

The secret of creating a garden that works well for your family is to start with a plan of the space, much as you would when designing a home. Pace out the entire area and make a rough scale drawing of the garden, including any existing features you want to (or have to) incorporate. Make some photocopies of this, to enable you to experiment with different designs without having to redraw it each time.

Once you have established all the basic elements, work out the sites for these elements, and add them to your scale drawing. If you are planting for the first time, remember that gardens can take up to ten years to reach maturity, so you will need to take into account how any new trees or shrubs will look both now and when they are fully grown.

Create areas of interest by demarcating specific spaces with trellises or hedges, an arch, an arbor, or a pergola. Changes of level are good ways of breaking up larger spaces, and children adore running up and down shallow steps into different areas. For subtle dividers, make walls from railroad ties, woven willow hurdles, bamboo screens, or trelliswork. Decorative devices such as these are pleasing to look and serve a practical purpose. Equally delightful are narrow paths flanked with lavender and rosemary or planted with chamomile to serve as a fragrant walkway.

Water features are always soothing. Options include a pond (see page 227), a miniature fountain, a wall fountain that issues water into a stone font, or a small electric recycling pump that pushes jets of water over large pebbles.

LEFT: Changes of level help to enlarge a garden visually and provide a range of interesting perspectives. Here, shallow brick steps lead up from a child's table and chairs to a sandbox to a peaceful enclosed area, ideal for an afternoon of quiet reading while the children make endless sand castles.

RIGHT: This tiny garden still manages to find room for an intimate outdoor dining table and an impressive herb bed, as well as a shed and a cold-frame. Containers are ideal on pavement and for small areas where flower beds would take up much valuable space – though they do need frequent watering.

BUILDING IN FLEXIBILITY

If you plan to stay in your family home for the foreseeable future, it is worth treating the garden in the same way as the house, by choosing major elements that can be adapted as the children grow up and your needs change. For example, a permanent wooden play structure driven deep into the earth may be great when children are young, but it will have lost its attraction by the time they have left primary school. A jungle gym designed to be reassembled for use as a pergola for climbing roses,

FAR LEFT ABOVE: Eating alfresco is pure pleasure, whether or not it is among olive groves and sunflowers. Here a grapevine twists invitingly around stone pillars which support a sun-shading slatted roof.

LEFT: Even in a small urban garden there is often room for a swing, a sandpit, a small patio for trike-riding, and one or two flowerbeds for the parents to enjoy. Planning the space carefully will mean you can always fit in more than you thought possible.

wisteria, or a vine, however, is more practical. It can even be converted back to its original use when grandchildren appear on the scene.

A fiberglass pond liner sunk into the ground can be used as a wading pool initially and then converted into a proper pond, complete with fish and plants, when the children have outgrown it. A built-in sandbox can be transformed into a planting trough or water feature.

LOW-MAINTENANCE GARDENS

Most gardens tend to be more or less forgotten for much of the year, as they always seem to be at the bottom of the list of things to do. Then come the first warm, sunny days of the year, and suddenly nine months of neglect are followed by a frantic weekend of manic pruning, weeding, and digging. At times like this, a low-maintenance garden comes into its own, and it is invaluable when children are young and time is short.

Grassing over large flower beds, or at least making them smaller, reduces the workload considerably. In the remaining beds, pack in as many shrubs as possible, including ground-cover plants. Shun annuals (except the ones the children plant – see page 231) and biennials in favor of

perennials, and choose types that will not need staking or tying up. Avoid too many container-grown plants unless you want to spend much of your time watering them.

Mediterranean flowers and shrubs can thrive on very little water, and so are ideal for low-maintenance plans and for parts of the world, or times of year, in which water is in short supply. In areas with mild winters, some of the sturdier desert-growing plants such as cacti and other succulents look stunning in bold groupings, yet can be practically ignored. Keep them out of reach of young children, though, since prickles are sharp and allergy-inducing.

If you are planting a hedge, it is sensible to opt for one like laurel or holly that will only need trimming once a year, rather than a fast-growing type like privet that requires trimming three times a year. (Unfortunately, the slow-growing types also take longer to reach a reasonable height.)

PLAY AREAS

The modern child is less likely than previous generations to play outside on the street, in the fields, or at the park without adult supervision. Apart from the safety reasons, there are also more distractions indoors now, such as the computer and the television, to prevent them from getting enough exercise and fresh air. A family garden or backyard therefore provides an important opportunity for children to let off steam, indulge in some really messy play, and commune with nature. If the yard is fairly large, they can also run around, hide, make dens, and happily wear themselves out.

A specific play area furnished with a swing, jungle gym, sandbox, and tree house or playhouse is child-heaven – and the stuff of fantasy for families who live in urban apartments or homes where the garden is more a patio than a meadow. But whatever the size of the garden, at least one of these elements can usually be incorporated without too much difficulty.

SWINGS

A swing is perhaps the single most popular play apparatus for children. It is also, however, the one piece of equipment that every park possesses, and the swings at parks are usually bigger and more fun than the domestic variety. If there is no room at home for a swing, regular trips to the park become all the more exciting. A swing needs a certain amount of clearance around

it if passing children are not going to be injured, so make sure it will provide pleasure rather than danger if you are planning to install one.

Swing heads are available that attach to a sturdy wall, allowing space to swing in an enclosed garden. Or if you have a big old tree, strong rope threaded through a wooden seat can be employed to create a rustic swing. Rubber seats are the safest, though, since they cause less injury than wood or plastic versions, both of which can splinter on hard impact.

JUNGLE GYMS

Jungle gyms are versatile and popular with both genders. As mentioned, if they are purpose-built from timber struts they lend themselves to adaptation as pergolas, arbors, or dividers when children are older. They can also be designed to incorporate swings, mini-playhouses, viewing platforms, climbing ropes, rope ladders, and slides. They should be sited within view of the house so that you can keep an eye on children using them. Jungle gyms can be left out in the garden all year and in winter have increased novelty value since they are not used so often.

If you are building a structure from scratch, make sure that you use sturdy wood, that the supports and stakes are within national safety standards, and that there is a soft landing onto bark chippings, special nonslip matting, or sand. Also check the structure regularly for wear and tear, particularly swinging-rope or rope-ladder attachments.

If building your own jungle gym is not an option, you might consider a purpose-made steel structure. This usually comes in a basic kit that can be added to and adapted as children grow.

SANDBOXES

Sandpits are hugely popular with both children and cats, so make sure that an exposed box is covered when not in use, to prevent

unwanted visitations. This will also stop rain and leaves from getting into it.

While a gaudy plastic container with a molded cover in which water games can be played is undoubtedly practical, a sandbox that blends into its surroundings makes more visual sense. For example, a patio could have a sandbox edged with colored tiles. Stepping stones, hefty boulders, logs, and railroad ties are also good edging materials. A sandbox should be at least 4 feet

ABOVE: A well-designed garden house can be a playhouse, guest room, workroom, and garden shed, all rolled into one. The raised deck surrounding it is a feature children adore and also makes the building more versatile.

FAR LEFT: Jungle gyms, forts, and tree houses made from rustic poles are constructions that children find irresistible – the rougher the better.

ABOVE: A trampoline in the garden is always attractive to children of all ages – almost as good as the parental bed for jumping up and down on.

LEFT: In a Japanese-inspired garden, a bark-chipped play area mingles effortlessly with other types of surfaces. When the swing has been outgrown, the space beneath it would lend itself to a water feature or a pebble walkway.

219

LEFT: A large sandpit is always popular with children and their friends. Make sure it is covered at night and replenish the sand annually.

RIGHT: A treehouse need not be an elaborate affair. This simple platform and wooden ladder are enough to promote adventure in an urban garden.

(1.2 meters) square. Fill it with washed or silver sand, not builder's sand.

It is tempting to site a sandbox as far away as possible from the house so that the kitchen floor does not become gritty when the children pad back indoors, but toddlers need to be watched to ensure they are not imbibing bucketfuls of sand. Make sure you can see the sandbox from the kitchen even if it is not near the back door.

As far as children are concerned, the best position for a sandpit is near a water source, such as a wading pool, an old sink, or even an old barrel sawed in half and filled with water. The water source should be close to an outside tap so that minimal traipsing is required to fill it up. Water and sand always conjure up sand castles, miniature dams, and flotillas of small boats, yachts, and water wheels.

PLAYHOUSES

Siting a sandbox next to a playhouse allows sand pies to be taken into the playhouse for cooking in the pretend oven, then "eaten" at a table, either inside the playhouse or outdoors. A painted picket fence enclosing the whole area and creating a mini-garden is the ultimate in small-world play and will keep children happy and well occupied for many an hour.

There are lots of different types of playhouses, ranging from simple foldaway, hinged hardboard or plywood panels to a converted shed or even a purpose-made miniature home, complete with gingham curtains, integral shutters, window boxes and a door knocker. Whichever type you choose, it will provide your children with many years of pleasure.

WILLOW TUNNELS AND WIGWAMS

A natural alternative that blends into the garden background very well is a willow tunnel. Anchor willow shoots firmly into the ground, then weave them into the required shape and tie them for stability. Because it roots very easily and grows quickly, it may produce greenery in just one year.

Wigwams are good temporary playhouses, in the garden as well as indoors (see page 238). Other alternatives are garden tents, blankets draped over chairs, extralarge cardboard boxes, and play tunnels.

TREE HOUSES

Tree houses provide the perfect setting for children's adventures and imaginary games. They may be as simple as a sturdy platform supported by planks or tree trunks and edged with trellis, or as fully formed as a little house on stilts nestled among the branches of a tree.

Simple will usually suffice, especially if rounded off with a couple of pirate flags or a weathervane, and a rope ladder or wooden steps for access. A fishing net slung across the top makes a good ceiling and provides a spot to store flashlights, treasure maps, binoculars, and a lunch box.

Retreating to a tree house for serious games of pirates, spies, or Moms and Dads is a great childhood occupation. The nest-like structure feels at once secure but special, a place away from the daily routine and grown-ups.

If you are not inclined to build a tree house yourself, specialist companies can advise on the suitability of your trees for the various structures they sell. Fruit trees are ideal for modest, low-level tree houses.

WHEELED TOYS

Ride-on toys, especially bicycles, play a big part in children's lives. Youngsters who live in the country or have a large garden tend to learn to ride on two wheels much sooner than apartment-bound children who can only practice during specific visits to an open space, a pedestrian-free sidewalk, or a quiet cul-de-sac under adult supervision. Paved areas make good cycle tracks, as do front drives or quiet pathways, and are also suitable for tricycles, scooters, and pedal cars. Storing bikes up on special hooks in a garden shed will keep them out of the way when not needed.

LEFT BELOW: A house or garage wall is a good space for installing a basketball hoop for group or solitary practice.

RIGHT: Paddling pools, however modest, are the sources of the best summer fun. Provide buckets and hoses, plastic watering cans, and plant sprays for additional water games and make sure there is a ready supply of dry towels for when the children start to shiver.

Play areas

To play most games in the garden, an area of lawn, unbroken by flower beds, is needed. Croquet, boules, horseshoes, garden skittles, and badminton are all good dexterous games that can be played on only a modest expanse of lawn.

Making messy pictures outdoors, as long as there is no breeze, is a good way of allowing artistic freedom without fretting about cleaning up. Set up a small table and chairs with newspaper and Play-Doh, or get out the PVA glue, glitter, lentils, and dried pasta, and watch a unique collage emerge.

Wet play is also best indulged in outdoors. Use an old dishpan and assorted plastic beakers, jugs, and watering cans for measuring and pouring and for general splashing.

No children's garden is really complete without a couple of discarded balls. Set up a small soccer net or paint a goal onto a garage wall with whitewash.

A basketball hoop can be attached above a garage door or on a side wall, where you can also site a special swing.

Pet grooming counts as a game too, as long as you have a very bubbly bath, one mud-spattered dog, and lots of grooming tools.

221

EATING AREAS

day you will be using it. You will need some form of shade for at least part of the time, even if it is just the dappled shade of a large tree. Alternatively, a sun umbrella is an economical and portable solution, while permanent options include a fixed or retractable awning, plus trelliswork, an arbor, or a pergola covered with climbers.

Shelter from wind may also be an issue, especially if you live near a coastline. Half-height walls, trelliswork, bamboo fences, willow hurdles, or oversized terracotta or stone pots containing miniature trees or topiary will provide protection and enclosure. An enclosed courtyard, walled garden, or easily convertible outbuilding works well as a cozy spot for alfresco meals.

Meals eaten out of doors in warm weather have a special magic. More pragmatically, alfresco meals relieve pressure on space indoors, simplify cleaning up where young children have eaten, and allow children more freedom when they, inevitably, finish eating before the adults.

Creating an area specifically for eating will make a natural focal point in the yard. Placed close to the house for easy access to the kitchen, it provides a gentle transition from indoors to out.

A SHADY, SHELTERED SPOT

When planning an eating area, take account of the direction of the sun at the times of

FAR LEFT ABOVE: There is little better in life than eating outside in warm weather, close to the sea yet sheltered by trees. Decking topped with large, thick cushions is all the seating that is required alongside this long, low picnic table. In bad weather, the feast can simply be moved into the conservatory.

LEFT AND ABOVE: Sausages clamped in a barbecue griddle are snapped up by eager children. A barbecue, whether it is a built-in brick type, a mobile one on wheels, a small hibachi-type, or a disposable version, provides a focal point for outdoor entertaining and makes family meals more fun, too.

LEFT: A Provençal tablecloth brings color to this long table. The colorful enamelware plates and plastic beakers blend in well with the jug and tablecloth and colored glassware. Although indelibly associated with Provence, all the elements that make up this idyllic scene can be successfully transplanted to another country in fine weather.

OVERLEAF: An attractively presented spread of fresh seafood, bread, and vegetables is irresistible to small hands, which can just reach the essentials.

BARBECUES

If you enjoy barbecuing, you will undoubtedly want to provide space for a barbecue near the eating area. It may be either built-in or freestanding but should not be sited too near windows belonging to you or the neighbors. Keep the cooking area free from overhanging trees or greenery. Pavement is preferable to grass on the ground under a barbecue. If you are building it yourself, try to include an area for storing food before and after serving and for sauces, marinades, and utensils.

GARDEN FURNITURE FOR ALL OCCASIONS

Furniture is a matter of preference, but bear in mind whether the table and chairs can stay outdoors all year or will need to be protected from winter weather. Certain items such as varnished wooden benches can happily survive bad winters, particularly if made from teak or iroko, but woven cane or softwood garden furniture needs to be indoors once the summer is over.

If you do a lot of family entertaining, you will need seating for children. Miniature picnic tables and benches are favorites with children. A low wall on a patio can double as a bench when softened by cushions. The simple picnic rug is always popular, but food and drink tend to tip over easily on such an uneven surface.

For families whose children have summer birthdays, the option of having parties outdoors is a welcome relief. With no worries about spilled food, broken ornaments, or greasy fingerprints, adults can relax and join in the fun. An entertainer could be called in, but games such as relay races, a treasure hunt, or identify-the-plants will often be appreciated just as much.

OUTDOOR LIGHTING

If you want to eat outside in the evening, good lighting is essential. Many homes have one outdoor light, but this may be too harsh to dine by. Garden lighting is now as sophisticated as that of the interior, so search around to find exactly what you require, and have it installed professionally.

You will probably want soft, low-level lighting for the eating area, with steps and perhaps the edge of the patio defined. Trees and foliage can be accented using uplighting, downlighting, or spread-lighting, or you could stick movable spiked spotlights into the ground. Ponds and fountains that are lit by night provide a fascinating shimmer.

Alternatives include lanterns suspended from stakes driven into the ground; garden flares, although they are not practical in high winds; nightlights secured in sand in the bottom of brown paper bags; and candles inside hurricane lamps. Some pot-bound candles contain insect repellent.

Outdoor entertaining

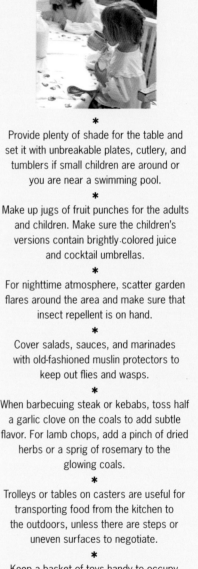

*

Provide plenty of shade for the table and set it with unbreakable plates, cutlery, and tumblers if small children are around or you are near a swimming pool.

*

Make up jugs of fruit punches for the adults and children. Make sure the children's versions contain brightly-colored juice and cocktail umbrellas.

*

For nighttime atmosphere, scatter garden flares around the area and make sure that insect repellent is on hand.

*

Cover salads, sauces, and marinades with old-fashioned muslin protectors to keep out flies and wasps.

*

When barbecuing steak or kebabs, toss half a garlic clove on the coals to add subtle flavor. For lamb chops, add a pinch of dried herbs or a sprig of rosemary to the glowing coals.

*

Trolleys or tables on casters are useful for transporting food from the kitchen to the outdoors, unless there are steps or uneven surfaces to negotiate.

*

Keep a basket of toys handy to occupy small children at a safe distance while any barbecuing is being done.

*

Always have plenty of paper towels on hand for the inevitable spills as children pass by on bikes or during boisterous games of hide-and-seek.

QUIET AREAS AND RETREATS

RIGHT: Building a tree seat is not too taxing but gives a great deal of pleasure. Design a seat that suits the size of the tree, its trunk, and the proportions of the garden, and be sure to use a good-quality hardwood such as teak so it will last a long time.

BELOW: Perfect as an instant recliner, a rope hammock fits in just about anywhere, even between an outside wall and a small tree. Position it in the quietest spot of the garden, away from the house and children's play area if possible.

sturdy rope and a strong seat, and be sure to hang it from a tree – and a branch – that will take an adult's weight.

Seats and benches are natural focal points in a garden, providing visual interest as well as inviting resting places. Simple stone benches or wooden garden seats (either painted, stained, or oiled) always look good, or you could improvise with an old tree stump or with railroad ties. Traditional painted cast iron or wrought iron benches can also look attractive, particularly the classic, less ornate versions. Place seats in sheltered spots but with the best possible view of the garden. If they are heavy, it is advisable to set them on

The appeal of a special place outdoors away from the house, even if it is just a shed, is alluring. Indeed, the potting shed has traditionally been the place to escape to, for a few hours of peace away from the hurly-burly of family life. As an area for quiet contemplation and guilt-free escape, the shed or garage exerts a strong pull on weary adults. (It can, of course, have an equally strong attraction for children, so make sure that all insecticides, slug pellets, weed killers, fungicides, fertilizers, and dangerous tools are locked safely away.)

RESTING PLACES

Sloping off to read in a hammock is a great escape if you can get away with it. Fruit

trees have especially sturdy branches that are often at just the right height for a hammock. The farther the trees are from the house, the better.

An arbor or other leafy bower enclosing a bench, seat, or chair is instantly restful. Train scented climbing roses, wisteria, jasmine, honeysuckle, or clematis over it for scent and color, and place pots of fragrant herbs close by.

Tree seats offer shade and shelter and are hard to resist. A slatted wooden hexagonal seat encircling a tree trunk creates a traditional scene and begs to be sat on.

It's always a shame that swings are designed only for children. Make a tree swing large enough to bear an adult using

a hard surface, since mowing right up to the base is not always possible.

Outdoor seating also allows adults to keep an eye on children while reading, puttering, or entertaining. It should not be too close to any secret dens, tree houses, or wigwams, though, since these require privacy to remain popular with youngsters.

Make sure you have some lightweight, portable chairs that can be moved around as need be, following the sun or the flowers. Seating placed close to scented flowers or a particularly beautiful flower bed will add to the tranquility when you are taking time out in the garden. Water is an acknowledged soother, so even a fold-up chair placed next

LEFT: A semi-enclosed structure such as this summerhouse not only provides a sheltered spot to sit, but also serves as an architectural feature in a garden.

BELOW: Rather than providing shade from the hot sun, this simple verandah attached to a log cabin offers a cozy retreat hidden deep in the woods. Sturdy tree trunks form the pillared supports and informal rattan furniture is arranged to make the space feel like a real room – only the view is better.

to a small pond of weaving fish will induce relaxation. You may even mentally redesign the whole garden while you sit there, momentarily forgetting about the domestic chaos inside.

BETWEEN HOUSE AND GARDEN

Being both shaded and partially enclosed, a verandah offers a cool retreat in the summer or a sheltered spot when the weather is poor, making it an excellent time-out zone. Rocking chairs, hammocks, swing seats, and deep cane sofas are perfect here.

Similarly, a conservatory, with doors flung open, plants spilling out, and a comfortable chair placed enticingly close to the entrance, makes an irresistible resting spot. In fact, the conservatory often becomes the favorite room in a home, allowing the family to enjoy the garden whatever the weather. As a bridge between indoors and out, it provides a flexible area in which to work, relax, entertain, or play while surrounded by nature.

FAMILY GARDENING

The garden is one area of the home where everyone can have their own space, however tiny, and work together to create something

ABOVE: Harvesting home-grown apples is one of those traditional rituals enjoyed across the generations.

RIGHT: Planting spring bulbs or even just messing around in the soil between the flowers is what children enjoy best about a garden. An early interest in the outdoors can lead to a lifelong love of gardening and nature and a deep-rooted ecological awareness.

that all can benefit from. Clear away the bikes, balls, and scattered sand at the end of a warm day, and you can reclaim the garden in the same way that you revive a battle-scarred living room by clearing away toys and lighting a log fire in the fireplace.

Using plants that are fast-growing and tough will encourage children to participate in the rituals of sowing, growing, pruning, and harvesting. It will also help them to appreciate the importance of the seasons, of nature and nurture, while providing you with a good supply of produce and flowers.

CHILD-FRIENDLY PLANTING

While you may want to preserve one or two flower beds filled with delicate plants, it is best to invest in tough, quick-growing shrubs so that children can wander through the garden without having to worry about

damaging the plants. Bamboo provides fast-growing, instant cover for adventuring young ones, as do willow, elder, and dogwood. Hazel and privet make good screens and dividers if you want to preserve a special place for delicate plants and flowers. Just make sure that there is at least one rough-and-tumble place.

PETS AND WILDLIFE

Pets and wildlife go hand in hand with a busy childhood, so you may need to give over some space in the garden to rabbit or

guinea-pig runs. Chickens are another possibility. They do need daily tending, but the eggs are always useful (if you can find them), and there is something heart-warmingly absurd about a hen picking and scratching its way around a garden, conjuring up noise, life, and normality wherever it strays. In the less conventional but still irresistible category are goats and ducks.

Nesting boxes, a bird-feeding table, and a birdbath are great assets in a garden, particularly where wildlife is in short supply. Teach children which foods will attract different species of bird. Ponds are another great source of fascination across the generations. Fish, frogs, newts, water striders, water boatmen, and dragonflies flitting between and underneath water lilies and other water plants are a magnet for the eyes of young and old alike.

Designating an area of the garden for wildflowers that naturally self-seed is often a rewarding exercise. Left to their own devices, swaying poppies merge with wheat-grass, cow-parsley, and vibrant violas to present a cohesive meadow of color.

PLANTS TO AVOID

Some plants are highly poisonous and should be avoided while children are young or curious enough to pick and eat fruits, flowers, and berries. It is generally safer to discourage young children from eating anything from the garden. The worst species include foxgloves, euphorbia, laburnum, yew, nicotiana plants, deadly nightshade, monkshood, daffodils, and juniper. Avoiding all slightly toxic plants is not really practical, so keep a close eye on children until they are past the try-anything-once stage.

grown in a separate "kitchen garden," or among flowers and shrubs or in large pots. Some, such as lettuces, carrots, radishes, and strawberries, can even be grown in window boxes.

Even if it is a matter of simply placing a few pots on a balcony or windowsill, the harvest always tastes better when you have

grown it yourself. Tomato plants, runner beans, zucchini, lettuces, potatoes, and carrots all thrive without too much effort.

A fun way of supporting runner beans is to grow them up tall canes forming a wigwam large enough for a child to fit inside. Mark a circle in the earth and push the canes firmly into the ground around this circle, leaving an opening for a doorway. Lash them together securely at the top, then plant the beans around the outside.

GROWING FLOWERS

Children enjoy growing flowers, too, and a small flower bed devoted to children's plants will always be a hit. Edge it with large sea shells or interesting-colored stones for extra visual appeal. Encourage the children to select and plant their own favorite flowers – they could even sow the seeds in drills shaped like their initials.

The process of growing seeds, nurturing them, and reaping the benefits is a revelation to children who always appreciate

GROWING YOUR OWN FOOD

Growing food in the garden brings immense satisfaction for adults and sheer delight for children. Most people have fond memories of climbing fruit trees as children to taste the crops, whether they were ready or not. But even if you have no fruit trees, children can help to grow vegetables and soft fruits. Choose types that your family all enjoy, and try to arrange the sowing schedule so that you have bumper crops when children are home from school (but not when you are all away on vacation!).

If possible, allow each child his or her own growing area, for which they have complete responsibility. Food crops can be

ABOVE LEFT: An unused bread oven has become an outbuilding for garden storage in the countryside.

ABOVE: Cutting your own Christmas tree is a big treat when you have young helpers to make sure you have chosen the biggest, best specimen.

RIGHT: Runner beans trained up a garden outbuilding that doubles as work space and shed demonstrate the versatility a garden can offer as a place to grow produce and flowers and also serve as an extension to the home.

RIGHT: In the doghouse, but barely so. This home-made kennel festooned with vibrant orange and red nasturtiums is proof that even the most functional items in a garden can blend into the surroundings in a decorative way.

instant results. In the case of nasturtiums and sunflowers, they are not often disappointed. In fact, sunflowers are so obliging that you can instigate a race between siblings or your child's friends, to see whose sunflower grows the tallest.

Flowers can be grown up wigwams in the same way as runner beans. Grow Galaxy sweet peas or climbing nasturtiums up tall wigwams that the child can fit inside, and Bijou sweet peas or black-eyed Susans up doll-sized wigwams.

Another fun idea is to hollow out a coconut shell, paint a face on it, fill with soil, and plant creeping Jenny, periwinkle, or stone crops in it. Hang the coconut in the garden where everyone can admire its lush crop of hair, and don't forget to water it.

A "child's garden mixture" of annual seeds will also prove popular, as will cornflowers, poppies, godetia, candytuft, and marigolds. To complete the children's sense of satisfaction, encourage them to use their flowers in arrangements for the house – you may be pleasantly surprised at the floral artistry that emerges.

SHARING CHORES

Children love participating in a family dig, so harness their enthusiasm by enticing them into helping with general chores. They will probably enjoy picking up unwelcome snails or bugs (though maybe not slugs) and tossing them into the compost bin, and also digging holes in which to plant shrubs and then filling the holes with water from the

watering can. Clearing leaves in the autumn is more of a pleasure when children join in, gathering up your premade piles into trash bags. Give them pruning shears when they are at an age not to pinch their hands, and you will have a willing dead header for several years. Weeding can be pleasurable, too, when your helper inquires, "Are these naughty plants or good ones?" Just make sure they are not inadvertently ripping out your newly divided primroses.

Buy children their own gardening notebooks so they can record their successes and failures. A pair of sturdy gloves, a wheelbarrow, and small garden implements will encourage their enthusiasm, as will an apron, a flower press, and a camera (to prove how tall the champion sunflower was).

the farrells, **a country garden**

Susie and Peter Farrell have such an extended family that their only realistic option when looking for a new home was to design and build their house to accommodate themselves and five children. In a small village in England's Cambridgeshire countryside, they bought a building plot on which Peter designed and built a new home from scratch, using indigenous stone and a traditional facade. The stone from which Peter built the house was gathered from a nearby derelict home. In fact, it is said that all the stonework in their village emanates from the ruins of the local castle from which it was plundered a few centuries ago.

Once the home was complete, the Farrells purchased an adjoining field to create one enormous garden comprising several distinct areas. This has enabled them to combine their passion for gardening with a seriously adventurous play area for their children, who at that time ranged from toddlers to teenagers.

Above: Shallow stone steps flanked by low brick walls and matching pairs of pots lead from the house past the eating area toward the lawned area of the garden.

Above left: Gathering the runner beans turns into a game of hide-and-seek for Esme.

Below left: French windows open out from the plant-filled conservatory onto a gloriously rich collection of trees, shrubs, and flowers.

Right: The outlook from an upstairs bedroom window provides a perfect bird's-eye view of various areas of activity and division within the whole garden.

Now that both the house and garden are finished, the Farrells have more time to devote to their kitchen design business. In a joinery workshop close to the house they oversee construction work and have recently renovated the country kitchen of the cookbook writer and broadcaster Delia Smith.

In the space of just six years, their garden has matured from a forlorn meadow, complete with a stream at one end of the plot and several well-established fruit trees, to a sprawling, welcoming garden with several individual areas, each with their own function and feel. Comprising more than two acres of land in total, the space is any child's dream, not to mention a heady prospect for a keen gardener. A colorful, well-tended country garden gradually eases into a walled orchard that in turn curves down to an unkempt *Wind in the Willows* area at the furthest point from the house. Here, a n elongated pond links a series of playhouses and tree houses in what can only be described as a child's play heaven.

The most popular playhouse for the children and their visitors has always been Ratty's House. It was designed for the 1994 Chelsea Flower Show in London and transplanted to the Farrells'

meadow later that summer. A turf roof identifies it immediately and, with water nearby and a tree-trunk bridge linking it with a tree house across the riverbank, the whole scene wants only for Toad and Ratty themselves.

With so many different elements to the garden, there is something to occupy each family member for hours at a time, with no threat of boredom or diminished discovery, so the entire family spends as much time as possible outdoors. Susie adores gardening and has helped to plan and construct several gardens for the Chelsea Flower Show. Her workroom and drawing board are on the first floor of the house, by a large bay window overlooking the garden, so she always has a sense of the outdoors with her as she works. The living room, too, opens onto the garden, and in the summer the doors are left permanently open so everyone can traipse in and out at leisure.

At the top of the garden, close to the house, is a cultivated space with carefully tended lawns, elegant flower borders, a gazebo, a potting shed, and a patio filled with containers of box and plantain lilies. Here, quick-growing shrubs allowed the garden to mature as

Above left and right: Esme and Rory, the two youngest children, are developing a passion for gardening, helping to repot and tend the vegetable patch. This helps to keep the large family supplied with fresh produce throughout the year.

Runner beans, potatoes, carrots, basil, and rhubarb are among the crops that flourish in this old-fashioned, enclosed kitchen garden. The runner beans are trained over a wigwam of canes to create a tunnel of bright green leaves and scarlet flowers.

House Rules

* *When space gets tight, build a playhouse or tree house – the children will eventually move in.*

* *However small the garden, create different areas within it for pots, people, and play.*

* *Grow your own vegetables and herbs – children can help, eat the crop, and learn to economize.*

* *Devote an area to a children's vegetable plot.*

* *Keep part of the garden wild, as a haven for children and wildlife and as a space to encourage threatened wildflower species.*

* *Greenhouses and sheds do not have to be unsightly work areas in a garden. Design them so they enhance the space.*

swiftly as possible, while providing a practical, low-maintenance planting scheme. With such a busy family life, even keen gardeners like the Farrells find they must bend to convenience. They try to keep the lawns and flower beds adjacent to the house as immaculate as possible, so that an overall feeling of order and calm pervades the immediate vicinity of the house. Further down the garden, the gentle slide into informality, followed by the wild, uncultivated children's play area and general undergrowth, is neither a shock nor a visual horror.

Close to the back of the house and the kitchen door is a round garden table topped with a large sun umbrella and surrounded by metal chairs, an ideal spot for eating. During the summer, breakfast is eaten outdoors, en masse, and the same area is used for evening drinks and quiet meals.

A bank of lavender gives off a delicious scent and leads the eye down to the walled garden, where herbs mingle with cultivated vegetables. An element of self-sufficiency is more a necessity than a hobby with so many mouths to feed. Tomato plants, runner beans, lettuces, and potatoes are all grown in abundance, while the

Above left: A greenhouse is both a place to nurture delicate plants and cuttings and a beautiful addition to the garden itself. Trailing vine wanders across one side of the roof and generous terracotta pots sit on either side of the entrance.

Above center and right: A garden the size of this means there is never any time just to sit and appreciate all the hard work it takes to maintain it. The younger children hide away in Ratty's House, a *Wind in the Willows* extravaganza of tree trunks and ivy.

"With the additional plot of land, the garden has become more than an extension of the home. It is a series of spaces as versatile and entertaining as the house itself."

greenhouse is home to a large, rambling grapevine. Both the greenhouse and the large wooden potting shed are used by all members of the family. Rory, who is four years old, particularly enjoys helping with the planting. When the various fruit trees in the orchard have shed their crop, the children are encouraged to bag up the fruit and sell it locally.

From this working part of the garden, a stone arch and shallow stone steps lead down to the children's "wilderness" garden. En route are more plum and apple trees, a large wooden table for outdoor eating on warm days, and all the playhouses.

Susie calls this section of the garden the "blue painted village," as the variety of activities that take place here remind her of a theme park. When her eldest daughter celebrated her eighteenth birthday, the various playhouses doubled up as additional bedrooms, enabling thirty people to spend the night – a serious sleepover by anyone's standard.

Entertaining outdoors is one of the pleasures of having a large garden. During the summer, the Farrells tend to cook enormous barbecues, gathering the family and all their friends in one place. They also eat many family meals down by the pond, in the "wilderness" area, and the children often take sandwiches and other provisions down to the tree houses and sleep there for the night – or at least until the wildlife starts producing unnerving noises in the small hours or Cluckie, the pet chicken, decides that there is one visitor too many.

Above and right: Tree houses, swings, and wild zones keep children happy for hours.

Left above and below: An elegant gazebo and a beautifully tended herbaceous border are the adult antidote to adventurous play elsewhere in the garden.

CHILDREN'S wigwam

A wigwam is the perfect place for a sheltered picnic, a pretend tea party, or simply an important powwow. Quick to make and easy to store, it can be used outdoors or inside and is an ideal "instant diversion" when children need a change of scenery or a new activity on a rainy day. Decorate the duck or canvas with colorful handprints, cotton tassels, letters and numbers, or animal motifs. Stencils and stamps are fun and easy for children who want to create their own style of decoration to use.

RIGHT: Fast-growing plants such as sunflowers, nasturtiums, marigolds, zucchini, and runner beans growing up a bamboo teepee provide instant delight in a children's garden. Once hooked, children will often tend and harvest their own plots without prompting.

FAR RIGHT: This wigwam was painted freehand using acrylic paints in several different colors and mixes. Zigzags, crosses, and spots are all easy motifs for children to apply themselves. Once the painting is finished, leave to dry (preferably in the sun) for a few hours.

YOU *will need*

* String, pencil, and thumbtack
* Paper, tape, and scissors
* 7½yd (7m) of canvas or duck, or half that amount if using extra-wide fabric that is at least 68in (173cm) wide
* Sewing machine and matching sewing thread
* ¼in- (6mm-) wide rope, about 2ft (50cm) long
* 6 bamboo canes, 78in (2m) long
* Acrylic or fabric paints
* Paintbrushes
* Stencils or stamps
* 4⅔yd (4.2m) of ¾in- (2cm-) wide thick ribbon

1 Tie the ends of a piece of string to a pencil and a thumbtack so that the length between them is 68in (173cm). Tape pieces of paper together to form a rectangle at least 68 x 134in (173 x 340cm). Hold the thumbtack in place halfway along one long edge, and draw a semicircle as shown; cut out. Unless you are using extra-wide fabric, cut the canvas or duck in half crosswise, place the pieces with right sides together, and pin and stitch a ⅝in (1.5cm) seam along one long edge; press the seam open. Use the paper pattern to cut out a semicircle from the fabric.

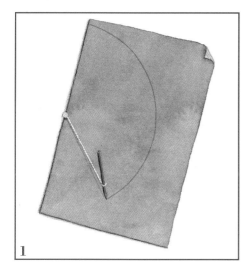

2 With the rope, tie the canes together 1ft (30cm) from the ends. Halfway along the straight edge of the fabric semicircle, cut out a small semicircle to just fit around the canes. Press under and stitch a ½in (1.25cm) double hem on all edges. Do any stamping or stenciling on the fabric now.

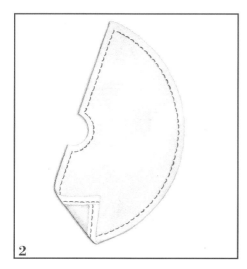

3 Place the fabric over the framework. Fan out the canes at the base so the fabric front edges meet and slightly overlap. Using pins, mark positions for ties at the opening edges and at each pole, near the bottom and also halfway up. Cut 12 pieces of ribbon 1ft (30cm) long and four pieces 6in (15cm) long. Remove the cover and stitch the short ties at the marked spots on the opening, two on the right side of one edge and two on the wrong side of the other. Fold the long ties in half and stitch to the wrong side at the marked spots. Assemble the wigwam, knotting the ties around the canes, and do any hand-painting.

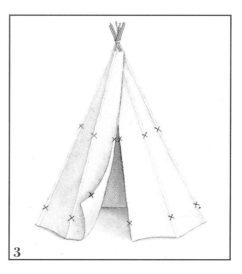

CHILDREN'S birdhouse

BELOW: The ceremonial hanging of the birdhouse is inevitably followed by hours of serious bird-watching while you wait to check that birds don't find your design too much of a physical challenge.

RIGHT: Multiple houses are more of a garden feature for both humans and feathered friends.

Children adore birdhouses, and these look particularly charming in the garden. Although birds might use them for roosting in fall or winter, they will not be used for nesting until spring. The instructions are for the large birdhouse, but the same method is used for the smaller ones. The size of the hole determines which birds will use it: 1in (25mm) for blue, marsh, and coal titmice, 1⅛in (28mm) for great titmice, and 1¼in (32mm) for nut-hatches and house and tree sparrows. If you build more than one birdhouse, use different-sized holes to attract different species, since birds such as titmice do not like having others of the same species as near neighbors. Secure it at least 6ft 6in (2m) off the ground, on a tree, post, or wall.

In the autumn, after the birds have left the nest, unscrew the base and clean out the box. It should not be inspected at any other time, or the birds might abandon it. Simply site the birdhouse in view of the house and watch from a respectful distance.

YOU will need

* ½in- (12mm-) or ⅝in- (16mm-) thick exterior plywood: 1 front and 1 back piece, 12in (300mm) square; 2 side pieces, 4 x 6in (100 x 150mm); 1 base piece, approximately 10½ x 4in (276 x 100mm), which will be cut to fit
* Jigsaw, tape measure, and drill
* Aluminum screws and screwdriver
* ¼in- (6mm-) thick planed stripwood, cladding, or fencing slats 1⅜in (35mm) wide, for roof: approximately 10ft (3m), which will be cut to fit
* Galvanized nails and hammer
* Water-based wood preservative (for any untreated wood)
* Wood stain or paint and brush
* Scrap pieces of wood for door and windows
* Scrap piece of wood or batten, for attaching to post (optional)
* Wire and piece of old hose or tire, for hanging on tree (optional)

1 Cut out the slightly curved roofline on the plywood front and back. In the front, cut out a hole 1–1¼in (25–32mm) in diameter, depending on the birds you wish to attract (see above). Position it halfway between the sides and 6¾in (170mm) from the bottom edge.

2 Measure, drill, and countersink holes along the side and bottom edges of the front and back pieces. Assemble the birdhouse by screwing the sides to the front and back. Cut the base to fit and screw it to the front and back. Cut the roof slats so that there will be a slight overhang at both the front and back. Measure the positions of the nails (which, for each slat, should be covered by the adjacent, overlapping slat) and carefully drill pilot holes in all the slats to avoid splitting the wood. Starting at the bottom of one side, nail the slats in place, overlapping the slats to cover the nail heads and finishing at the apex of the roof. Repeat for the other side of the roof, with the last slat overlapping the edge of the slat on the other side.

3 If the wood is untreated, paint the outside of the birdhouse with water-based preservative. There is no need to paint the inside. Stain or paint, as desired. Leave the inside and the entrance hole untreated. Cut out pieces for the door and windows, paint or stain them, and then nail them in place. Decorate with more screws or nails, adding one to resemble the doorknob. Make a small platform from scrap wood and fix it to the top of a post sunk into the ground, then screw up through the platform into the base of the birdhouse; or fix it to a piece of wood mounted on the side of a post. Alternatively, drill holes in the back of the birdhouse and attach it to a tree with wire encased in a piece of old hose or tire, to prevent damage to the tree. If you decide to hang the birdhouse on a tree, make sure it is well away from branches where cats can lie in wait for birds.

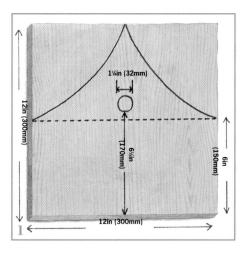

DECORATED pots

BELOW: Children's pots livened up with a variety of vertical and horizontal stripes in a medley of colors for a vivid, almost tribal look.

RIGHT: Blues, grays, and greens are used in random stripes and neat diamonds as a striking foil to lemon-yellow daffodils.

FAR RIGHT: Where a more subtle approach is called for, simply painted or etched pots with a white base make understated companions for leafy herbs or plants with silver-gray foliage.

Transforming a common-or-garden terracotta pot is so simple yet effective that children find it as satisfying as adults. Once the pots are painted, fill the children's version with easy-care plants for the children to nurture. Pansies, nasturtiums, and sunflowers all grow relatively quickly, as do herbs such as parsley and chives.

For this project "long Tom" pots were used but the same techniques can be applied to any size or shape of terracotta pot. The etched pot is decorated by scratching the pattern into a coating of exterior filler; this hardens to a tough, nonporous surface, serving the dual purpose of protection and decoration.

The striped pot, which is not covered with filler, is painted with acrylics, using masking tape to create the stripes. Select different widths of masking tape according to the size of pot and the width of stripes desired. If you wish, you can vary the width of the painted horizontal stripes, placing them randomly rather than regularly down the pot.

YOU will need

ETCHED POT:

* Terracotta "long Tom" pot
* Exterior filler such as Tetrion (in powder form)
* Burnt umber acrylic paint
* 2in (5cm) flat decorator's brush
* Sharp craft knife or wooden skewer
* Matt acrylic varnish and brush (optional)

STRIPED POT:

* Terracotta "long Tom" pot
* Masking tape
* White emulsion paint
* Acrylic colors of your choice (optional)
* Flat artist's brush
* Polyurethane varnish and brush

1 For the etched pot, dilute the exterior filler with water, following the manufacturer's instructions, until it is the consistency of thick cream. Add a small amount of burnt sienna acrylic paint until you have achieved the shade you want. The color will darken slightly once dry, so aim for a couple of shades lighter than the one you want. Use a flat paintbrush to apply two or three coats of the mixture to the pot. Leave to dry for about one hour. (Do not leave any longer, or the filler will set hard and you will not be able to work on it.)

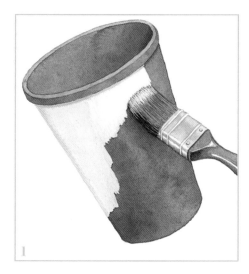

2 Draw the design to be etched on the filler-covered surface, then use a sharp craft knife or wooden skewer to scratch the design into the filler. Leave to dry. The unvarnished pot will be safe outdoors, but you can apply a coat of matt acrylic varnish to give the pot a slight sheen.

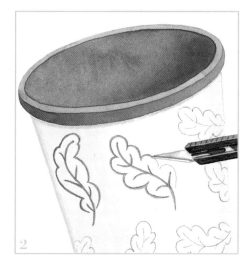

3 For the striped pot, apply strips of masking tape at regular intervals around a terracotta pot. In the remaining gaps, apply a coat of white emulsion and leave to dry. Apply one or more colors (or simply another coat of white emulsion) once the white undercoat has dried and then paint on simple motifs in a further color or colors – swirls, dots, circles, and borders all work well. The pots also look good with just the stripes painted on. Carefully remove the strips of masking tape when the paint is completely dry. Protect the painted surface against rain with a coat or two of polyurethane varnish.

243

COMPOST bin

Recycling garden waste and organic matter is an important part of maintaining a working garden. Make up this compost bin in a weekend and the family will use it for years to come. The bin needs to be a reasonable size so the contents can get hot enough in the center to decompose, but not so big that air cannot get to the center or so high that you cannot use it easily. This bin is 36in (92cm) square and 39in (99cm) high. Only the bottom retaining board is fixed in position at the front; to allow easy access, the other retaining boards are just slotted between the front pairs of posts one by one as the compost heap builds up.

YOU *will need*

* Sawn, pressure-preserved softwood:
  6 x 1in (150 x 25mm) boards:
  9 long boards, 36in (915mm) long;
  6 medium boards, 35in (890mm) long;
  4 short boards, 34in (865mm) long;
  6 or 7 retainer boards, 34in (865mm) long;
  6 posts, 2 x 2 x 48in (50 x 50 x 1220mm)
  Ask your lumberyard or supplier to cut the wood to size.
* 100 long zinc-plated nails or screws
* Piece of wood to use as spacing bar, ½–¾in (12–20mm) thick
* Steel tape measure
* Steel ruler
* T-square
* Marking gauge
* Pair of G-clamps
* Drill or hammer, and screwdriver

1 Lay two of the posts flat and position a short board across them, flush and square at the ends. The outer edges of the posts should be 34in (865mm) apart. This board will form the bottom row of the back of the bin. Secure the board to the posts using G-clamps. Fix in position with long nails or screws.

2 Next, stand the frame upright and place a long board along the adjacent side, flush with the post; secure it with a G-clamp and nail or screw it to the post. Repeat for the other side with a second long board. Place another post inside one of these boards, flush with the other end. Check it is square at the top using another long board, and nail or

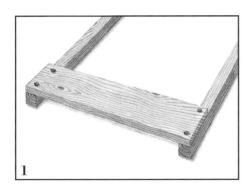

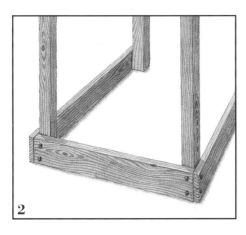

screw the post into the board. Repeat for another post and the other side board. Rest a retainer board against the front posts on the inside, but do not fix it in place yet.

3 Allow for the ventilation gaps by placing a spacing batten on top of the back board, then lay a long board across it. Repeat the process with one medium board on each side. Continue working in this way, one row at a time, so that the back boards are alternately short/long lengths, and the sides are alternately long/medium lengths, until you reach the required height. This bin is six boards high, plus spacing. Each time a new board is added, check the structure is still square by holding a spare board at the top, flush with the vertical posts.

4 Fix the front retainer board to the backs of the front posts with screws or nails. Place the remaining two posts behind the board, leaving a 1½in (40mm) gap between them and the front posts. Fix these posts to each side board, screwing or nailing them from the outside.

5 The remaining front retainer boards will be slotted between the posts as the compost heap builds up inside.

FAMILY LIFE: **a survival guide**

Family life is really the seven ages of man distilled into intense periods of utterly differing lifestyles. Just as you think you are nearly a grown-up, with a first home under your belt, a bit of overseas travel, and a bank account that nearly balances, you give it all up and start a family. Suddenly your life is completely transformed by the arrival of the next generation. Your days are at once dulled by repetitive routine and enriched by having children to nurture.

FIRST-HOMERS

Thinking of starting a family? Do the decorating. Enjoy that endless leisure time. Lie in bed all morning with breakfast and the newspapers. Savor the silence. On a weekend take one day to catch up on all your phone calls, letter-writing and domestic admin. Go to the movies, stay up all night, go shopping all day, eat with friends, take weekend breaks in sophisticated cities. It will be your last chance for a while.

BABYHOOD (0–2)

Buy a nightlight, a good book, and a comfy chair. Fill the cupboard with comfort food to eat when exhaustion beckons. Put away and label baby clothes when they are outgrown; you may need them again. Keep a baby thermometer and basic medicines on hand near the nursery, along with the doctor's and local emergency numbers, and

a baby-listening device. After a few weeks, get out of the house as much as possible. Make friends with parents of similarly aged babies – you'll find you suddenly have a lot in common. Routines make life easier but don't be a slave to them. Babies are transportable – to friends' houses, shops, and even galleries or museums. Postpone the cinema and theater for now – you probably couldn't stay awake anyway.

PRESCHOOL (3–5)

Remember that it is impossible to over-stimulate preschool children. Forget the chores and take everyone out for the day. Rediscover the joys of making and doing, baking and cooking, for and with the rest of the family. Construction is big: wooden blocks, paper lanterns, and dress-up clothes will all benefit from the input of parents and children alike. Little craftmakers emerge at this age – as do baby brothers and sisters. Just as life is becoming more manageable, you do the whole baby thing again, only this time with double the exhaustion. At this point many say enough is enough: two children will do nicely. Some, though, see this merely as a beginning, and go on to have more children. These people usually need to move house quite soon.

EARLY LEARNERS (6–12)

You never forget the day your first child starts school. Weep, celebrate, or contemplate – your life will now gradually lapse back into a less manic phase. You may go back to work, or perhaps change your working arrangements so you can attend the beckoning school gate at least part of the week. When the children come home, make learning fun, and try to reinforce what they are doing at school (if you can get them to divulge it). Prepare for the transition from cute new reader to independent child. For a child at the higher end of this age group, set out physical and moral boundaries if you want them to respect you, and vice versa.

TEENAGERS FROM HELL (13–18)

It's all true. Your children hate you. Their life's not fair. Take a deep breath, chant "It's just a phase" 100 times each morning, and try to find a smidgeon of common ground. If all else fails, go on vacation for a weekend (but check your household insurance first).

Teenagers were invented to remind you how hard it is to deal with hormones running riot and also to make you nostalgic for a simpler way of life, an era that was undeniably different from the present. Under no circumstances should you try to join in and be groovy with the younger generation. Even if you do like some of the same rock music, never admit it, as they will hold you in contempt, probably in public.

EMPTY-NESTERS

Where did the last 18 years go? You quite miss the unbearable music, the mess, the enormous phone bills, and the strange, monosyllabic friends. What next? For a start, clear the bedroom and the loft. Reorganize the home for occasional visits from offspring and companions. Redecorate poster-scarred teenage rooms in a way that says, "You are welcome any time, but so are our friends and relations." Silently vet potential partners but try not to comment. Move to a smaller house if you must but remember the next stage....

FULL CIRCLE

Grandparents, us? Bring out the embarrassing photos of your babies in front of the grandchildren. Talk of shared memories of childhood. Ladle time and affection on grandchildren – these are precious years in which to consolidate family ties. Start downsizing gradually. Consider the location of your house and maybe move to a smaller plot, or else make your home more low-maintenance and user-friendly, moving ovens and fridges to eye level, for example. Do you live in a sensible location? Are you close to family and friends? Can you walk everywhere if you find yourself unable to drive? Get someone else in to do the decorating. Most of all, enjoy your leisure time.

suppliers and addresses

To ensure safety in your home, below is a list of resources to keep you and your children out of harm's way.

SAFETY GUIDANCE AND CHILDPROOFING

Canada Safety Council
1020 Thomas Spratt Place
Ottawa, Ontario
K1G 5L5
Tel. (613) 739-1535
www.safety-council.org/

Canadian Child Care Federation
30 Rosemount, Suite 1000
Ottawa, Ontario
K1Y 1P4

Ontario Safety League
21 Four Seasons Place, Suite 1000
Etobicoke, Ontario
M9B 6J8
Tel. (416) 620-1720
www.osl.org

For decorating ideas and ingenious ways to spruce up your home, contact one of the companies below. Many have catalogs and/or stores near you.

FABRICS

Ashley House
1838 West Broadway
Vancouver, B.C.
Tel. (604) 734-4131

Dream Designs
956 Commercial Drive
Vancouver, B.C.
Tel. (604) 254-5012

Primavera Interior Furnishings Ltd.
Toronto, Ontario
Tel. (416) 921-3334

Valerianne of Vancouver
1445 Bellevue
West Vancouver, B.C.
Tel. (604) 925-9698

3109 Granville Street
Vancouver, B.C.
Tel. (604) 732-9646

CARPETING, FLOORING AND TILING

Country Floors
321 Davenport Road
Toronto, Ontario
M5R 1K5
Tel. (416) 922-9214

World Mosaic
1665 West 7th Avenue
Vancouver, B.C.
Tel. (604) 736-8158

FURNITURE

Belle Epoque Furnishings
1066 Yonge Street
Toronto, Ontario
M4W 2L4
Tel. (416) 925-0066

Ikea Canada
800-661-9807 mail order
Burlington: (905) 681-1044
Calgary: (403) 273-4339
Edmonton: (403) 433-6000
Montréal: (514) 738-5556
Ottawa: (613) 829-0160
Toronto: (416) 222-4796
Vancouver: (604) 273-2051
www.ikea.com

Mobler Imports Ltd (Across Canada)
3351 Sweden Way
Richmond, B.C.
Tel. (604) 270-3535

10550 Mayfield Road
Edmonton, Alberta
T5P 4X4
Tel. (403) 444-1199

Norwalk: The Furniture Idea
980 Cambie Street
Vancouver, B.C.
Tel. (604) 681-6363

1655 United Boulevard
Coquitlam, B.C.
Tel. (604) 540-4733

UpCountry
Toronto, Ontario
Tel. (416) 586-1370

GARDENING AND OUTDOOR ACCESSORIES

Dominion Coal Gardenland
Toronto, Ontario
Tel. (416) 489-5498

Revy Home and Garden Warehouses
2727 East 12th Street
Vancouver, B.C.
Tel. (604) 253-2822
Head Office 888-4111

Sheridan Nurseries
(416) 798-7970 for stores in Ontario

Southlands Nursery
6550 Balaclava
Vancouver, B.C.
Tel. (604) 261-6411

Teatro Verde
Toronto, Ontario
Tel. (416) 966-2227

The Avant Gardener
2235 West 4th Avenue
Vancouver, B.C.
Tel. (604) 736-0404

1460 Marine Drive
West Vancouver, B.C.
Tel. (604) 926-8784

The Natural Textile Company Inc
2571 West Broadway
Vancouver, B.C.
Tel. (604) 736-2101

Thomas Hobbs Florist by Maureen Sullivan
2127 West 4th Avenue
Vancouver, B.C.
V6M 1Z6
Tel. (604) 263-2601

Weal and Cullen
(various locations in Toronto)

HARDWARE AND PLUMBING

Crème de la Crème Vintage Plumbing Inc.
Toronto, Ontario
Tel. (416) 701-1021

Home Depot
800-654-0688 for stores across Canada

Reno Depot
888-443-4839 for stores in Québec

Revy Home Centres
Head Office 888-4111

HOUSEWARES AND LINENS

Au Lit Fine Linens
630 Mount Pleasant Road
Toronto, Ontario
M4S 2N1
Tel. (416) 488-9662

Casa Rustica
1131 Hamilton Street
Vancouver, B.C.
Tel. (604) 681-9772

Chintz and Company
950 Homer Street
Vancouver, B.C.
V6B 2W7
Tel. (604) 689-2022

1720 Store Street
Victoria, B.C.
V8W 1V5
Tel. (250) 381-2404

1238 11th Avenue SW
Calgary, Alberta
T3C 0M4
Tel. (403) 245-3449

10502 105th Street
Edmonton, Alberta
T5H 0K8
Tel. (403) 428-8181

Cruickshank's
1015 Mount Pleasant
Toronto, Ontario
M4P 2M1
Tel. (416) 750-9249

Divine Decor
4133 Dundas St. W
Etobicoke, Ontario
M8X 1X2
Tel. (416) 236-7356

Du Verre
280 Queen Street W.
Toronto, Ontario
M5V 2A1
888-DU VERRE (388-3773)

Ethan Allen Home Interiors
Stores located in Coquitlam,
Calgary, Edmonton, and two
in Ontario
800-228-9229 for information
Head Office: Tel. (203) 743-8000

Elte Carpet and Home
80 Ronald Avenue
Toronto, Ontario
M6E 5A2
Tel. (416) 785-7885

Georgia Interiors
2210 Cambie Street
Vancouver, B.C.
V5Z 2T7
Tel. (604) 875-0045

Jacaranda Tree
569 Mount Pleasant Road
Toronto, Ontario
M4S 2M5
800-561-0606

Jordans Interiors
1470 West Broadway
Vancouver, B.C.
Tel. (604) 733-1174

1539 United Boulevard
Coquitlam, B.C.
Tel. (604) 522-9855

La Cache
346 Queen Street W.
Toronto, Ontario
M5N 2A2
Tel. (416) 979-9567
(Locations across Canada)

Lightheart and Company
100-535 Howe Street
Vancouver, B.C.
V6C 1M9
Tel. (604) 684-4711

375 Water Street
Vancouver, B.C.
V6B 5C6
Tel. (604) 685-8255

Livingspace Interiors
1550 Marine Drive
North Vancouver, B.C.
Tel. (604) 987-2253

1100 Mainland Street
Vancouver, B.C.
Tel (604) 683-1116

Pacific Linens
Capilano Mall
60-935, Marine Drive
North Vancouver, B.C.
Tel. (604) 980-8922
(Locations across Canada)

Pier 1 Imports
22113 Yonge Street
Toronto, Ontario
M5B 1M4
Tel. (416) 363-2131
Also, 13 stores located in ON,
8 in Québec, Dartmouth/NS;
Dieppe, Westmoreland Co./NB
800-447-4371 for information

Robin Kay Home and Style
1670 Cypress St.
Vancouver, B.C.
Tel. (604) 731-1199

1569 Marine Dr.
West Vancouver, B.C.
Tel. (604) 925-6611
(Stores also in Calgary, Banff,
and four in Toronto)

Scantrade International
60 Horner Ave
Toronto, Ontario
M8Z 4X3
Tel. (416) 259-1127

LIGHTING

bianca luce
1074 Davie Street
Vancouver, B.C.
Tel. (604) 681-7723

Compagnie D'Eclairage Union
Montréal, Québec
Tel. (514) 340-5000

Old House and Home
2507 West Broadway
Vancouver, B.C.
Tel. (604) 731-2516

Sescolite Lighting Centres
Toronto, Ontario
Tel. (416) 651-6570
Burlington, Ontario
Tel. (905) 632-8659

PAINT

Benjamin Moore
(available at paint dealers
across Canada)
800-304-0304 for information
www.benjaminmoore.com

General Paint
(604) 253-3131 for stores in
Western Canada
www.generalpaint.com

Para Paints
(available at paint dealers
across Canada)
800-461-7272

Pratt and Lambert Paints
(available at paint dealers
across Canada)
800-289-7728 for information
Selectone Paints
800-875-9935 for locations

**HOME FURNISHINGS
BY MAIL ORDER**

B.B. Bargoon's
800-665-9227 for shop-at-
home service

Once Upon a Time...
Toronto, Ontario
Tel. (416) 698-2480
timecaps@interlog.com

index

Page numbers in *italics* refer to photographs.

acknowledgments

Conran Octopus would like to thank the following photographers and organisations for their kind permission to reproduce the photographs in this book:

1 Edina van der Wyck (arch: Josh Schweitzer); 2 Gross and Daley (arch: Chuck Dietsche and Dan Costa); 5 Richard Imrie; 6 Left Andrew Cameron/Wedding & Home/Robert Harding Syndication; 6 Center Paul Ryan/International Interiors; 6 Right Maura McEvoy; 7 Left Hotze Eisma (des: Ellen O'Neil); 7 Center Earl Carter; 7 Right Bill Reavell/Homes & Ideas/Robert Harding Syndication; 8 Timothy Soar/The World of Interiors (arch: Chris Cowper); 9 Christian Sarramon; 10 Karsten Damstedt Jorgensen/Bo Bedre, Denmark; 11 Robin Matthews; 14 Above Verne Fotografie; 14 Below Peter Mauss/Esto; 15 Spike Powell/Elizabeth Whiting Associates; 16 Above Jerome Darblay; 16 Below Tom McWilliam/House Beautiful, © May 1996/The Hearst Corporation All rights reserved; 17 Eric Morin; 18 Alan Weintraub/Arcaid; 19 Claire de Virieu/Inside; 20 Above Simon Brown/The Interior Archive; 20 Below Albert Roosenburg; 21 Philip Bier/View; 22 Above Lu Jeffery (des: Rachel & Harvey Cooke); 22 Below Marie-Pierre Morel (sty: G. Lesigne); 23 Above Verne Fotografie; 23 Below Richard Felber; 24 Ken Sparkes; 25 Alexander van Berge; 26-31 Scott Francis/Esto (arch: Walter Chatham); 32 Richard Imrie/Conran Octopus; 33 Richard Imrie; 34 Above Geoff Lung/Vogue Living; 34 Below Robin Matthews; 35 Brian Harrison/Country Homes and Interiors/Robert Harding Syndication; 36 Left Christian Sarramon; 36-7 Jean Francois Jaussaud/Inside; 37 Right Pascal Chevalier/British Vogue/The Condé Nast Publications Ltd; 38 Above Neil Lorimer/Elizabeth Whiting Associates; 38 Below Ron Sutherland; 39 Henry Wilson/The Interior Archive (des: Brett Muldoon); 40 Simon Brown/Homes & Gardens/Robert Harding Syndication; 41 Jean-Marc Palisse/Madame Figaro; 42 Richard Imrie/Conran Octopus; 43 Above VTWonen; 43 Below Simon Brown/The Interior Archive (des: Clodagh Nolan); 44 Jessica Strang (des: Nic Thomas); 45 Lizzie Himmel; 46 Left Giovanna Piemonti; 46 Dennis Brandsma/VTWonen; 47 Right Ray Main/Mainstream; 48 Left Antoine Rozes; 48 Right Home/Inside; 49 Jan Baldwin courtesy of Sue Williams; 50 Left Albert Roosenburg; 50 Above Right Verne Fotografie; 50 Jean-Marc Palisse/ Madame Figaro; 51 Above Fritz von der Schulenberg/The Interior Archive (des: Caroline Clifton-Mogg); 51 Below Right Gross and Daley; 52 Left Mark Daley/Esto; 52 Above Joshua Greene; 52 Below Fritz von der Schulenberg/The Interior Archive (des: Juliette Mole); 53 Lizzie Himmel; 54 Left Richard Imrie/ Conran Octopus; 54-5 Elizabeth Zeschin; 55 Right Dennis Brandsma/VTWonen; 56 Left Henry Wilson/The Interior Archive (des: Emma Kennedy); 56-7 Jerome Darblay; 57 Below Ray Main/Mainstream; 58 Above Simon Brown/The Interior Archive (des: Penny Rich); 58 Below Jean-Marc Palisse/Madame Figaro; 59 Trevor Richards/Homes & Gardens/Robert Harding Syndication;

60 Left Rodney Hyett/Elizabeth Whiting & Associates; 60 Center Dolf Straatmeier/VTWonen; 60-1 Rodney Hyett/Elizabeth Whiting & Associates; 61 Right Hotze Eisma; 62 Above Mark Daley/Esto; 62 Below Christian Sarramon; 63 Scott Francis/Esto; 64 Left Paul Ryan/International Interiors (des: Frances Halliday); 64-5 Hans Zeegers/VTWonen; 65 Right Christian Sarramon; 66 Mark Burgin/Belle Magazine (arch: Elizabeth Watson Brown); 68 Above Richard Imrie; 68 Below Left Geoff Lung/Vogue Entertaining; 68 Below Right Scott Frances/Esto; 69 Above Jerome Darblay; 69 Below Simon Brown/The Interior Archive (des: Sebastian Conran); 70 Mark Luscombe-Whyte/Homes & Gardens/Robert Harding Syndication; 70-1 Pieter Estersohn/LachaPelle (representative); 71 Below Dennis Brandsma/VTWonen; 72 Above Hans Zeegers/VTWonen; 72 Center Geoff Lung/Vogue Living; 72 Below Maura McEvoy; 73 Peter Mauss/Esto, as seen in Metropolitan Home July/Aug 1995; 74 Left A. Lorenzen/Camera Press; 74 Center Yves Duronsoy/Inside;

74-5 Scott Frances/Esto; 75 Right Christophe Dugied/Madame Figaro; 76-81 Simon Brown/Conran Octopus; 82-3 Verity Welstead/Conran Octopus (sty: Cathy Sinker); 84 Christian Sarramon; 85 Chris Drake/Country Homes & Interiors/Robert Harding Syndication; 86 Anthea Sieveking/Collections; 87 Verity Welstead/Conran Octopus (sty: Cathy Sinker); 88 Left Gilles de Chabaneix/sty: Tine Rozensztroch/Marie Clarie Maison; 88 Right-89 Verity Welstead/Conran Octopus (sty: Cathy Sinker); 90 Richard Imrie/Conran Octopus; 91 Richard Imrie; 92 Above Elizabeth Zeschin/She Magazine/Camera Press; 92 Below Hotze Eisma/VTWonen; 93 Dennis Brandsma/VTWonen; 93 Above Elizabeth Zeschin/Camera Press; 94 Center Metropolitan Home/Inside; 94-5 Jacques Dirand/The Interior Archive; 95 Jonathan Pilkington/The Interior Archive (des: Sly); 96 Above Simon Watson; 96 Below Hotze Eisma; 97 Above Michael Crockett/Elizabeth Whiting & Associates; 97 Below Otto Polman/VTWonen; 98 Above Marie-Pierre Morel/sty: Catherine Ardouin/Marie Claire Maison; 98 Below Edina van der Wyck (arch: Josh Schweitzer); 99 Left Richard Imrie; 99 Right Mads Mogensen; 100-1 Spike Powell/Elizabeth Whiting & Associates; 101 Right Melanie Acevedo; 102 Above Geoff Lung/Vogue Living; 102 Below Gross and Daley; 102-3 Home/Inside; 104 Hotze Eisma/VTWonen; 105 Jan Baldwin (des: Roger Oates); 106 Above Hotze Eisma;

106 Below Hotze Eisma/ VTWonen; 106-7 Geoff Lung/Vogue Living; 107 Right Jan Baldwin (des: Roger Oates); 108 Left Dennis Brandsma/VTWonen; 109 Albert Roosenburg; 110 Left Alexander van Berge; 110 Right Dennis Brandsma/VTWonen; 111 Han Zeegers/VTWonen; 112 Above Melanie Acevedo; 112 Center Dennis Brandsma/VTWonen; 112 Below Ingalill Snitt; 113 Hotze Eisma/VTWonen; 114 Scott Frances/Esto (arch: Marcy Wong & Donn Logan); 116-120 Richard Imrie/Conran Octopus; 122-123 Verity Welstead/Conran Octopus (sty: Cathy Sinker); 124 Above Luc Wauman; 124-125 Verity Welstead/ Conran Octopus (sty: Cathy Sinker); 126 Tom Leighton/Homes & Gardens/Robert Harding Syndication; 127 Verity Welstead/Conran Octopus (sty: Cathy Sinker); 128 Above Marie Pierre Morel/sty:Catherine Ardouin/Marie Claire Maison; 128 Below-29 Verity Welstead/Conran Octopus (sty: Cathy Sinker); 130-1 Alexander van Berge; 131 Richard Imrie/Conran Octopus; 132 Above Jerome Darblay; 132 Below Geoff Lung/Vogue Living; 133 Christian Sarramon; 134 Left Jerome Darblay; 134-5 Verne Fotografie; 135 Right Jerome Darblay; 136 Left Jerome Darblay; 136 Right Pieter Estersohn/LachaPelle (representative); 137 Ian Parry/Abode; 138-9 Verne Fotografie (arch: Wim de Puydt); 139 Right Simon Brown/Conran Octopus; 140 Alexander van Berge; 141 Above Melanie Acevedo; 141 Below Luc Wauman; 142 Above Left Eric Morin; 142 Above Right Jan Verlinde; 142 Below Christian Sarramon; 143 Dennis Brandsma/VTWonen; 144 Above Hotze Eisma; 144 Center Jan Baldwin (courtesy Sid and Cathy Benson); 144 Below Jerome Darblay; 145 Christian Sarramon; 146 Above Luc Wauman; 146 Below Yves Duronsoy; 147 Dominic Blackmore/Domain; 148 Above Simon McBride; 148 Below Jerome Darblay; 148-9 Hotze Eisma; 150 Left Richard Imrie/Conran Octopus; 150-1 Luc Wauman; 151 Right Jan

Baldwin (courtesy of Sid and Cathy Benson); 152-3 Christian Sarramon; 154 Above Simon Upton/Homes & Gardens/Robert Harding Syndication; 154 Below Simon Upton/Homes & Gardens/Robert Harding Syndication; 155 Simon Upton/Homes & Gardens/Robert Harding Syndication; 156-159 Simon Brown/Conran Octopus; 160 Above Verity Welstead/Conran Octopus (sty: Cathy Sinker); 160 Below Alexander van Berge; 161 Verity Welstead/Conran Octopus (sty: Cathy Sinker); 162 Tibault Jeanson/The World of Interiors (Elizabeth Selse); 163 Luc Wauman; 164 Verity Welstead/ Conran Octopus (sty: Cathy Sinker); 165 Verity Welstead/Conran Octopus (sty: Cathy Sinker); 166 Above Yves Duronsoy; 166 Center Living Textiles; 166 Below-67 Verity Welstead/Conran Octopus (sty: Cathy Sinker); 168-9 Richard Imrie/Conran Octopus; 170 Above Alexander van Berge; 170 Below René Gonkel/ Kinderen; 171 Dominic Blackmore/ Homes & Ideas/Robert Harding Syndication; 172 Richard Waite; 173 Nicolas Tosi/Madame Figaro; 174 Above Hotze Eisma/VTWonen; 174 Below Kinderen; 175 Above James Wedge (des: Jane Cumberbatch); 175 Below René Gonkel/Kinderen; 176 Left Ken Sparkes; 176 Right Kinderen; 177 Above Andrew Wood/The Interior Archive; 177 Below Charlie Colmer/Country Living (des: Dragons of Walton Street); 178 Above A. Gelberger/Agence Top; 178 Center Ouders; 178 Below Edina van der Wyck (arch: Josh Schweitzer); 179 Pascal Chevalier/British Vogue/ The Condé Nast Publications Ltd; 180-1 Simon Brown/Conran Octopus; 182 Above William Waldron/Inside; 182 Below Jerome Darblay; 183 Alexander van Berge; 184 Above Alberto Emanuele Piovano; 184 Center Hotze Eisma/VTWonen; 184 Below Hotze Eisma/VTWonen; 185 Jonathan Pilkington/The Interior Archive (des: Sly); 186 Karsten Damstedt Jorgensen/Bo Bedre, Denmark; 186 Right Jessica Strang;

188 Above Melanie Acevedo; 188 Below Sandra Lousada/ Collections; 189 Left Dominic Blackmore/Homes & Ideas/Robert Harding Syndication; 189 Right Russell Sadir/Ideal Home/Robert Harding Syndication; 190 Left Domininc Blackmore; 190 Right Paul Ryan/International Interiors (des: Frances Halliday); 191 Above Richard Davies (des: Future Systems); 191 Below Hotze Eisma/VTWonen; 192 Above Maura McEvoy; 192 Below Dolf Straatemeier/VTWonen; 193 Above Andreas von Einsiedel/Homes & Gardens/Robert Harding Syndication; 193 Below Camera Press; 194 Above Hotze Eisma/VTWonen; 194 Below René Gonkel/Kinderen; 195 Above Left Maura McEvoy; 195 Above Right VTWonen; 195 Below Paul Ryan/ International Interiors (des: John Michael E Keblad); 196 Above René Gonkel/Kinderen; 196 Center Simon Brown/Homes & Gardens/ Robert Harding Syndication; 196 Below Simon Brown/Homes & Gardens/Robert Harding Syndication; 197 Above Rodney Weidland/Australian House & Garden; 197 Below David Churchill/ Arcaid (arch: Stickland Coombe Architects); 198-203 Hotze Eisma/ Conran Octopus; 204 Ikea; 205 Sallyanne Craig (des: Pip Thompson); 206 Above Mads Mogensen; 206 Below Left Tom Leighton/Homes & Gardens/Robert Harding Syndication; 206 Below Right Mads Mogensen; 208 Fernando Bengoechea; 209 Sylvie Lancrenon/sty: Lauwe de Chombart/Marie Claire Idées; 210 Left René Gonkel/Kinderen; 211 Right Sylvie Lancrenon/sty: Lauwe de Chombart/Marie Claire Idées; 212-13 Karen Bussolini; 213 Right Richard Imrie/Conran Octopus; 214 Above Melanie Acevedo; 214 Below Richard Imrie; 215 Mads Mogensen; 216 Above Fritz von der Schulenburg/The Interior Archive (des: Mimmi O'Connell); 216 Below Brian Carter/The Garden Picture Library; 217 Left Jerry Harpur (des: Michael

Balston); 217 Right John Glover (des: Susy Smith); 218 Hotze Eisma; 219 Above Left Jan Verlinde; 219 Above Right Richard Imrie; 219 Below Gary Rogers; 220 Above Gil Hanly; 220 Center Steven Wooster/The Garden Picture Library; 220 Below Melanie Acevedo; 221 Above Marie-Pierre Morel (sty: G. Lesigne); 221 Below Ian West/Bubbles; 222 Above Left Ron Sutherland; 222 Above Right Solvi Dos Santos; 222 Below Left & Right Georgie Cole/Vogue Entertaining; 223 Richard Imrie; 224-5 Ingalill Snitt; 226 Above John Miller/The Garden Picture Library; 226 Below Mads Mogensen; 227 Above John Glover; 227 Below Fritz von der Schulenberg/The Interior Archive; 228 Above Left Mirjam Bleeker/Naterlie Taverne; 228 Below Jennie Woodcock/ Bubbles; 228-9 Andrew Lawson; 230 Above Sara Wilson/She

Magazine/Camera Press; 230 Center Jerry Harpur (des: Mirabel Osler); 230 Below Curtice Taylor; 231 John Glover; 232-36 Juliette Wade/Conran Octopus; 238-9 Christopher Boas; 239 Touch Design; 240 Earl Carter; 241 Above Chris Meads; 242-3 Verity Welstead/ Conran Octopus (sty: Cathy Sinker);

244 Richard Imrie/Conran Octopus; 245 Marc Broussard/sty: Catherine Taralon/ Marie Claire Idées; 246 Above Ouders; 246 Center Maura McEvoy; 246 Below Earl Carter; 247 Richard Imrie/ Conran Octopus; 254 Simon Brown/Conran Octopus; 255 Gross and Daley (arch: Chuck Dietsche and Dan Costa); 256 Richard Imrie/ Conran Octopus.

Every effort has been made to trace the copyright holders. We apologise in advance for any unintentional omission, and would be pleased to insert the appropriate acknowledgment in any subsequent edition.

PROJECTS

The following projects were specially made for Conran Octopus:

Aprons, papier-mâché bowl, etched pots: Anjie Davison
Family bulletin board, stamped curtain, folding screen, bathroom shelf, lamp shades, ceiling mobile, painted pots: Emily Jewsbury
Plaster plaques: Helen Fickling
Blue daisy throw: Plainfeather
Embroidered bed linen: Mary Norden
Painted game table: Pip Thomson